Locating Anthony Trollope

A Life in View

*To Joanna,
With my best wishes
Pamela Barrell*

Locating Anthony Trollope

A Life in View

Pamela Marshall Barrell

JANUS PUBLISHING COMPANY LTD
Cambridge, England

First published in Great Britain 2022
by Janus Publishing Company Ltd
The Studio
High Green
Great Shelford
Cambridge CB22 5EG

www.januspublishing.co.uk

Copyright © Pamela Marshall Barrell 2022
British Library Cataloguing-in-Publication Data
A catalogue record for this book is available from the British Library

ISBN 978-1-85756-931-5

All rights reserved. No part of this publication may be reproduced, stored in a retrieval system or transmitted in any form or by any means, electric, mechanical, photocopying, recording or otherwise, without the prior permission of the publisher.

The right of Pamela Marshall Barrell to be identified as the author of this work has been asserted by her in accordance with the Copyright, Designs and Patents Act 1988.

Cover Design: Janus Publishing Company Ltd

Cover Image: John Tordoff

Printed and bound in the UK by KnowledgePoint Limited, Reading.

Anthony Trollope, collage by John Tordoff

Contents

List of illustrations	xi
Foreword by Quentin Letts	xv
Introduction	xvii
Early Years	1
16 Keppel Street, Russell Square	1
St George's Church, Bloomsbury Way	4
The Family Move to Harrow	7
Illots Farm, Harrow on the Hill	7
Julians, Harrow on the Hill	8
Harrow Weald	10
Back to Illots Farm	14
Wider Family	15
Paternal Ancestry	15
Casewick	15
Cottered	18
Rushden	20
Julians at Rushden	21
Maternal Ancestry	25
Heckfield, Hampshire	25
Fulham	28
Exeter	29
Education	32
Harrow School	32
Sunbury	37
Winchester	37
Fanny's Visit to America	41

School Holidays/Lincoln's Inn	44
Bruges	48
Thomas Anthony Trollope L.LB	52
St Martin's le Grand, St Paul's	57
An Overview of the Post Office, Anthony's Eventual Successful Career and the Introduction of Post Boxes	60
Lodgings in London	65
Northumberland Street, Marylebone (now Luxborough Street)	65
Monken Hadley	67
Trollope's Illness in Northumberland Street	72
Ireland	75
Banagher	76
Drumsna	76
Carrick-on-Shannon	77
Kingstown, now Dun Laoghaire	81
The Cliffs of Moher	81
Mallow	83
Clonmel	83
Rotherham	87
Penrith	91
Rose Trollope	94
Salisbury and Winchester (*The Warden* and Barchester Novels)	97
Somerset House	102
Waltham Cross	105
Hunting	111
London Clubs	115
Beverley	119
Politics and the Houses of Parliament	123
Railway Stations and Speculation	126
The Palliser Novels	131
Recurring Themes	138

Oxford and Cambridge	138
Horse Racing and Newmarket	139
Aristocracy	140
Freemasonry	141
Violence	143
Hats, Beards, Boots and Shoes/Observations	145
Strong Women	152
Cecilia Meetkerke	152
George Eliot	152
Kate Field	154
Other Women	158
Publications, Periodicals and Printers	159
Method of Writing	166
Art and Illustrations	169
Criticisms and Reviews	175
Trollope's Response to Criticisms	177
Villino Trollope in Florence and Death of Fanny	179
Liverpool and SS *Great Britain*	182
Australia	189
Montagu Square	194
Library	199
Further Travels	204
Post Office Travels	204
Egypt and the West Indies	204
North America	205
South Africa	207
Holiday and Research Travels	207
Europe	207
Scotland	208
Yorkshire and the Lake District	209
Norfolk and Suffolk	213
Iceland	219

South Harting	224
Garlant's Hotel, Suffolk Street	229
John Tilley	233
Kensal Green Cemetery	236
Recollections and Letters	239
Obituaries	243
Minchinhampton, Gloucestershire	245
Descendants	248
Westminster Abbey	251
Acknowledgements	255
Sources	257
List of Publications by Anthony Trollope	259
Index	265

Illustrations

Frontispiece: *Anthony Trollope*, collage by John Tordoff	v
House on the corner of Keppel Street and Gower Street	3
Wall plaque near Keppel Street	4
St George's Church, Bloomsbury Way	5
Illots Farmhouse, Harrow on the Hill	9
Garden and rear of Julians, Harrow on the Hill	12–13
Casewick, Uffington	16–17
St John the Baptist Church, Cottered	19
St Mary's Church, Rushden	20
Julians, Rushden	22–23
St Michael's Church, Heckfield	26
Possible model for 'Aunt Jemima's House' in Exeter	30
Modern line-up of post boxes in Exeter	31
Modern boys at Harrow School	33
Harrow School	35
Outside the graffiti wall at Winchester School	40
Victorian horse trough at Carey's Walk, Lincoln's Inn	46
Carey's Walk, Lincoln's Inn	47
Steps of the Chateau d'Hondt, Bruges	51
Encyclopaedia Ecclesiastica	55
Modern Jerwood Library, Trinity Hall, Cambridge	56
The Lord Raglan tavern, rebuilt 1852, incorporating parts of Roman wall, still next door to St Martin's le Grand	59
Selection of historical designs for post boxes	62–63
Workhouse and graveyard as viewed by Trollope from his room at Northumberland Street	66

Emily's tomb at St Mary the Virgin Church	68
Grandon, Monken Hadley	71
Taylor's Bar, Drumsna	78
The Courthouse, Carrick-on-Shannon	79
Newly restored Victorian bandstand located between the two piers at Dun Laoghaire	81
Irish novels	84–85
Old Bank, Rotherham	89
Plaque at the entrance to the driveway of Carleton, Penrith	92
Sleigh as displayed in the Museum of Life in Hull, Yorkshire	96
Barchester novels	98
St Cross/Hiram's Hospital, Winchester	101
Rear of Waltham House and garden	108–109
Typical hunting meet	113
Whist table at the Athenaeum	117
Bandstand at Beverley, near Hull, Yorkshire	120
Houses of Parliament	124
Heritage train	128
WH Smith, Paddington Station	129
Ruined folly at Waltham Abbey	135
Copped Hall with folly	136–137
Emblem of Freemasonry	142
Young Men Brawling outside a Gentleman's Club by Gwen Raverat	144
Palliser novels	148–149
Map of area local to Trollope (turned by 90 degrees) showing correlation with his own depiction of Barchester	150
Trollope's Barsetshire: redrawn from the sketch-map made by the novelist himself	151
Doorway of Smith, Elder and Co at 32 Cornhill	160
Periodicals	162–163
Columbian Hand Press at Cambridge University Press	165
A typical Victorian writing desk	167

Staircase and entrance hall of the former Royal Academy, Somerset House, now the Courtauld Institute	173
Villino Trollope, Florence	181
Albert Docks, Liverpool	185
First-class cabin leading off ballroom of SS *Great Britain*	187
Hull of SS *Great Britain*	188
Plaque on basement wall of 39 Montagu Square	194
No. 39 Montagu Square, Marylebone	195
Trollope's bookplate	201
Former library at Waltham Cross	202–203
Ruins of Bolton Abbey, Yorkshire	209
Stepping stones to the Strid	210
A typical commercial inn, opposite the Town Hall, Leeds	211
King's Head, Bungay, shortly before demolition	213
Shelves of novels, travel books, short stories and biographies	216–217
Late-Victorian station at Wemyss as it is today	221
Drinking fountain and horse trough said to be commissioned by Trollope	225
Water tower at North End, South Harting	227
Stage Door of Haymarket Theatre overlooked by Garlant's Hotel	230
John Tilley's House at 73 St George's Square, Pimlico	234
Tomb and inscription at Kensal Green Cemetery	237
Greylands, Minchinhampton	247
Doorway of Westminster Abbey	253

Foreword

Postal surveying and Ireland were a perfect combination for the would-be novelist. Trollope's work for the Post Office – the Irish stress the first syllable of that second word – took him by horseback through many a county. Lucky devil, he saw more of Ireland and her people than almost any Irishman. Location, location, location, say estate agents. The slogan stands good for students of literature, too. Novels are works of imagination but they are moulded by experience, particularly place. Trollope the Post Office traveller encountered myriad towns and villages and they got his mind smoking like peat on a parlour fire.

   The Macdermots of Ballycloran, his first book, opens with a description of a ruined house. This was based, as Pamela Marshall Barrell writes, on a visit Trollope made to Drumsna, Co Leitrim, off the Dublin–Sligo road. One evening Anthony and a friend strolled along a country lane and found a wrecked mansion, Headford House. '*Oh, what a picture of misery or useless expenditure, unfinished pretence and premature decay!*' Those words affect me greatly. My mother's family used to be something in Co Cavan but my grandfather died young in 1949 and the venture never recovered. One afternoon in 1983 I accompanied my grandmother and mother on a visit to the family's old house. Like Headford, it had fallen to ruin. The roof was gone, the garden had overgrown and as we picked our way through the brambled mess and inspected the crumbling walls, some still with wallpaper visible, I was overcome by melancholy. We found the chicken shed. '*It smells exactly as it did*,' exclaimed my grandmother. The house had once been a prosperous farm but all that effort, all that '*useless expenditure and unfinished pretence*', was in disarray.

   It is the duty of the novelist to rebuild human pretence, to reconstruct from the rubble. Trollope did that. What a bounty he made from an unsettled childhood, from his peregrinations and from the thousands of acquaintances he struck while criss-crossing the British Isles. Abroad, too: there were trips to Iceland, Italy, Australia, South Africa and more, all before the invention of EasyJet. Was it restlessness that drove him? Or itchy interest in his fellow creatures and their fleeting lives? '*The quest for experience was undiminished*,' one biographer put it. Maybe it was a quest for material for the next novel.

Pamela's book is the work of, to use the word in its old sense, an *amateur* – an infectious enthusiast driven by artistic pleasure.

Trollopians are a delightful and learned lot. My late uncle, John Letts, helped to start the Trollope Society. Pamela's modestly worn expertise is typical of what one would encounter at the society's dinners. I hope members will not take umbrage if it is suggested that Anthony himself, had he attended a Trollope Society dinner, would have found characters to jackdaw for his next novel. But not, please, a Ferdinand Lopez. That black-moustached adventurer, as you will remember, hurls himself into the path of an onrushing locomotive at Tenway Junction. The description in *The Prime Minister* finds Trollope at his most urgent and exciting. Tenway Junction! The very name sets one's mind pumping like the piston of an express train '*coming round the curve at a thousand miles an hour*'. We learn here that the junction was probably based on Willesden Junction, which today is served by Overground and Underground services, complete with bing-bong Tannoy announcements, safety markings and posters promoting the ingratiating mayor of London. Tenway today surely lacks something of the steam-whooshing romance it had in coal-smutted Victorian days. We can therefore be glad that Anthony Trollope captured it – and so much else – in his magnificent fiction, ensuring that our ancestors' 'expenditure and pretences' were not lost to posterity.

Quentin Letts

Introduction

I became a devotee of Anthony Trollope's writings – forty-seven novels, numerous short stories, biographies and travelogues – in the mid-1970s, and have read and re-read them ever since. I therefore began this 'view of his life' with the object of visiting places associated with him, seeing where he was born, brought up and lived as an adult, and from where he travelled, worked and hunted, in an effort to see him not just as a monumental man of letters, but as a human being placed in his own time and social stratum. It is extraordinary how most places I visited have changed very little since 1815, the year of his birth, enabling me to see both the context and how many of these sites provided inspiration for his novels. I found myself asking questions as to why and how he viewed his childhood, and particularly how other members of his family felt during that time: I wanted to know their perspectives and emotions, as well as Anthony Trollope's.

Trollope began writing novels in the 1840s after having married and established a career in the Post Office, sensitively reflecting the times and areas he lived in. They are mainly love stories, with characters' dilemmas and choices as to whether to marry for love or, when desperate for funds, to marry for money, land and position. Along the journey there are many twists and turns, with topical themes such as clerical intrigue, politics, hunting, club life, and also the genteel poverty of the upper classes, the rise of the middle classes, and violence and deprivation among the lower classes.

Trollope's character has been described variously as loud, outspoken, bluff, blustery, gruff and *like a whirlwind*, in other words a front hiding a sensitive and kindly-natured man able to write sensitive and gentle novels. He wrote many times of how happy his life had been since moving to Ireland, but in later life after ill health forced him to give up his passion for hunting and his youngest son moved to Australia, he became depressed. Perhaps he began to see his life as a mirror image of his childhood; his son's going away reflected his mother's absence, and a need to supply money to both his adult sons contrasted with his own childhood lack of money. Perhaps this depressing time caused him to compare his adult life with his childhood situation, suggesting that when he began his *Autobiography*, instead of remembering or even mentioning happy times, he dwelt solely on the dubious ones.

His *Autobiography* is in two parts: the first dwelling solely on his portrayal of a miserable and wretched childhood – deserted by his mother and left in the care of a bad-tempered failure of a father – and the second chronicling his literary works with dates and times. However, I feel there are many inconsistencies throughout the first part of his *Autobiography*. He famously and feelingly wrote about the pain of walking several miles per day to and from school, at a time when walking or horse-riding were the only possibilities, and indeed throughout his life he continued (happily) to walk vast distances, often up to 24 miles (*'at a 6 mile-an-hour stride'*) on Post Office business, as well as many times for pleasure. At the same time, he grew up seeing his own father walk to and from Harrow to Lincoln's Inn daily. His worries about being muddy and dirty were perhaps also exaggerated as he was known for being scruffy at the height of his adult success, wearing, for instance, a stained pink hunting coat. There is no doubt Trollope was uncomfortable at school, even ostracized as a Day Boy, but I hope to show that his sufferings were probably exaggerated as he failed to mention the schoolfriends he made and kept throughout his life. As his recall of events outside school and his novel writing skills were very sharp, I feel it is unlikely that he was mistaken when writing his *Autobiography*, and therefore hope to show that when looking back, as a sensitive adult, he had learnt to understand and appreciate the pain and difficulties his parents faced, and consequently I believe he camouflaged the fact that the real reason for his and his family's miseries was a lack of money, and therefore a genuine social embarrassment.

I also seek to find answers to many other puzzles, omissions and inconsistencies, such as Trollope's failure to mention the sadness of the death of his brother Arthur or the playfulness of his two younger sisters with their tutor during his early childhood; his aunts, uncles and grandparents; and his mother's gregariousness during the time she was at home. When circumstances changed, leading to her long absence, it was obviously an upsetting time, as was his father's illness, but again I hope to uncover some of the reasons for the improbable assertion of the necessity of spending school holidays alone at Lincoln's Inn daily and his failure to mention her letters.

There have also been assertions of an affair with the young American Kate Field, upon which I hope to add to doubts already expressed by others. It is true that he wrote her an ambiguous letter (which he also did to other ladies as part of his ebullient character), together with what is believed to be a long description of her in his *Autobiography*. Disappointingly, his son omitted this when he published the book posthumously, meaning we can never know for certain, although I hope I can show in my findings why I believe it to be implausible.

Introduction

Anthony Trollope's *Autobiography* was also startling to his contemporaries: the Reverend Dr Donald Macleod, editor and fellow writer, wrote: '*... we were surprised by the picture he* [Trollope] *draws of the hardships of his early life. For no trace of sorrow, no memory of disappointment, could be detected in that bluff and cheery presence*'; and his cousin's wife and contemporary Cecilia Meetkerke regretted its '*misleading reticence*'; while biographer Michael Sadleir said '*Of self-portraiture he was very sparing*'. The *Autobiography* is undoubtedly puzzling, but by visiting his familiar haunts and walking in his footsteps, linking them to other writings and circumstances, I hope I can disprove at least some of the unhappy stories.

I have been fascinated and thrilled by my travels with Anthony Trollope and, although he is as intriguing as ever, his insights into other human feelings and behaviour remain wholly relevant in today's world and will always remain so.

Trollope's own writings have been my main source, together with his brother Tom's *While I Remember*, coupled with quotations and contemporary letters, and my own and friends' observations.

Pamela Marshall Barrell B.A.
www.artsviews.co.uk

Early Years

16 Keppel Street, Russell Square

Although known as a Victorian writer, Anthony Trollope was actually born on 24th April 1815, two months before the Battle of Waterloo, when George III reigned, followed by George IV in 1820, then William and Mary. It wasn't until 1837 that Queen Victoria ascended the throne, when Anthony was 22 years old. Keppel Street was in a fashionable upper-middle-class area mainly occupied by judges, lawyers and barristers. It was named after Admiral Keppel, a prominent figure in the Austrian war of succession, and is no longer residential, the London School of Hygiene and Tropical Medicine taking up one side of the road and UCL Hospital the other. Just around the corner of Keppel Street and Gower Street there are still the same tall, narrow-fronted houses, with a dining room on the ground floor and a main drawing room on the floor above, both fronting the street.

Anthony's mother, Fanny, née Frances Milton, became a prolific writer, while his father, Thomas Anthony, was a barrister of Middle Temple with Chambers in Old Square, Lincoln's Inn. Anthony was the fifth child, with older brothers Thomas Adolphus (Tom) born 1810, Henry (1811) and Arthur William (1812), and a sister, Emily, who was born and died in 1813. As Anthony was born just two years after her death, he must have been extra welcome. His sisters Cecilia and another Emily were born later, in 1816 and 1818. Anthony began his *Autobiography* in 1876 but it was not published until after his death in 1882, and contained the words:

> *In writing these pages, which, for the want of a better name, I shall be fain to call the autobiography of so insignificant a person as myself, it will not be so much my intention to speak of the little details of my private life, as of what I, and perhaps others round me, have done in literature; of my failures and successes such as they have been, and their causes; and of the opening which a literary career offers to men and women for the earning of their bread.*

This perfectly describes the concentration on his writing career with very few facts about his earlier life. His elder brother Tom, in contrast, details in his memoir *While I Remember* a very happy childhood and upbringing. The family lived in *'genteel poverty'* and Tom describes eating breakfast at 7 a.m. in a back-drawing room to save lighting an extra fire. Only two tallow candles were used to light both this room and the front drawing room, barely reaching the outer corners and needing frequent snuffing by snufflers kept on a plated tray. Wax candles at half-a-crown a pound were considered *'an extravagance not to be thought of ...'*. The family dined mainly on mutton, as do characters in not only Anthony's novels but also those of Dickens and Thackeray. However, the family maintained a servant dressed in the Trollope family livery and Tom and Henry read their Eton Latin grammar on their knees in front of a sofa before the parents came downstairs.

Tom also mentions that they dined at 5 o'clock, *'rather a late hour'*, because their father was industrious and laborious. From about 6 years old, both Tom and Henry were considered capable, on their own, of *'... walk*[ing] *from the house to Lincoln's Inn, so as to arrive in time to walk back with* [their] *father'*. During the walk home they recited Latin and their morning's *'poetical achievements'*. Their father, a Wykehamist and Fellow of New College Oxford with a Vinerian Scholarship (i.e. having top marks in the Bachelor of Civil Law examination), *'was very strict in instilling education into all his children'*. He also pointed out houses in nearby Russell Square, Bedford Square, Red Lion Square and Bloomsbury Square, occupied by prominent legal luminaries.

Although Anthony Trollope did not wish to include details of his home life, and in any case would have been too young at this time to remember many details, he must nevertheless have absorbed general happiness as several of his fictional characters live in the area: Mrs Furnival in *The Three Clerks* *'... in a genteel drawing room near Cavendish Square remembered with regret the small dingy parlour in Keppel Street'*; Lady Anna in the book of that name lodges with the barrister Sergeant Bluestone around the corner in Bedford Square for her 'safety' (i.e. hidden away from her lover, Daniel Thwaite), and daringly takes a carriage – for a two-minute ride – to him in Great Russell Street. Further in the novel, when Lady Anna's mother, the Countess, resides in Keppel Street she attempts to shoot the tailor:

> *By this time they were all in the parlour ... 'Daniel Thwaite', said the Countess, 'if you do not leave this, the blood which will be shed shall rest on your head,' and so saying, she drew nigh to the window and pulled down the blind. She then crossed over and did the same to the other blind, and having done so, took her place close to a heavy upright desk* [containing the gun], *which stood between the fireplace and the window.*
>
> (*Lady Anna* 1874)

House on the corner of Keppel Street and Gower Street

Little Louey in *He Knew He Was Right* is snatched outside the derelict Parker's Hotel between Mowbray Street and Gower Street, and the Ball family also live there when Mrs Mackenzie laments that *'the rent is ninety pounds, and the taxes twenty-two, ... and there's the taxman come now for seven pound ten, and where I'm to get it unless I coined my blood I don't know'*.

Anthony would have been constantly reminded of the area throughout his life: Dante Gabriel Rossetti was brought up at no. 7 Gower Street at the same time as the Trollope family (perhaps providing family conversation about artistic pursuits). Later the Pre-Raphaelite movement was founded in 1848 in that same house, influencing some of Anthony's characters' disapproval of Pre-Raphaelite paintings. His future friend and illustrator John Everett Millais had also lived in Gower Street since the age of 19 in the 1830s, at no. 83, and at one time Charles Dickens lived in the area. Close to the nondescript brown plaque commemorating Anthony Trollope's birthplace on the wall of UCL in the former Keppel Street is a plaque for the family's neighbour, Richard Trevithick (1771–1883), pioneer of high-pressure steam, and more recently the building housed MI5. George Orwell used the UCL Art Deco Senate House as the base for the 'Ministry of Truth' in *1984*, and the BBC filmed *Sherlock* in a nearby house instead of 221B Baker Street.

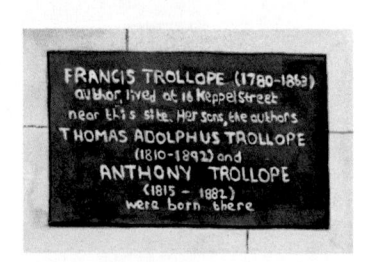

Wall plaque near Keppel Street

St George's Church, Bloomsbury Way

Shortly after his birth, Anthony was christened at St George's Church as his brothers had been before him. The church was a short carriage trip away, mainly across what was still open fields. It was built on land described as '*Ploughfield*', bought for £1,000 from Lady Russell, widow of the Whig Lord John Russell.

This Anglican church was one of twelve New Churches, stretching from the West End of London to Greenwich. It was the last of six churches designed by Nicholas Hawksmoor, built by a Tory government in response to an expanding population and consequent growth of non-conformist chapels and other places of worship. Competition between the different forms of worship and their clergymen provided the background in novels written later both by Anthony and his mother.

The church is fronted by a large portico with a statue of George I perched proudly on top of a high stepped steeple, at the base of which are figures inspired by Pliny's description of the ancient world. The large vaulted and

St George's Church, Bloomsbury Way

brick-lined undercroft would originally have been used for burial purposes, but today somewhat incongruously houses the Museum of Comedy. The beautiful interior of the church betrays the fact that it was not built with the comfort of women in mind, as the narrow and curved staircase to the upper floor would have prevented women in circular skirts and multiple petticoats from ascending, a common factor in other churches built at that time.

The noticeboard outside shows a reproduction of William Hogarth's *Gin Lane*. Both *Gin Lane* and *Beer Street* form a pair of prints produced only sixty years earlier to highlight the poverty and drunkenness of a fallen section of society. They depict areas strewn with drunken bodies, with starving families giving their babies gin-soaked rags instead of food, in an attempt to stave off hunger and keep them quiet. They are a reminder of how even families living in *genteel poverty* in the 1800s, such as the Trollope family, lived precariously. Anthony later chronicled this precariousness and resultant downfall of several characters such as Lizzie in *The Eustace Diamonds*, Carrie Brattle in *The Vicar of Bullhampton*, and the Polish brother and sister duo Sophie Gordeloup and Count Pateroff, who lived '*off their wits*' in *The Claverings*.

In later life Anthony Trollope supported bold and forthright women and had he been alive in 1913 would probably have approved of St George's Church hosting the funeral of suffragette martyr Emily Davison. Later, Charles Dickens, close associate and competitor, used this church as a setting for 'A Bloomsbury Christening' in *Sketches* by Boz.

The Family Move to Harrow

Illots Farm, Harrow on the Hill

'*I was born in 1815, in Keppel Street ... and while a baby, was carried down to Harrow*' Anthony boldly stated in his *Autobiography*. This was not strictly accurate as according to Tom, two years older, they would have been 8 and 6 years old, implying that they moved in 1821. However, Anthony was probably still technically classified as a baby as until about 7 years old, young boys usually wore full length skirts overlaid by pinafores until formally 'breeched', i.e. fully toilet-trained and thus able to manoeuvre the customary long tight breeches by themselves.

It was becoming fashionable for families to move westwards out of London to more rural areas, but the main reason for the Trollope family move was so that all four boys, Henry, Tom, Arthur and Anthony, would be eligible to attend Harrow School as Day Boarders, where one of the tutors was a friend of their father. Strangely, Anthony did not mention that his brother Arthur died while living here three years later, aged 22, in 1824; possibly his family shielded him from grief due to his age, or perhaps Anthony's memory was too painful. Arthur's portrait by the family art tutor Auguste Hervieu is held in the National Portrait Gallery and shows a handsome, fair young man.

Both Tom and Anthony wrote that the move to Harrow was disastrous. Anthony described Illots Farm as:

> ... *a farm* [that] *was the grave of all my father's hopes, ambition and prosperity, the cause of my mother's sufferings, and of those of her children, and perhaps the director of her destiny and ours.*

The family rented Illots Farm from Lord Northwick. The house was set in 157 acres down a short but dark leafy lane from the top of the steep hill upon which sits Harrow on the Hill, where his father's brave intention was to continue his work at the Bar whilst managing the farm, a task for which he had no knowledge or skills. To make matters worse, instead of consolidating Illots Farm, the father compounded the difficulties by not only foolishly building an even larger house just 100 yards away further up the incline towards the village, again on rented land, but at the same time purchasing '*various dark gloomy Chambers in and about Chancery Lane*', where he also planned to carry on his practice as a barrister.

They called the second house Julians, after the house owned by his father's great-uncle Augustus Meetkerke, from whom the family, rightly or wrongly, expected to receive a large inheritance, which failed to materialize. The subject of inheritances and the need to marry for money are a constant theme in Anthony's novels.

In 1861 Anthony's book *Orley Farm* was based on Illots Farmhouse, and when Mr Ridley Hastings much later housed his Prep School in the same premises ('*so that boys did not have to enter Harrow too early*') he called it Orley Farm.

Julians, Harrow on the Hill

Julians is still a gracious 18th-century-style two-storey residence, in mellow curving yellow brick. Nowadays it has a large and incongruous extension in a solid, square high-Victorian manner, fortunately screened by mature trees, in what is still a secluded country lane. The garden has parterres and rose areas, and a terrace with sunken patio. There are big windows and French doors, a feature later used by many of Anthony's characters who step in and out or sit by the open doors on calm summer evenings, like Lily Dale in *The Small House at Allington* (1864), or Patience and Clarissa in *Ralph the Heir* (1871). The young Anthony must have enjoyed three or four years at home with his sisters Cecilia and Emily who, like most young ladies, would presumably have had tutors (for music, singing, painting and Latin), and, as Fanny was a very sociable person, there would have been a constant stream of visitors, friends and relatives, and neighbours. Christmases were known to be festive, when even Anthony's father joined in amateur theatricals, which may have been recounted in the 'Christmas at Noningsby' scene in *Orley Farm* (1862). Puzzlingly, Anthony does not mention this family atmosphere at all: perhaps he forgot about it and dwelt solely on harder times (unlikely), or he exaggerated to compete with Dickens as has been suggested by Nicholas Shrimpton of Oxford University Press (again unlikely as by then he enjoyed a successful career), or depression, as by the time he wrote his *Autobiography*, all his siblings apart from Tom had died and perhaps he could not bear their memory.

In the constant stream of visitors was a certain suave and insincere Reverend Mr Cunningham, whose presence and reputation spawned tensions and rivalries within the wider Harrow social circle. C P Snow in *Trollope: His Life and Art* (1975) describes '*a certain antagonism between the vicar, the Rev Mr Cunningham, and the clerical element of the school world*'. Mr Cunningham, known as '*Velvet-Cushion Cunningham*', was

Illots Farmhouse, Harrow on the HIll

'*Evangelical*' (from his book of that title) whilst the seven masters of the school were known to be '*high and dry*'. It was whispered that Cunningham's father had purchased his living in suspicious circumstances, and C P Snow asserts that the rivalry between Cunningham and Harry Drury (the Trollope family friend and Harrow schoolmaster) focused on class distinctions, the former being perceived as outwardly more '*gentlemanlike*' (even though he was the son of a London hatter), and the latter thought to be *'superior in talent, but essentially coarse'*.

The minutiae and subtleties of such social situations feature in novels by his mother Fanny, in *The Vicar of Wrexhill*, but also by Anthony, particularly with Evangelicalism and the insincere Emilius in *The Eustace Diamonds* (1872) and the slimy Mr Slope in *Barchester Towers* (1857), and frequent discussions as to whether or not a character is a *'gentleman'*.

The family of course would have kept horses and there was plenty of room for stabling; consequently they would have been able to travel to their relatives in Fulham, Cottered and Rushden in Hertfordshire, Exeter in Devon, Casewick in Lincolnshire and Heckfield in Hampshire, and indeed Tom chronicles walking to Fulham one Sunday morning for breakfast before joining his relatives at church.

Harrow Weald

When it became apparent that Mr Trollope's expected inheritance would not materialize, the family moved from Julians to what Anthony described as *'a hamlet in the large parish in the direction of Pinner'* in nearby Harrow Weald, three miles away, where his father:

> *... unfortunate that he was, took another farm. It is odd that man should conceive, and in this case a highly educated and a very clever man, that farming should be a business in which he might make money without any special education or apprenticeship.*

It does seem to be a poor business decision that with ever-decreasing funds the family continued to rent the original Illots Farm, Julians back at Harrow and the father's Chambers in Lincoln's Inn, while taking on yet another rented property further away at Harrow Weald.

In mitigation they rented out Julians to the Rev Cunningham, above, notwithstanding their disapproval of him, and were legally committed to the lease on Illots Farm. Tom, in his autobiography, thought that the second farm *'...did in some degree alleviate loss from the larger farm at Harrow, and that, could he have got rid of the latter, the Harrow Weald farm might have paid its way'*; conversely Anthony thought this was the final step towards ruin, as without knowledge of crops and seasons, and sufficient capital to prepare, and with the fact that crop yields nationally went down between 1800 and the 1850s, failure was inevitable:

> *The farmhouse was not only no more than a farmhouse but was one of those farmhouses which seem always to be in danger of falling into the neighbouring horse-pond. As it crept downwards*

> from house to stables and from stables to barns, from barns to cowsheds, and from cowsheds to dung-heaps, one could hardly tell where one began and the other ended! There was a parlour in which my father lived, shut up among big books, but I passed my most jocund hours in the kitchen, making innocent love to the bailiff's daughter.

This description may have been exaggerated, or poetic licence. Anthony's brother Tom thought it to be *'en noir'* and described the residence as having been once a very good house, although no longer in good condition and *'indeed a much better house than it would have been if its original destination had been that of merely a farmhouse'*.

Even small working farms would surely have needed workers, with plough/cart horses and their resultant stabling and stable-lads. Workers would have been needed to buy, till and sow seeds, pick, store and market crops, and look after machinery and horses, and an accountant/supervisor would have been needed to pay wages. Neither Anthony nor Tom mentioned such staff in their memoirs, possibly because of social distinctions, although Anthony's characters frequently consulted their father's man of business, such as Silverbridge and Lord Gerald in the Palliser novels, usually to request money (which of course Anthony could not do!). Not only Anthony but also his father would have needed at least a clean shirt to wear at Lincoln's Inn, meaning that staff inside the house must have washed and ironed clothing and bedding, and also collected firewood and lit at least one fire for cooking. Someone would also have had to draw copious amounts of water from a well, not only for the family but also for the horses.

It was at this period that their father became increasingly bad-tempered and suffered from severe headaches for which he used calomel, the standard remedy; presumably from the cumulative stress of managing two farms and practising law whilst also walking daily to Lincoln's Inn and back (13–14 miles each way via modern roads); even if there had been a shorter route across fields in the 19th century it would still have been a considerable feat before commencing a day's work.

To compound the family's problems, it was whilst living at Harrow Weald that Anthony's mother Fanny went to America for over three years, taking Henry, Cecilia and Emily and their tutor with her, leaving the father to manage all the properties and his legal work on his own. By this time Anthony and Tom were boarding at Winchester, but when his father and Tom also went out to America to visit Fanny for a few months, Anthony was left alone at school and possibly during school holidays. Understandably, he felt especially left out and neglected, even if, as I believe, there would have been necessary staff to attend to his basic needs.

Garden and rear of Julians, Harrow on the Hill

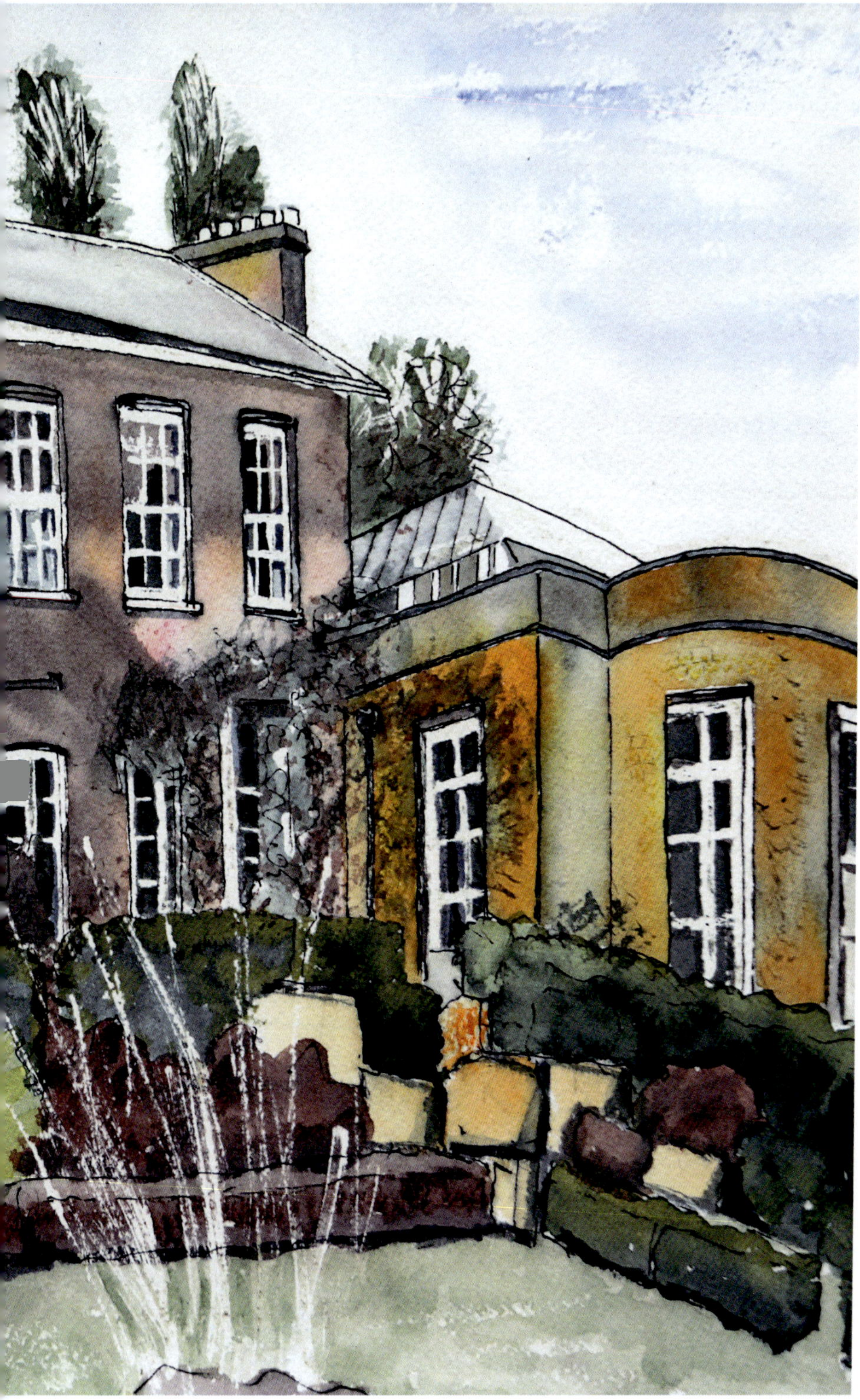

Back to Illots Farm

Whilst Fanny's trip to America was an abject failure per se, it enabled her to write the enduringly popular *The Domestic Manners of the Americans*, the first of many such travelogues and novels. The income earned was about £900 in the first year, and £250 p.a. thereafter, according to the RPI a sum worth £93,983.50 today. With this additional sum the family were soon able to return to Illot's Farm, where Anthony had about a mile to walk to Harrow School. After her own publication, Fanny was able to help find subscriptions for Anthony's father's book *Encyclopaedia Ecclesiastica*, which he had begun in her absence even whilst suffering increasing headaches, and holding down the Chambers and two unsuccessful farms: facts which Anthony mentioned only in scathing terms when relating his own loneliness and distress in his *Autobiography*.

Presumably, Anthony's (and his father's?) clothing improved, and their neighbour Colonel Grant became helpful and friendly towards them. However, Anthony still sadly said, '*I coveted popularity with a coveting which was almost mean*'. Once again, the house became a magnet for visitors, friends both old and new. Fanny's social circle included writers and clergymen; the poet Letitia Landon, an editor and contributor to the *Literary Gazette* sometimes called '*The Female Byron*'; dignitaries of the church, and the Rev Henry Milman, third son of Sir Francis Milman, physician to Queen Charlotte.

Nevertheless, his father continued to deteriorate until he either became psychotic or relapsed into speechless depression. It has been suggested that he was affected by and/or addicted to his prescribed doses of calomel and morphine, as were many famous Victorians, for example Elizabeth Barrett Browning and Wilkie Collins. He may perhaps have been in the early stages of dementia, which would not have been a recognized ailment at that time.

Wider Family

Anthony Trollope had many family connections whom he must certainly have visited during his childhood, and later as an adult, as the characters, and the landscapes and their buildings, greatly influenced his novel writing.

Paternal Ancestry

Casewick

The Trollope family seat of Anthony's great-grandfather was at Casewick (full name 'Casewick in the Bushes', pronounced Kesik), situated just outside the village of Uffington (a derivative of Uffa meaning tun or town), three miles east of Stamford in Lincolnshire. His father was a grandson of a younger son of Sir Anthony Trollope (1691–1784), 4th Baronet, a sheep farmer who bought the house in 1621 for the sum of £5,500 (£1,527,731 today). It is inconceivable that there would not have been family visits either way whilst they were living at both Keppel Street and Harrow, and as an adult, Anthony is recorded as hunting and staying with his cousin Sir John Trollope.

Casewick is on the site of a deserted medieval village named *'Casuic'* in the Domesday Book and described by Pevsner as *'one of the few houses in the country* [which] *fill one with such delight'*. It is one of three 'big houses' in the area: Uffington Manor being almost opposite, owned by the Earl of Lindsey, and Burghley House, a short distance away, owned by the political Cecil family. In 1934–45 John Betjeman and his new wife Penelope Chetwode lived in a farmhouse nearby, and his poem 'Uffington' describes the tension of village church bells: *'Tonight we feel the muffled peal/Hang on the village like a pall'*.

Uffington nowadays is a small village, with a public house (the Bertie Arms) and the church of St Michael and All Angels being the prominent features. I was privileged to meet two local farmers who told me of historic family rivalries, particularly between the Lindsey and Trollope families – a typical theme for many of Anthony's novels. The Earl of Lindsey and his family had the 'advantage' of living opposite the church: the huge gates to their formal park are exactly opposite the similar gates of the church, thus making a continuing line. Casewick, on the other hand, is a little way off with a more rural approach through grazing sheep and a ha-ha – but then the

Casewick, Uffington

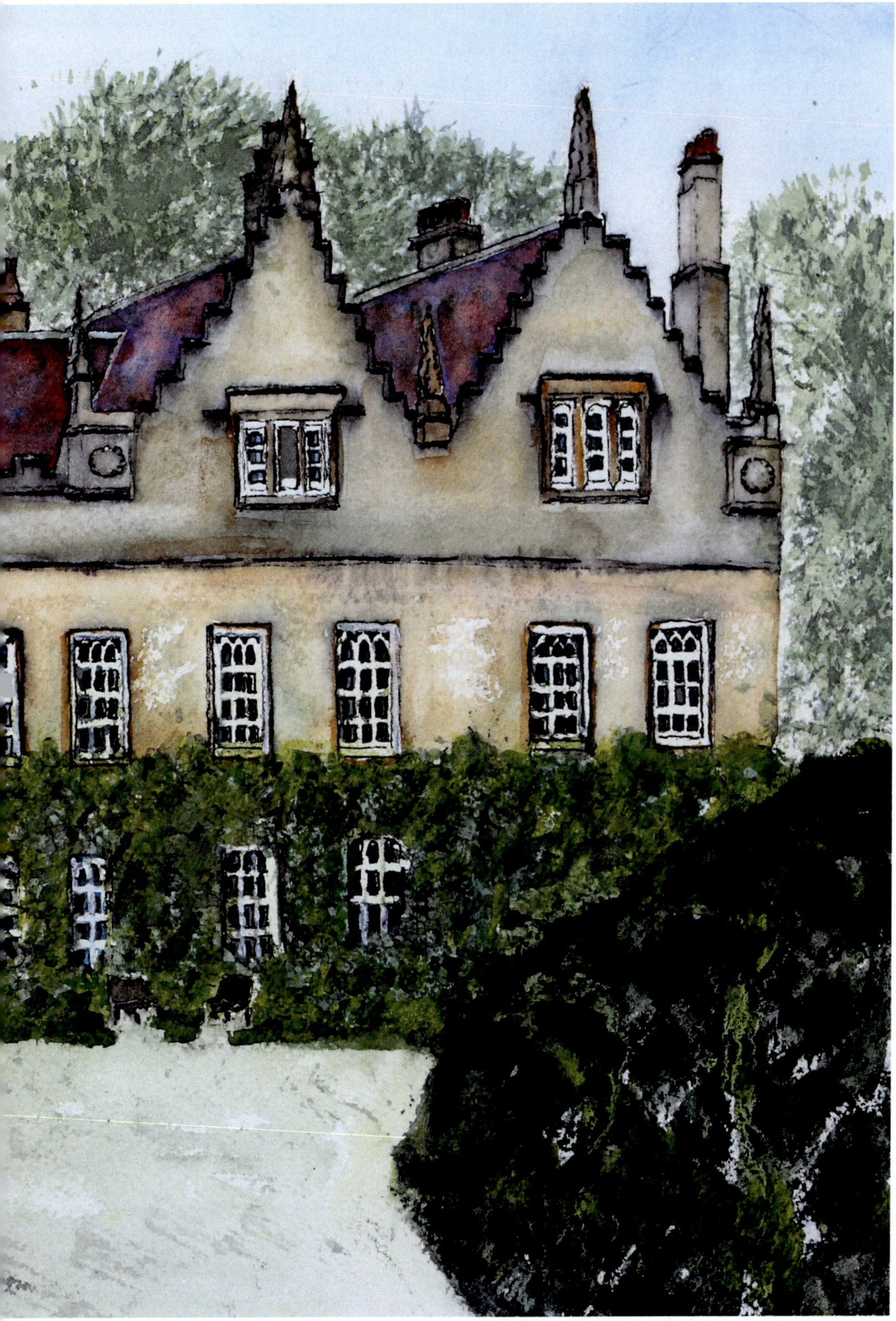

Trollope family had a whole chapel to themselves at the front of the church, now called the Trollope Chapel! The entrance to this is up in the choir stalls on the left, whereas the Lindseys were confined to two back pews, albeit larger than those for the general congregation. One of my informants had been a choirboy and remembered Lady Dorothy Trollope-Bellew sitting in the family chapel in the mid-1970s while the male members of the congregation were segregated on the right-hand side of the church and the female members on the left. Unfortunately, the Lindsey family seat burnt down in late 1904. In *The American Senator* (1877) Arabella went to the church which was:

> ... close to the house and the family pew consisted of a large room screened off from the rest of the church, with a fireplace of its own – so that the labour of attending divine service was reduced to a minimum.

A journey from Harrow to Casewick would have taken nine hours and twenty minutes by stagecoach to Stamford along the London to York Great North Road. It would have then been necessary to find a local coach or more likely one sent from the house for the last leg of the journey from Stamford to Uffington. Anthony's characters endure many such carriage rides, including on the continent. The Great Northern Railway (GNR) did not open from London to York until 1852 when Anthony would have been 39, and even so the route went via Peterborough rather than Stamford, making it necessary to stop at one of the nearby villages of Tallington, Syston or Essendine, and take a stagecoach from there. Either way was an arduous journey in the 19th century, meaning, of course, that visitors would necessarily stay at the house for a few days before attempting the return journey, and Anthony would therefore have absorbed the rivalries, and feasibly have attended the church services.

He would also have learnt that an ancestor of the Lindsey family had been Chancellor of the Exchequer and that several other family members were in Parliament. The scene was set for status, one-upmanship, Parliament and long journeys, all of which later occurred in his novels.

Cottered

Anthony's paternal grandfather, also called Anthony, was first cousin to Sir John Trollope, 6th Baronet. He died in 1806, before Anthony was born, leaving Anthony's father, Thomas Anthony, a small legacy enabling him to marry Fanny, his mother. His grandfather had been the rector for forty-four years at St John the Baptist Church in the village of Cottered, three miles from the coaching town of Buntingford (where the Angel Inn was the staging

St John the Baptist Church, Cottered

post for coaches travelling from London to Cambridge), and six miles from Baldock and Stevenage. The parish is situated between two Roman roads: Ermine Street (the present A10), and Stane Street (known locally as Back Lane). The latter was once thought to have been an important pilgrimage route to Walsingham in Norfolk. This and Bronze Age artefacts found nearby may explain the wall painting of St Christopher, patron saint of travellers, on the wall of the nave. Formerly known as St Mary's Church, the oldest part dates from the mid-14th century and has five bells. The description by Neville Chuck, in *Glimpses of Cottered*, is similar to the often overlong introductions to Anthony's novels, i.e. that the village was once divided into two manors, the Manor of Cottered also known as The Lordship, and Cheynes Manor, with several moated houses, inhabited both in the past and recently by notable families including a president of China and members of the Danish royal family.

Rushden

In 1770 Anthony's grandfather additionally became the vicar of St Mary's Church in Rushden, two miles away along a field-track. This parish (divided by hills and split into three separate areas) still comprises a population of only 200 people with a village hall and pub but no shops. His grandfather presumably took on this extra responsibility because of his marriage to Penelope Meetkerke, a marriage which produced six children who, although Anthony's own age, became his great-aunts and uncles. Penelope was the elder sister of Augustus Meetkerke whose family owned the estate of Julians in the village, after which Anthony's parents had named the ill-fated house they had recklessly built in Harrow in expectation of inheriting the estate. However, the myth is confusing as when this elder brother died, he left the estate in 1840 to another Augustus Meetkerke (born in 1819 and only four years older than Anthony), the sixth member of the family with the same name. The idea that Anthony's father thought he would inherit

St Mary's Church, Rushden

the estate in 1840 is strange, but perhaps the myth arose because he had expected to receive some marriage settlement on Fanny which, according to C P Snow in his biography *Trollope* (1975), he did not do, as he had omitted to sign the correct documents.

Julians at Rushden

This large house in Rushden, as featured in *Country Life* of 20th June 1947, is deeply secluded behind an extensive outer park with exotic and specimen trees, walls, pastures and arable land. The estate also includes the Lordship of Rushden and nearby Cumberlow Green (as mentioned in *Mr Scarborough's Family*) with a solid income from farmers' and cottagers' rents. Parts of the property are Jacobean with 18th-century renovations, and the red-brick stable block and formal gardens have Grade II, and Grade II Listed, walls and piers. The inner gardens include stables and yards, forecourt, iron gates, separate formal gardens and several lawns, one of which is approached by a flight of semi-circular stone steps from the house. A circular pond is aligned with the gateway leading to the kitchen garden, while another pond and orchard lie in a wooded area containing a chalk pit with icehouse.

In more recent times Randolph Churchill and Evelyn Waugh stayed in the house. It would indeed have been a wonderful property for the Trollope family to inherit and would have more than solved their financial problems. As Tom remembered visiting Julians many times, staying there and recounting evenings and breakfasts, it is inconceivable that Anthony did not visit also, especially as many of his novels feature 'large houses' with spacious grounds, such as Gatherum Castle in the Palliser novels and *Framley Parsonage*, and Courcy Castle in *Doctor Thorne*.

Anthony's brother Tom recounts visiting Adolphus Meetkerke in *While I Remember*, describing him as '... *being a good landlord, kindly natured, good sportsman, active magistrate, and good husband – but had a sort of "flavour of roughness" about him and his surroundings – pretentious*' – a character Anthony's readers would recognize. Tom also wrote: '*Aunt Meetkerke or properly great-aunt-in-law, admirable specimen of a squires[s], intimately acquainted with the poor in the parish, always came to breakfast in a green riding-habit, and passed most of her life on horseback.*' Again, readers of Anthony's novels would be very familiar with such a character, particularly Adelaide Palliser and Mrs Spooner in the Palliser novels. '*After dinner, in the long low drawing room with its faded stone coloured curtains and bookless desert spaces, she always slept, as peacefully as she does now in Julians' churchyard.*'

Julians, Rushden

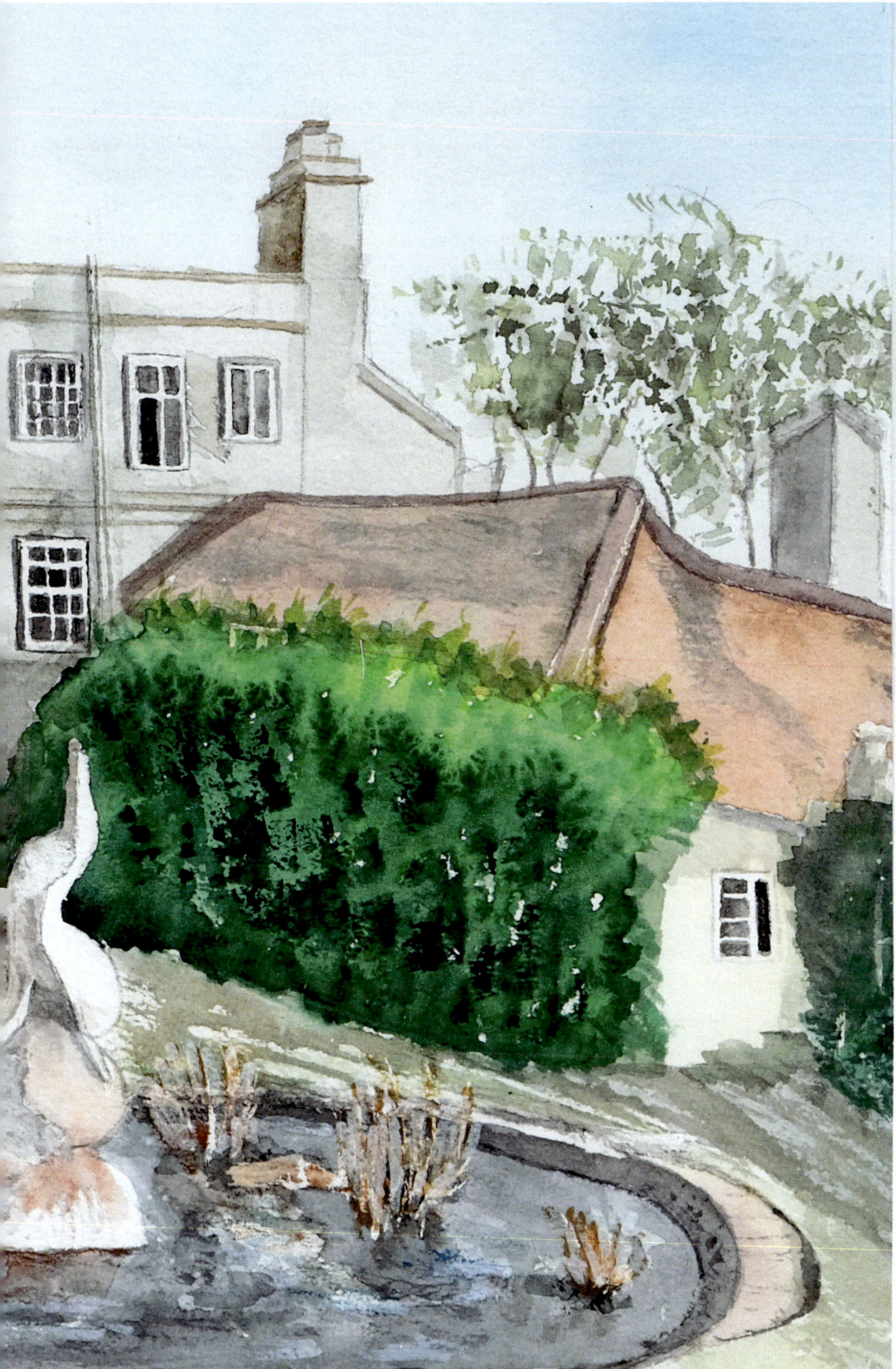

This prosperous and fertile area around Rushden, Cottered and Julians in Hertfordshire in the 19th century boasted a brewery, two pubs, a blacksmith, a wheelwright and a nearby watermill. Although his grandfather was dead at this time, as we shall see, Anthony must have been still aware of this community, and also the history of dissenters, Protestant non-conformists, Quakers and Congregationalists in the area and the building of a Congregational chapel, all situations encountered in his novels. Additionally, in 1855 a special hand-made postage stamp was issued in Cottered and later a post office was run from Flint Cottage, with the sub-postmaster William Pickett doubling up as the headmaster of Cottered School. In the nearby staging post of Buntingford there is also an almshouse, erected in 1684 by Bishop Seth Ward of 'SALISBURY & CHANCELLOR of YE MOST NOBLE ORDER OF YE GARTER', which probably entered Anthony's mind when considering the plot for *The Warden*.

In spite of omitting mention of family visits to Hertfordshire in his *Autobiography*, Anthony drew heavily on his detailed knowledge of the area for several novels set nominally elsewhere. For instance, *The Way We Live Now* (written as late as 1875 and set largely in Norfolk) echoes both his upbringing and this familiar area: Lord Buntingford is a constant figure, Lady Carbury (an authoress) lives in straitened financial circumstances, some of the action is centred in America, a flour mill is mentioned, and families spend time in their first-floor back drawing rooms. Again, several scenes in *Mr Scarborough's Family* (published posthumously in the magazine *All the Year Round* 27th May 1882 to 16th June 1883) are also reminiscent of the fictional village of Buston set in Hertfordshire with squire Mr Prosper living at Buston Hall (probably based on Julians above). Not long before he died in 1882 Anthony was looking back at his life, preoccupied with inheritance, his own Will, how to treat his wife and family fairly, and transferring his own concern for their provision to the '*rich and unconventional John Scarborough*'. Mr Scarborough shares many of his traits: two sons, considerable estate, fond of whist, and more afraid of incapacity than death, the only difference being that Anthony was a devout Christian while Mr Scarborough is an atheist. The book's hero, Harry Annesley, heir to Mr Prosper, worries that Mr Scarborough would take a wife and have children and thus disinherit him: '*In unhappy frame of mind he went down by the train to Stevenage, and was there met by the rectory pony carriage*'. Harry Annesley's father is the rector of Buntingford, and the preposterous Miss Thoroughbung represents the local brewers (see **Cottered** and **Rushden** above).

The watermill at the nearby village of Stotfold on the border of Hertfordshire could also have contributed ideas for the plot of *The Vicar of Bullhampton* (written 1868 and published 1870). Its name derives from drovers penning their horses (stots) in enclosures (folds) when breaking journeys on the Great North Road (now the A1). Anthony insisted his watermill was set near Salisbury (although in later life he told a friend it was in Somerset), but he would have known there were no flour and only woollen mills in the Salisbury area, hence his *'woolcarders'* (bedesmen) at Hiram's Hospital in *The Warden* (1855). However, he was most probably familiar with the now Grade II Listed flour mill in Stotfold (on site for over 1,000 years with new owner John Randall in 1866) as he would certainly have passed through either on a journey to Casewick, or for business or hunting reasons, as it fits descriptions in the book:

> *In front of the building there ran a road – which after all was no more than a private lane. It crossed the smaller stream and the mill-run by two wooden bridges; but the river itself had been too large for the bridge-maker's efforts, and here there was a ford, with stepping-stones for foot passengers.*

It is an easy and pleasant walk across the water meadows to the parish church of St Mary the Virgin (with its tower), and the vicarage (with its *'broad stone steps, with iron balustrades curving outwards as they descended'*) where *'The path ... crossed simply a corner of the church precincts, as it came at once upon a public footway leading from the fields through the churchyard to the town'*. There is also a Methodist and a Baptist church close by to provide inspiration for the Bullhampton rivalries. The incumbent vicars at Stotfold in the mid-19th century were Trinity Cambridge men; one had played cricket at Lord's and his successor became Canon of Gloucester Cathedral.

Maternal Ancestry

Heckfield, Hampshire

Heckfield is a delightfully small and tranquil village set in 862 acres nestling between Reading and the South Downs, on the Duke of Wellington's estate, a couple of miles from Hook station on the South Western railway line. The church of St Michael's is larger than one would expect, but Heckfield is described in the Domesday Book as being originally a busy thoroughfare with an annual fair. Anthony's maternal grandfather, the Reverend William Milton, became the rector aged 31 and remained so until his death at 82. As both Anthony's grandfathers were men of the cloth it is unsurprising that many of his novels are centred on clergymen and their families.

The young Reverend William Milton's father was a saddler who had managed to send his son to Winchester and New College, Oxford and thus to train as a clergyman. The College is still a patron of the parish and since

1379 has had the right to appoint the incumbent just as a similar college had the right to support Mr Harding in *The Warden* (1855). William Milton soon married Mary Gresley, who, like him, had come from a humble background, in contrast to the Trollope side of the family. A year after their marriage, with a living of £120 p.a., William engaged a curate and they moved back to his childhood area of Bristol where they had six children: Mary (1776), Fanny (Anthony's mother, 1779) and Henry (1784), who all lived, and three other children (Cecilia, John and Emily) who all died. Shortly after Henry's birth, Mary their mother died also, when Fanny was about 6 years old. Anthony Trollope often featured clergymen who were either absent from their parishioners (such as the Reverend Stanhope in *The Warden*) or were lazy and left all the work to the curate, although there is no suggestion that the Reverend Milton was lazy. On the contrary, he was scientifically and practically minded: he suggested to the ancient Society of Merchant Venturers that they convert the port of Bristol into a floating harbour. His idea was turned down but later implemented without any credit accorded to him, although his friend Jeremy Osborne had been secretary of the corporation at the time, but there was no rancour as the same Jeremy Osborne later witnessed his Will.

St. Michael's Church, Heckfield

Milton was also concerned with the number of accidents in crowded stagecoaches caused by breaking linchpins. His design for redistributing the centre of gravity of the total load by enlarging the height of the back wheels to 6ft, thus spreading the load 'low and far behind' and preventing deaths from toppling, is in the British Library. He organized a trial demonstration journey with a loose wheel and, when it fell off at 6 mph, the coach had enough momentum to carry on, turn round and return, enabling the coachman to collect the wheel quite safely. After being repaired, it could carry on again at 8 mph. Milton also invented a plate with a silver centre, aimed at preventing noise from scratching cutlery, perhaps necessary if the family were used to eating in silence (or at least until the servants had departed), such as do many of Anthony's later characters who similarly eat their meals in total silence.

Tom chronicles the family interest in stagecoaches and how, as a child after about 8 years old, one of his favourite ramblings was to the White Horse Cellar coaching inn in Piccadilly to watch coaches arriving or starting, particularly those going south and west. He thus knew their routes and speeds, and *'By this means, indeed, came my first introduction to English geography'*.

When William Milton's father died, he used his small inheritance to move the family to a more desirable area of Clifton, where Fanny and her sister Mary, now young ladies, enjoyed the social life and assembly balls (Miss Mackenzie in Anthony's book of that name enjoyed such balls in the fictional Littlebath). Many years later, a peer of the realm told Anthony that *'I danced with her* [your mother] *when she was Fanny Milton, and I remember she had the neatest foot and ankle that I ever saw'* (*Interviews & Recollections* edited by R C Terry). After being a widower for fifteen years the Reverend Milton married Sarah Partington and the family moved back to Heckfield. It is suggested that Fanny did not greatly approve of her stepmother.

The church of St Michael's has a large graveyard with imposing family tombs, including the Reverend William Milton's. There is also a memorial to him inside the church:

SACRED TO THE MEMORY
OF THE REVEREND WILLIAM MILTON, A.M. FORMERLY FELLOW OF NEW COLLEGE, OXFORD, AND FIFTY ONE YEARS VICAR OF THIS PARISH

EMINENT BOTH IN LITERATURE AND SCIENCE, HE ADDED TO THE EXEMPLARY DISCHARGE OF THE DUTIES OF A CHRISTIAN MINISTER THE ELEGANT PURSUITS OF THE SCHOLAR AND THE ACTIVE PROSECUTION OF EXTENSIVE DESIGNS FOR THE PUBLIC GOOD.

HE CLOSED AN USEFUL, AND HONOURABLE LIFE,
ON THE TWELFTH DAY OF JULY MDCCCXXIV,
IN THE EIGHTY FIRST YEAR OF HIS AGE.

> AS A FATHER, A HUSBAND, AND A FRIEND, DEEPLY HAS HIS LOSS
> BEEN FELT AND LONG WILL HIS REMEMBRANCE BE CHERISHED
> HIS REMAINS ARE DEPOSITED IN THE ADJOINING CHURCH-YARD
> ON THE EAST SIDE OF THE CHANCEL DOOR.

Tom described him as '*an excellent parish priest after the fashion of his day* [i.e. caring, kind, liberal] *with a sort of Horatian easy-going geniality about him*' and '*never being satisfied of anything when it seemed practicable to improve it*'. He also said that he preferred visits to Heckfield rather than Julians at Rushden because the village was '*situated in an extremely pretty country*', but that '*the main reason for the preference was that the old Bristol saddler's son was a far more highly-cultured man than the Hertfordshire squire*'.

The church is secluded behind trees and surrounded by a small cluster of equally secluded but magnificent residences. Beside the church is the beautiful early-Georgian house Highfield Place, built around 1819 with cellars which are much older. In the early 20th century this was the home of former Prime Minister Neville Chamberlain (famous for declaring '*peace in our time*' just before the Second World War) and is now a hotel. The building has several of Anthony's favourite large bay windows all around, with mature gardens having uninterrupted views over the ha-ha to Heckfield Heath and Riseley Common. One mile away is Stratfield Saye House, the family seat of the Dukes of Westminster. Later Horatio Walpole would live at nearby Park Corner and the Shaw Lefevre family also lived locally. The young Anthony must surely have visited Heckfield, attended church, seen the notable dignitaries, and viewed Stratfield Saye House in all its splendour, and been aware also that the Duke of Wellington preferred his smaller and simpler residence at Apsley House in London (perhaps a later model for the character of Plantagenet Palliser).

The Reverend William Milton declared in his Will that he wished his books, papers, Bristol Cup, and the remainder of his silver plate be given in equal portions to his three children and '*give moreover to my daughters £300, after taking into account what I have already advanced to my daughter Francis* [Fanny] *on her marriage to Anthony Trollope and what I have also advanced about the same time to my daughter Mary*'. £300 would be the equivalent of about £25,000 today.

Fulham

Fanny's younger brother Henry lived with his wife, Mary Anne, at Fulham, only nine miles away from Harrow, and again the young Anthony's family must surely have exchanged regular visits. Indeed, as stated earlier, Tom's memoir describes visiting Fanny's brother and family at Fulham one

Sunday morning, all alone, before breakfast by walking from Harrow to Fulham. He then did *'ample justice'* to the *'very solid and varied breakfast'* before accompanying the family to Fulham church and, despite standing up during the sermon, could not stop himself *'falling asleep and jerking awake with a bow'*.

Again, Anthony's novels contain many references to Fulham: in *Ralph the Heir,* the barrister Sir Thomas Underwood's daughters, Patience and Clarissa, live at Popham Villa on the banks of the Thames at Fulham where young men in turn visit them and spend pleasant evenings sitting out by the river. Five miles away, Lady Cantrip entertains at The Horns at Richmond, while Mrs Montacute Jones has a *'great garden party'* at Roehampton two miles further away from Harrow; and in *The Duke's Children* Miss Boncassen holds her river party twelve miles further towards Hampshire at Maidenhead, such places all being on the way to Heckfield when travelling by coach.

Exeter

Whilst Anthony's mother's cousin, Miss Fanny Bent, lived just outside Exeter at 8 York Buildings in the parish of St Sidwell's, local folklore suggests that what is now the Headmaster's House for Exeter Cathedral School fits the description of the fictitious home (*'behind the cathedral'*) of Jemima Stanbury in *He Knew He Was Right* (1869): as she *'...lives in a large brick house with beautiful gardens in the Cathedral Close'*.

Like Fanny Bent, Aunt Jemima is *'a maiden lady very much respected, indeed, in the city of Exeter'* and *'In the matter of politics she had long since come to think that everything good was over. She hated the name of Reform'*. She also hates modern fashions, especially crinolines and chignons which she calls *'those bandboxes which the sluts wear behind their noddles'*; Anthony confessed that *'she allowed herself the use of much strong language'*. This indomitable character was prone to making Tom giggle when walking up the nave of the cathedral and was fearless in climbing towers in Europe and accompanying Henry in climbing rocks on geological expeditions – nothing of which was mentioned in Anthony's *Autobiography*.

Anthony and family often travelled to Devon to visit Fanny Bent, as it would not be far away from the Milton family in Heckfield, and the children spent many school holidays with her which was not mentioned by Anthony in his *Autobiography*, nor the fact that she frequently gave them pocket money and helped financially when later they fled to Bruges. Anthony's mother often turned to Fanny Bent for help, and particularly when Henry was too ill with TB to travel with them to Bruges, she escorted him down to Exeter to leave him in her care.

Pamela Neville-Sington in *Trollopiana* no. 39 (Journal of the Trollope Society, 1997) says that aunts and *'honorary'* aunts feature in at least twelve of Anthony's novels, including the unscrupulous Lady Monk, and the formidable Marchioness of Auld Reekie. She pointed out that they made marvellous plot-devices with their many quirks of character, and that in both real life and fiction they often stepped into the role of surrogate mother when so many died either in childbirth or of tuberculosis (as in Anthony's own family) or suffered sudden financial misfortune. In *He Knew He Was Right* the fatherless Dorothy Stanbury goes to live in Exeter with her cantankerous aunt Miss Jemima Stanbury to ease her mother's and sister's financial burdens.

Possible model for 'Aunt Jemima's House' in Exeter

Wider Family

In *While I Remember* Tom described her as:

Very plain in feature who, dressed with Quaker-like simplicity and an utter disregard for appearance ... [she] was as well known in Exeter as the cathedral towers. She had a position and enjoyed an amount of respect which was really singular in the case of a very homely-featured old maid of very small fortune ... she was a thoroughgoing Churchwoman and Conservative ... she had a strong sense of humour.

Anthony's fictional Aunt Jemima was '*... a little woman, now nearly 60 years of age, with bright grey eyes, and a strong Roman nose, and thin lips, and a sharp-cut-chin*'.

Through the Palace Gate beside the house is a fine square with large Georgian houses around the green, most of which are now converted into offices. Alas, instead of the '*iron box*' denounced by Miss Stanbury as unreliable in preference to the Post Office, there is a bank of three modern post boxes in Barnfield Road to deal with the increased mail.

It is clear from the above that even when very young, Anthony's childhood memories influenced many of his characters and their daily lives and situations; his absorption of their surroundings enabled him to understand his characters' lives and emotions.

Modern line-up of post boxes in Exeter

Education

Anthony's parents' strong belief in the importance of education stemmed from the fact that the only careers open to young men of their class involved the church, law, Oxford or Cambridge, or the military (unless inheriting a family estate), and therefore part of the reason for the move to Harrow was that as parishioners all the boys would be eligible to go to Harrow School as Day Boarders, before going on to Winchester. Also, one of the masters, Henry Drury, was a friend of Anthony's father. Unfortunately, lack of funds, debts and resultant health issues necessitated many changes to the Trollope family plans.

Harrow School

> ... as [his father] *had friends among the masters at Harrow, and as the school offered an education almost gratuitous to children living in the parish, he ... determined to use that august seminary as a 't'other' school for Winchester, and sent three of us there, one after the other, at the age of seven.*

So said Anthony in his *Autobiography*, explaining that the boys, including Arthur before he died, were able to attend with very low fees by living in the parish, implying that his father had made at least one sensible decision at the time of their move. Tom, in his autobiography, did not paint such a degrading financial picture as Anthony, but of course being older, when he first attended Harrow the family were relatively successful and happy; by the time Anthony joined the school in 1823, the family's financial problems had begun to accumulate. Tom did, however, comment that the Headmaster, despite being incredibly fat '... *was able to give a flogging and liked to start the week with one ...*'

There had been a school at Harrow since 1243, but in 1615 a rich farmer, John Lyon, formally founded and financed a '*little school with some boarders*' as a memorial to his own dead children; by the time Anthony and his brothers attended, Joseph Drury had developed it into primarily a boarding school. Being a Day Boarder amongst full boarders today would be considered quite normal, staying at school for prep and dinner and going home at about 8 p.m., but in a very socially conscious 19th-century society, it would have highlighted a general financial insecurity and been something of a social stigma. Anthony was particularly sensitive and aware of this social disability, and I suggest his misery at having to walk to and from school was not the walking per se (as stated above – although without street lighting it would have been scarily dark in winter – his father walked from Harrow to Lincoln's Inn daily) but rather the real stigma in those days of being a Day Boy. Characters in his novels are minutely aware of other characters' social standing, income, friends' and relatives' incomes, which members of 'Society' they knew, and which person they should marry in order to obtain a fortune. Coincidentally, in 2019 when needing to check the way to the school from the station, I asked a couple of passers-by: one responded '*Ah, the posh boys*' and the other '*Oh, the rich ones*'! Although the school is co-ed today, there are cascades of boys in smart pale grey trousers, navy blazers and straw boaters swarming around. It seems fashionable for them to have their hands in their pockets, something I imagine Anthony would not have been able to do as the fashion for tight breeches at that time would have made it impossible.

The village of Harrow on the Hill, up a steep incline from the station and modern thoroughfare below, is quite unspoilt with curving narrow streets, narrow alleyways and steps down to roads on lower levels, amongst mainly late-Victorian or Edwardian buildings. The magnificent school buildings take up most of the area at the peak, with houses, library, schoolrooms and two churches. The school originally consisted of one large room on

Modern boys at Harrow School

the ground floor holding a different class in each corner, the youngest two classes being at one end and two senior classes at the other end. Apart from a white marble fireplace, the room still has its small, high windows and dark oak panelling up to two-thirds of the walls – panelling now full of carvings by successive pupils. It is extremely dark nowadays on winter afternoons, and when lit by candlelight would have been particularly gloomy.

Anthony would have studied from 6 a.m. to 6 p.m., with a short break for lunch, and two new monitors (prefects) chosen each week. The Headteacher overlooked everyone from a high wooden seat and lectern, below which was a low stool where boys bent over for their canings – for which they could choose their own type of birch from a cupboard containing a selection.

One day, when the masters were upstairs having lunch and the children downstairs having theirs, a child carved his name above the heavy door and was of course expelled on the spot, but despite punishments successive boys followed the example until the whole space was filled and Anthony crammed his name meticulously into a corner, sideways from top to bottom – A TROLLOPE (reinforcing the suggestion that he stayed at school for lunch – see below). Other names include Byron, Sheridan, Peel, Spencer Perceval, with the name PALLISER perhaps giving future inspiration for Anthony's well-known Palliser novels, coupled with a later Reverend Palliser who baptized his own children. As mass expulsion was impractical and whipping unsuccessful, it eventually became a tradition for every boy's name to be professionally carved on boards displayed in their boarding houses. Outside the front of the school is the Milling Ground where Anthony, bullied for many years by a boy called Lewis, eventually lost patience and challenged him: they reputedly fought ferociously for an hour. It is said that Lewis' injuries were so great that he took three days to recover.

Anthony's belief that he was '*big and awkward and ugly*', and '*skulked about in a most unattractive manner*' was reinforced by the Headmaster stopping him in the street once and asking him:

> ... *with all the clouds of Jove upon his brow and all the thunder in his voice, whether it was possible that Harrow School was disgraced by so disreputably dirty a little boy as I! Oh, what I felt at that moment! But I could not look my feelings. I do not doubt that I was dirty; but I think that he was cruel. He must have known me had he seen me as he was wont to see me, for he was in the habit of flogging me constantly. Perhaps he did not recognize me by my face.*

Harrow School

Anthony always maintained he learnt nothing at all at school except Latin and omitted to mention a school prize for English: Lord Bessborough lamented years later that Anthony had beaten him to a prize he had especially hoped to achieve (*Harrow School*, Howson and Warner, p. 72). Today, Anthony's achievements are commemorated in his coat of arms housed in the nearby Speech Room. He also said he had no friends, but he remained on good terms with some of his contemporaries who knew him later as a famous man. Sir William Gregory of Coole, an Anglo-Irish Squire and later Governor of Ceylon, in his memoir stated:

> *I avoided him, for he was rude and uncouth but I thought him an honest brave fellow. His faults were external; all the rest of him was right enough. But the faults were of that character for which schoolboys will never make allowances and so poor Trollope was tabooed ... He gave no sign of promise whatever, was always in the lowest part of the form ...*

However, only a few years later Anthony was a frequent guest at Coole and they hunted together. When both were in their sixties, Anthony stayed for weeks with him in the Governor's mansion in Ceylon. Another school friend, Thomas Henry Baylis QC, author of *The Rights, Duties and Relations of Domestic Servants, their Masters and Mistresses* (1857), wrote:

> *I entered the school [Harrow] at the age of eight, and left as a monitor at sixteen; I was first a home-boarder [Day Boy], but afterwards went into Oxenham's House. While a home-boarder we lived at Greenhill Green, and Anthony Trollope, whom I remember well, used to call for me on his way to the school. I used to sit next to him in the Sixth Form. I think he much exaggerated his Harrow sufferings; they were less than other home-boarders who went young to the school: they were often sadly bullied and pursued with stones on their way home.*
>
> *Anthony Trollope: His Work, Association and Literary Originals* (THS Escott, 1913)

Byron's illegitimate 4-year-old daughter, Allegra, is buried under the porch of the nearby St Mary's Church, as the Reverend John Cunningham, being a governor of the school, did not allow her to be buried in the graveyard – perhaps in protest, Anthony's heroines often read Byron, and his *Autobiography* states: 'In our own century what literary names stand higher than those of Byron, Tennyson, Scott, Dickens, Macaulay, and Carlyle?'

It was this same Reverend John Cunningham whose Evangelicalism was satirized in the slimy Mr Slope in the Barchester novels and by his mother Fanny in *The Vicar of Wrexhill*.

Film buffs will of course know that Harrow School is often used by film companies, e.g. for parts of *Harry Potter* and *The Crown*.

Sunbury

In early 1825, Anthony was briefly moved to a private school at Sunbury kept by Arthur Drury, brother of his Harrow tutor Henry Drury. Although still without pocket money, he felt that he lived '*more nearly on terms of equality with other boys than at any other period during* [his] *schooldays*'. However, even there he complained he was wrongly punished for a misdemeanour and not allowed out until he had written a long sermon. Although he received an apology, he still remembered the incident fifty years later in his *Autobiography*:

> ... it burns me now as though it were yesterday. What lily-livered curs those boys must have been not to have told the truth! – at any rate as far as I am concerned I remember their names well, and almost wish to write them here.

He then went back to Harrow School before going on to Winchester.

Winchester

Like Henry and Tom before him, Anthony began boarding at Winchester aged 12, from the spring of 1827 to the summer of 1830, one and a half of those years overlapping with Tom. He stated that during their schooldays he felt his brother to be '*of all my foes, the worst*': '*I have been flogged oftener than any human being alive. It was just possible to obtain five scourgings in one day at Winchester, and I have often boasted that I obtained them all*'.

Tom was designated Anthony's tutor and ruler and, as Anthony described it, exacted obedience by thrashing him with a big stick as '*part of his daily exercise*', although of course this is not how Tom remembered it, and Anthony again forgot to mention in his *Autobiography* that by the time he left he was a monitor.

According to Tom, the Entrance Examination consisted of '*Well, boy, can you sing?*' '*Yes, sir.*' '*Let us hear you*'. Boy speaks in ordinary voice. '*Very well, boy. That will do! – Exam over.*'

Daily routine consisted of rising at 5.30 a.m., chapel at 6.30, school at 7.30, followed by bread, cheese and 'bobs' (huge jugs) of beer in the afternoon. Dinner was in the evening, except Sundays when it was served in the middle of the day and any spare roast beef was given to twenty-four old women who weeded the college quad (see Hiram's Hospital in *The Warden*, below).

In the college is a graffiti wall, with a clear spidery carving of 'A TROLLOPE' alongside those of his contemporaries in a similar fashion to that at Harrow, although unfortunately the second 'O' has eroded away.

Both boys felt they left Winchester, as they did Harrow, as: *'fairly good Latin scholar[s], and well grounded .... In Greek; and very ignorant indeed of all else'*. In later life Anthony forgot any beatings and admitted that *'few brothers have had more of brotherhood'*. Both became successful writers and were able to confer with and influence one another.

It was in 1827, just after Anthony began at Winchester, that Fanny went to America, and Anthony (and Tom) presumably spent their holidays at Harrow Weald. However, a year later in September 1828 Anthony's father took Tom with him to visit her and the other children, leaving Anthony alone at Winchester. According to Tom in *While I Remember*, they stayed with Fanny for *'between five and six months'*. This would have left Anthony alone at Winchester over the Christmas holiday period which seems particularly sad, and perhaps the following Easter as well. However, the college archivist, Suzanne Foster, says there are no records of his staying on during the holidays, and that he was quite likely taken home by the Headmaster or second master. I write this during the Covid lockdown of 2020–1 when many boarders at my grandson's school could not go home for Christmas and stayed instead with a master or schoolfriend. Although it is believed that Christmases in the 1820s and 1830s were not celebrated as they are today, with the first Christmas card not being sent until 1843, Suzanne Foster found A K Cook's book *About Winchester College* (Macmillan and Co., 1917), which states that:

> ... at the end of the 17th cent there was a break from school work at Christmas, but by no means everybody went home. By 1768 this break had become a real holiday, lasting three weeks, extended to four in 1791 after a successful solicitation by epistle for their extension.

It is conceivable of course that relatives collected Anthony, or even a stable hand from the farm at Harrow Weald.

The college pupil lists (known as 'long rolls') show that Anthony left in the spring or summer of 1830, a little while before Fanny's return in 1831.

During this time, the teenage Anthony was extra sensitive and conscious of his clumsy appearance: he recorded that his father forgot to send him money, and was deeply embarrassed that not only were his college bills unpaid and tradesmen told not to allow him credit, but also that '*Boots, waistcoats, and pocket-handkerchiefs, which, with some* slight superveillance, were at the command of other scholars, were closed luxuries to me', and he wore his shabby patched clothes. He was also deprived of the essential one shilling a week pocket money, called a 'battel', which other boys received in order to pay for any extra attention needed from servants – he thought that this would have been humiliatingly obvious to all the other boys and staff.

> *I suffered horribly ... I could make no stand against it. I had no friend to whom I could pour out my sorrows ... ah! How well I remember all the agonies of my young heart; how I considered whether I should always be alone; whether I could not find my way up to the top of that college tower, and from thence put an end to everything?*

Ironically, Anthony would have been intelligent enough to join the sixth form and continue to Oxford aged 19, as his father had earlier wished all three boys to do (only Tom managed to go, briefly, to Alban Hall), but as there was no money for this, in 1831 he returned once again, humiliatingly, to Harrow School as a Day Boarder. Having left Harrow briefly for Sunbury and returned, and a second time for Winchester, he now returned once again for a further 18 months. However, his life might have been very different if he had remained at Winchester, as over 60 per cent of pupils became High Anglicans and priests of the Church of England. Anthony may not have been as successful at such an occupation as he was at writing novels, and he would probably have rejected the Oxford Movement like his character Archdeacon Grantly in *Barchester Towers*.

However, Anthony almost certainly exaggerated problems in his *Autobiography*, specifically his complaint about the twelve miles per day he was forced to walk from Harrow Weald, all alone, to and from Harrow School. The distance from Harrow Weald to Harrow School by road is 2.6 miles, and as the boys usually had only between 10 and 30 minutes for lunch it would have been unrealistic for him to walk that distance home, eat lunch and return within that time. This means he would probably have walked to school once in the morning and back in the evening, making a total of perhaps five miles per day and, as stated earlier, walking or horse-riding in that era were the only modes of transport and therefore quite usual. If he really did go home for lunch as he said, it would 'only' make a total of eight miles by modern roads, and in the Victorian era there would probably have been short cuts across fields or, as he put it, 'muddy lanes', and a reason for always being splashed with mud and grime.

> *What right had a wretched farmer's boy, reeking from a dunghill, to sit next to the sons of peers, or much worse still, next to the*

sons of big tradesmen who had made their ten thousand a-year? The indignities I endured are not to be described.

Nevertheless, it would have been dreary and particularly so in the dark winter months without street lighting, and the terrain as he described it would have been very muddy. Schools are still located to serve students within a radius of 4–5 miles' walking distance (although parents now use their SUVs), and school lunch breaks at Harrow School still comply with those 10–30 minutes. Anthony was certainly selective in his *Autobiography* about his boring and uncomfortable walk from Harrow Weald but however many miles he walked he found them to have been an advantage in later life as whilst walking he wove stories and characters in his head which he later drew upon in his novels.

I did not manage to walk the route Anthony would have taken to school from Harrow Weald, but I retraced the footsteps he would have taken from Julians and Illots Farm, along a short dark and wooded lane (probably less than a quarter of a mile long) before emerging into the main thoroughfare, and presumably at that period there would have been neighbours also walking or driving their carriages up and down, together with farm carts and tradesmen.

Outside the graffiti wall at Winchester School

Fanny's Visit to America

Fanny's visit to America was initially unfortunate, both for her and for Anthony, although it later sparked the beginning of both their successful careers as writers. Understandably, it was difficult and upsetting for Anthony at the time, but as shown earlier, he learnt how to weave stories in his head whilst walking to school, and the fact that he had to leave Winchester and go back to Harrow saved him from going on to Oxford and ultimately entering the ministry.

Also as stated above, it was in 1827, whilst the family residence was at Harrow Weald and Anthony and Tom were boarding at Winchester School, that Fanny made the visit with her friend Fanny Wright, a ward of General La Fayette. Her decision was made partly with the altruistic idea of improving the lot of the slave population in the southern states, partly to find employment for the eldest son, Henry (perhaps the ministry, military or education were unsuitable for him), and partly to earn some money. In addition to Henry, she also took the young girls Cecilia and Emily with their tutor, Auguste Hervieu.

Predictably, things did not go according to plan, so she moved on to Cincinnati with the equally grand idea of creating an emporium of bazaar, lecture hall and athenaeum. Inevitably this venture also failed as the building was improbably situated in the middle of an uncultivated field several minutes' walk away from town, without a roadway. To compound the failure her husband spent money they could ill afford by buying unsuitable trinkets and shipping them out for her to sell. She lamented having to sleep on the floor and sell something expressly to buy Cecilia some shoes. The intended American experience was an abject failure, and after three years she returned with the children, including Henry, who had not found any employment. Whether or not she had intended at the outset to stay for this length of time is unknown, but as various setbacks occurred during her time there, she probably stayed longer than anticipated. She wrote constant letters, and Frances Eleanor Trollope later recorded one sent to Tom saying: '*My poor dear Anthony will have outgrown his recollection! Tell him not to outgrow his affection for us! No day passes, hardly an hour – without our talking of you all.*'

This was obviously the most upsetting time for Anthony and would have coloured his later judgement, especially during the school holidays, and most particularly when his father took Tom to visit her, leaving him alone at Winchester. However, once again there are some inconsistencies in his account. Why, if he was at Winchester during the Christmas (and possibly Easter) holiday, had he to go to Lincoln's Inn, all alone, during his father's absence? If this episode referred to a later holiday once he was back at Harrow School, it would still be unusual as there would have been staff running the house and farm. When the family later fled to Bruges, they took two servants with them, implying that at least two must have been employed, and maybe more. Also, his numerous relatives would surely have visited him, or most likely invited him to stay with them.

Anthony was scathing of his father in his *Autobiography*, for his many mistakes and bad judgements, but his father did also work incredibly hard within his limits – running two farms, practising law, walking to and from Lincoln's Inn, researching his own writings, worried sick about money, a long time without a wife or older children to confer with and suffering intense headaches – perhaps addicted as we have seen, or perhaps suffering a breakdown, or perhaps in the early stages of dementia.

There were, however, some jolly times as Tom recounts how he and Anthony, at some point during this time, having the exact amount between them of 2 shillings entrance money, walked fourteen miles to Vauxhall Pleasure Gardens, danced all night, and walked the fourteen miles back – not only did they choose to do so for pleasure but also on empty stomachs.

Whatever the truth, whether this period was exaggerated or falsely remembered, it is accurate to say that writing retrospectively during a bout of depression, Anthony genuinely felt abandoned, unloved and uncared for, and never forgot this perceived period of neglect. This may explain his adult projection of an over-boisterous, noisy, exuberant character, whilst being inwardly reserved and hiding his real feelings. Children in Victorian families were born in large numbers and people were resigned to the fact that many died in infancy. C P Snow suggested he developed a Nordic stoicism at this time: things could hardly get worse, and it was '*dogged as does it*', an expression he gave to Mr Crawley in *Framley Parsonage* (1861). It is also often commented that the single-minded Mr Crawley was reminiscent of his father.

Fortunately, Fanny's experiences in America were not wholly unsuccessful: she achieved her goal of making money when she wrote the first of many travelogues on her return in autumn 1831. Accordingly, *The Domestic Manners of the Americans* (1832), described as both snobbish and funny, was very popular in England but understandably not so in

America, as it complained of people putting their feet up on the tables, spitting and being vulgar. She went on to write for more than twenty years, in *'receipt of considerable income from her writings'*. Thirty years later Anthony wrote his own book on America from a different perspective.

School Holidays / Lincoln's Inn

As we know, whilst his mother was away Anthony spent his school holidays with his father, then a practising Chancery barrister, in his Chambers at 23 Old Square (built 1500), behind New Square (built 1680) in Middle Temple, before transferring to larger ones at Lincoln's Inn.

But also, as stated above, when his father and Tom joined his mother and sisters in Cincinnati for five or six months from September 1827, Anthony claimed he spent his whole summer holiday alone in these Chambers, reading Shakespeare, this being the only reading material he could find. I find this puzzling as by Tom's account they returned from America in February or March 1828, but if he was wrong and Anthony was alone in the summer holiday, it would still be unusual for him to need to go to Lincoln's Inn (a long walk as we have seen above) without his father, as the family had supportive relatives and staff. Anthony also had at least one school friend from Harrow living nearby. Perhaps he was referring to occasions when he accompanied his father to Lincoln's Inn at times when he necessarily went out for a spell to visit a client.

However, we know Anthony did accompany his father on several previous occasions and described the dark dingy rooms where a pupil had previously committed suicide. These holidays were generally monotonous and dismal enough; if he really did go alone, they would have been particularly so in otherwise deserted Chambers:

> There is, I think, no sadder place in the world than the waiting-room attached to an attorney's chambers in London. In this instance it was a three-cornered room, which had got itself wedged in between the house which fronted to Lincoln's Inn Fields and some buildings in a narrow lane that ran at the back of the row. There was no carpet in it and hardly any need of one, as the greater part of the floor was strewed with bundles of dusty papers.

Although Anthony later called himself 'an idle, desolate hanger-on, that most hopeless of human beings, a hobbledehoy of nineteen, without any idea of a career, or a profession, or a trade', he was already, even as a teenage schoolboy, building up his store of memories. Many of his novels contain characters and places based on his early experiences of his time at Lincoln's Inn: Sir Thomas Underwood in *Ralph the Heir* (1871) worked, lived and slept in his gloomy Chambers with a decrepit manservant-cum-assistant; while waiting for her cousin and future husband, John Ball, Miss Mackenzie visited similar Chambers in *Miss Mackenzie* (1865) and stood under the Carey's Walk gateway to Lincoln's Inn:

> She was to meet Mr Ball there, and also to meet Mr Ball's lawyer. Of course she consented to go, and of course she was on Mr Slow's staircase exactly at the time appointed.
> Of what was she thinking as she walked around Lincoln's Inn Fields to kill a quarter of an hour which she found herself to have on hand, we will not now enquire ...
> They were still standing on the pavement, where the street comes out from under the archway. She was gazing into his face, and he was looking away from her over towards the inner railings of the square, with heavy brow and dull eye and motionless face.

Anthony's father is portrayed as the crochety and stubborn Reverend Josiah Crawley with his disputed cheque in *The Last Chronicle of Barset* (1867); and perhaps Louis Trevelyan in *He Knew He Was Right* (1869), and most novels contain inheritance squabbles or discussions about Wills (*Mr Scarborough's Family*, 1883; *Orley Farm*, 1862), or tenant and other legal disputes. There are many lawyers: the flimsy Mr Getemthruit (*Three Clerks*, 1858), the serious Judge Stavely (*Orley Farm*) and the formidable criminal Lawyer Mr Chaffanbass (Phineas Finn's trial at the Old Bailey in *Phineas Redux* (1873) and Messrs Slow & Bideawhile (*Orley Farm*, *Miss Mackenzie* and *The Way We Live Now*).

Although he criticized his father many times in his *Autobiography* for his stubbornness, lack of attention to detail and foolishness in financial affairs, Anthony nevertheless treated fictional characters based on him with kindness and respect, such as Mr Crawley ('*dogged as does it*') and the amiable Sir Thomas who treated his family calmly and fairly, even if a little remotely.

A jokey legal epigram may also have been later remembered by Anthony as influencing the behaviour of his characters:

> To cause delay in Lincoln's Inn
> Two different methods tend:
> His Lordship's judgements ne'er begin,
> His Honour's never end.

('His Lordship' refers to the Earl of Eldon *'whose every hour is dedicated to learned dullness'* (Mr Getemthruit?) and 'His Honour' refers to Sir Thomas Plumer *'for the delays in Chancery ... a disposition to hesitate ... because he was anxious not to do an injustice'* (Mr Chaffanbrass?).

Jeremy Bentham criticized such lampooning, believing instead that delays in decision-making were inevitable due to the surge in legal cases from increasing population and commerce, with the addition of Appeals from the union with Ireland, a topic of special interest to Anthony. Another source of inspiration for his dramatic courtroom scenes and legal characters might later have been his own court appearance after uncovering misdemeanours in Irish post offices.

Just inside Carey's Walk gate (below) is the necessary drinking fountain and horse trough.

Victorian horse trough at Carey's Walk, Lincoln's Inn

Carey's Walk, Lincoln's Inn

Bruges

After Fanny's return to Harrow, once more providing the family with merriment, it was finally realized that even with the money coming in from her successful book, debts were continuing to pile up, and if Mr Trollope was not moved away, he would find himself in the Marshalsea prison (like Dickens' father).

Consequently, in 1834 they fled to Bruges (Belgium being the home of radicals, writers and free thinkers, and a typical refuge for people fleeing from debt), where they stayed for twenty months. Just in time, Anthony was commandeered to drive his father in the gig to Tower Bridge for the Ostend boat, the thirteen-hour crossing being the cheapest way. As his father had been severely seasick earlier when crossing to America, he was probably also sick whilst crossing to Belgium. As Anthony drove home, he met a neighbour who informed him that the bailiffs were confiscating their possessions: as they took items from the front of the house, neighbours such as Colonel Grant (whose daughter married Peregrine Birch, Clerk in the House of Lords and future friend of Anthony, again dispelling the ideas of loneliness and isolation) rescued others from the back of the house. After Fanny quickly took Henry to Exeter to stay with Fanny Bent, the rest of the family followed to Bruges.

Once there, as Pamela Neville-Sington wrote in *Trollopiana* no. 55 (2001), they rented the Chateau d'Hondt, a three-storey unfurnished suburban villa just outside the walls. For a penniless family, it remains an unexpectedly superior property, described by Fanny as being:

> ... very large, ... in order to make believe that it is furnished ingenuity is obliged to do the work of money and I am plotting and planning from morning to night how to make one table and two chairs do the work of a dozen.

Since then, the Chateau has fortunately and beautifully been kept by the same family for a century, and has imposing rooms with connecting doors, a large marble fireplace, and a graceful spiral staircase. Cecilia and Emily helped make the house pleasant. Then Henry arrived, feeling ill, and Tom soon returned to England to take up a teaching post.

At first all seemed well, and Anthony enjoyed his summer there. Released from his schooldays, he wrote: '*As well as I can remember I was fairly happy for there were pretty girls at Bruges with whom I could fancy that I was in love*', and Fanny maintained her sociable nature by entertaining a multitude of guests, both Belgian and English. They were particularly amused by a Monsieur Grascour who, with Anthony's extraordinary memory, materialized many years later in *Mr Scarborough's Family* (1883):

> *... he would have been taken as an Englishman were his own country not known. He had dressed himself in English mirrors, living mostly with the English. He spoke English so well that he would only be known as a foreigner by the correctness of his language.*

However, once again distress followed the family, this time in a particularly tragic way. First Henry and then his father became ill with tuberculosis, while Emily also began to exhibit symptoms. Feeling compelled to earn enough money to send Henry to a warmer climate, the standard cure in those days, Fanny began writing her third novel, *Tremordyn Cliff* – a mirror of Henry's condition. Together with two female servants she watched over him by day and wrote in the early mornings and after eight in the evenings, aided by green tea and sometimes laudanum. Anthony wrote:

> *The doctor's vials and the ink-bottle held equal places in my mother's rooms. I have written many novels under many circumstances, but I doubt much whether I could write one when my whole heart was by the bedside of a dying son. Her power of dividing herself into two parts, and keeping her intellect by itself clear from the world, and fit for the duty it had to do, I never saw equalled.*

Henry died a lingering death in 1834 aged 23, and ten months later, on the afternoon of 23rd October, the father, Thomas Anthony, died aged 62 after increasingly erratic fits of rage: a decent age according to Victorian perceptions. Anthony's novels often describe a 50-year-old as '*an old man*' or even a '*stooped old man*'; he once described Fanny as '*an old lady of fifty-five*'.

Henry and Thomas Anthony are buried near one another in the Protestant area of the cemetery outside the Catherine Gate of the town.

In 2001 some members of the Trollope Society visited the chateau, guided by Pamela Neville-Sington, when another member, Allen Holliday, discovered that in Chapter III of Anthony's third novel, *La Vendée* (1850), he describes: '*a large square building, three storeys high, with seven front windows to each of the upper storeys, and three on each side of the large door of the ground floor. Eight stone steps of great width led up to the front door*'; and '*between the top step and the door there was a square flagged area of considerable space*', exactly fitting the chateau as it still is today. La Vendée is set in Poitou during the French Revolution and was not well received at the time. As Anthony did not remember various happy times in his *Autobiography* it is remarkable that he should remember such detail twenty years later, although in mitigation he may have had the opportunity to see the building again on later visits abroad either for the Post Office or holidays. His neglected play *The Noble Jilt* (1851), also set in Bruges around the time of the French Revolution, did not have a good reception either and has largely been forgotten.

He also used his knowledge of Belgium when Phineas Finn in the book of that name fights a duel with Lord Chiltern on '*the sands at Blankenberg, a little fishing town some twelve miles distant from Bruges*', and Gertrude in one of his last books, *Ayala's Angel*, published in 1881 not long before his death, elopes to Ostend with Captain Benjamin Batsby in search of a non-existent clergyman who specialises in such runaway weddings,

Meanwhile Anthony was offered a commission in an Austrian cavalry regiment in Brussels, for which he needed to speak French and German. In order to acquire free linguistic skills, he became a classical usher (teaching assistant) for thirty boys at a school kept by Henry Drury, a former Harrow schoolmaster; an unlikely occurrence if, as he said, he had indeed had a bad relationship with his former schoolmasters. Predictably, after taking the boys out for a couple of walks, Mrs Drury declared that the '*boys' clothes would not stand any further experiments of that kind*'. However, Anthony was saved from military duties when his mother approached her dearest friend Mrs Freeling, wife of Clayton Freeling, whose father, Sir Francis Freeling, then ruled the Post Office. Consequently, aged 19, Anthony was sent back to London to begin a career that became most fortuitous for him.

While Anthony was sent back to London to begin his new career, conversely Tom (now a private tutor in London) travelled alone in the opposite direction back to Bruges for both their brother's and their father's funerals.

We have a glimpse of Anthony's character and seeming coolness in relation to his family, as when writing more than forty years later and looking back over so great a lapse of time, he said he could tell the story at first almost as calmly as he could a scene of intended pathos in fictions, '*but the scene was indeed full of pathos*', but then tenderly and more understandingly: '*becoming alive to the misery of the blighted ambition of his father's life, and becoming alive also to the evidence of the strain which his mother endured*'. Although he could do nothing but go and leave them in Bruges, at least he was comforted by the idea that he would no longer be a burden. Perhaps he had begun to appreciate the difficulties they too endured: '*a fallacious idea, as it soon proved*' because he was unable to manage his own finances in his early career at the Post Office and ran into debt.

Steps of the Chateau d'Hondt, Bruges

Thomas Anthony Trollope L.LB
Late Fellow of New College, Oxford, Barrister-at-Law

It is true that all who knew Anthony's father considered him to be austere and *'difficult'* but I wonder if this is undeserved. He was regarded as an utter failure in life, with no successful achievements: a failure in his financial dealings, a failure in his marriage settlements, a failure in his farming attempts, and by all accounts a failure as a barrister as his extreme grumpiness drove clients away.

However, he fathered seven children and strove to provide for the four who were still alive at the time of his death. He had wanted to give the boys the best education (even though he could not afford to give them full board); he arranged the move to Harrow on the Hill expressly so they could attend Harrow School and follow on to Winchester. He hoped they would go on to Oxford and enter one of the few respected Victorian professions. Tom described him as *'a very especially industrious and laborious man'* who was very strict about their education and did not let anyone sit *'idling'* without assigning them another task. He was believed to be as *'learned a Chancery lawyer as was to be found'* and was *'respected'* but not *'popular'*, with either his colleagues or his family.

Victorian fathers generally took all the financial decisions, but it was certainly monumentally unwise to rent so many properties at once: two uneconomic farms and one house to live in, one house rented out, and two premises in Lincoln's Inn; but it has to be remembered also that his wife was away for three years leaving him in sole charge of Anthony, as well as Tom in the school holidays. Fathers of his class would usually have left the care of children to their wives and nannies, meaning he would lack experience in arranging clothing and noticing whether they were growing out of clothes and shoes. In households such as theirs, sewing and dressmaking would usually have been done by a seamstress or, in very poor households, by the women of the family, as is the case with many of Anthony's later characters. Anthony's father would have been unable to stitch or *'turn'* clothing or sheets such as occupied Lucy and her aunt Mrs Dosett in *Ayala's Angel* (1881), or even wash his own clothes. As we have seen, there must have been at least a skeletal indoor staff to maintain the house, and outdoor staff to manage the farms and horses, presumably needing supervision.

He also walked many miles daily, practised law, and came home to work on his own writing project, an encyclopaedia of ecclesiastic terms. This workload would probably stretch any person and cause stress headaches, especially one addicted to the cure. The family readily said he grew more and more irritable and aggressive, and Anthony, though conceding that he was well educated and hard-working, wrote:

> ... the worse curse to him of all was a temper so irritable that even those he loved the best could not endure it. We were all estranged from him, and yet I believe he would have given his heart's blood for any of us. His life as I knew it was one long tragedy.

It is known today that extreme irritability can be a forerunner of dementia, a disease which may not have been recognized at that time. It would certainly account for Thomas Anthony's lapses in judgement and irritability. In *Trollopiana* no. 55 Pamela Neville-Sington describes how in Anthony's novel *La Vendée* (1850), the old and infirm Marquis sitting by the fire watching his daughter embroider in cold or wet weather, and being dragged out to sit in the garden amongst the birds when it was fine and warm, could perhaps be Anthony remembering his father in Bruges passing the time with his daughters Cecilia and Emily. His periods of docility and aggressiveness would fit with the progression of the disease, which could have coincided with the assumed TB.

Around 1830, despite struggling with his Chambers, his farms, his debts, health and loneliness, he began to write an *Encyclopaedia Ecclesiastica*, or *A Complete History of the Church: containing a full and compendious explanation of all ecclesiastical rites and ceremonies; a distinct and accurate account of all denominations of Christians, from the earliest ages of Christianity to the present time: together with a definition of terms usually occurring in ecclesiastical writers*. He continued writing right up to his death in Bruges in 1834 when he reached 'F' for 'Funeral Rites'. The ambitious undertaking was to be a:

> ... full and accurate account of the several subjects it will embrace, than has hitherto been given to the public ... The work will be illustrated with Lithographic Engravings giving an accurate representation of the different Monastic Orders, and will be printed in Four Volumes, Each of which is intended to be published in two parts. The price to subscribers will be One Pound each Part; the first of which will be put to the press as soon as a sufficient number of subscribers may warrant the undertaking.

When Fanny returned from Cincinnati before fleeing to Bruges, the tutor Auguste Hervieu prepared accompanying illustrations, and Fanny diligently found 105 subscribers. These were friends, family, clergymen including deans and bishops, and several college masters and libraries, including Winchester, Trinity College, Oxford, Trinity Hall, Cambridge, the Warden of New College Oxford and the Principal of Magdalen Hall.

Thomas Anthony conceded that he needed help from various quarters, and also wrote of his labours:

> The labour I have taken upon myself I feel may well be described 'an Herculean task', & it was long before I ventured to take the field. It having however been suggested to me by some of my clerical friends, & encouraged by the booksellers telling me that something of the kind was much wanting I first set about it/by way of trial but/without any fixed determination of prosecuting the work. In this manner I at length got thro' the 2 first letters A & B in a rough & unfinishd manner. These papers were put into the hands of Murray, & by him into those of a clergyman, who I have since found was lately one a learned professor of Oxford, & who was pleased to turn a favourable account of them to his employers. From this time I have turnd my attention more seriously to the subject. I have felt how desirable it would be to procure some coadjutors in this undertaking, & have made some no few overtures to some clerical friends; but hitherto with't success. In London every body is either idle, & chooses to continue so; or fully occupied; & country clergymen tell me, with much apparent truth, they have not a sufficient stock of [reference] books. Indeed I feel it would be impossible to execute any parts of the work, unless with an access to books, which the Libraries of London or one of our universities cd. /alone/ afford.
>
> I shall be glad to attend to the task you have given as to the translation of the Saxon ~~Chronicl~~ Constitutions; tho' I do not think a full exposition of these wd suit the nature of the work. Yet an abstract of them/such/ as you afterwards allude to might perhaps be well introduced.

The text begins with 'ABADDON, name given to Hebrew Tongue by St John in the Revelation to the king of the locusts or the angel of the bottomless pit ...', followed by:

> ABBA, a Syriac word signifying a father; and hence figuratively a superior, who might be honoured as a father with respect to age,

dignity, or affection. Thus in the Syriac, Coptic, and Ethiopian churches ... ABBA, is also a title of honour bestowed by the Jews upon certain? Rabbins, called Tanaites ... ABBACY, the rights or privileges of an abbot or abbess ...

and further followed by ABBE, ABBESS, ABBEY or ABBATHEY, ABBOT, ABECEDARII, ABELLIANS up to page 578 ending with FRENCH PROPHETS, FRIENDS, Society of.... FUNERAL RITES ...

Pamela Neville-Sington also pointed out that although *The Gentleman's Magazine* mentioned '*the clever novels and travelling sketches*' of his '*celebrated*' widow, Mrs Trollope, they made no mention of his own *Encyclopaedia Ecclesiastica* and even his own family failed to be complimentary. Tom did not suppose '*that any human being purchased the book because they wished to possess it*'; and that his father's death had, at least, '*delivered his subscribers from further demands on their purses*' (possibly a reference to the episode with the bailiffs), while Anthony supposed the volume to be '*buried in the midst of that huge pile of futile literature, the building up of which has broken so many hearts*'. However, had their father lived he would have been gratified to find that facsimiles of his book are now in all major universities and libraries around the world (and also available in paperback). On offering a paperback copy for sale, the Amazon website describes the book as being culturally important and part of the knowledge base of civilization

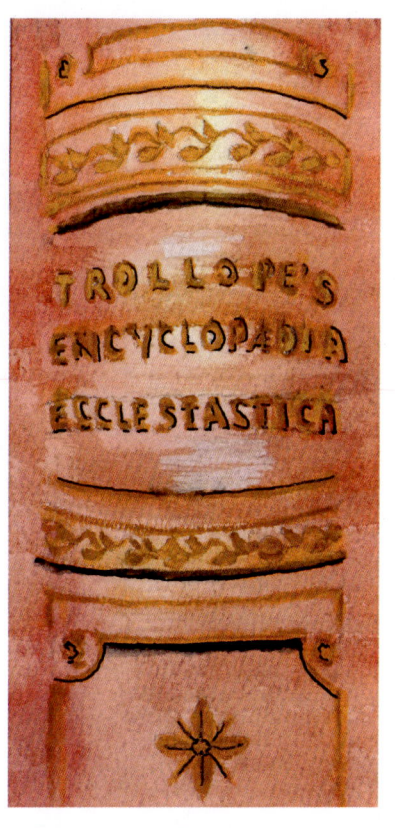

Encyclopaedia Ecclesiastica

Not as well known, his *A Treatise on the Mortgage of Ships as Affected by the Registry Acts, and on the Proper Mode of Effecting Mortgages on Property of this Nature, and on the Liabilities of the Mortgage* is also currently on sale as a paperback.

Modern Jerwood Library, Trinity Hall, Cambridge

St Martin's le Grand, St Paul's

When Anthony Trollope, aged 19, joined the Post Office on 4th November 1834 on a salary of £90, it was a large government-led institution with a central core of 'old school' masters, one being Sir Francis Freeling, later Secretary to the Post Office, who organized systems for Minutes, Reports and the Royal Mail Archive. The present London home of the British Postal Museum and Archive is named Freeling House in his honour. His son Clayton was Secretary at the Stamp Office and Clayton's wife was the friend of Anthony's mother, Fanny.

> ... I went to my friend Clayton Freeling, who was then Secretary at the Stamp Office, and was taken by him to the scene of my future labours in St Martin's le Grand. Sir Francis Freeling was the Secretary but he was greatly too high an official to be seen at first by a new junior clerk. I was taken, therefore to his eldest son, Henry Freeling, who was the assistant secretary, and by him I was examined as to my fitness.

Accordingly, Henry Freeling asked him to copy some lines from *The Times* newspaper as an entrance exam. In keeping with Anthony's particular clumsiness, especially in dipping a quill pen into an inkwell, he only produced a series of blots and mistakes. Remarkably, he was permitted to copy out some more text at home to take back for inspection the following day. When asked if he could do arithmetic, he said, '*A little*'. His brother Tom ensured he completed the copy overnight, but no one remembered to inspect it, and so he formally commenced his duties as a Junior Clerk in the Secretary's Office, an experience replicated in *The Three Clerks* (1858). Anthony's official appointment record reads:

> I beg to submit to your Lordship the name of Anthony Trollope as a Junior Clerk in the Secretary's Office ... Mr Trollope has been well educated and will be subject to the usual probation as to competency.

Despite his copying abilities (or lack of!) his job was to copy letters from ten in the morning until six in the evening. In addition to frequent blots, his timekeeping was appalling, and he used extended lunch breaks to play cards with fellow clerks. He was as discontented and rebellious as he had been in his schooldays and struggled to fit in with his colleagues. Unsurprisingly the office smelt of alcohol, as the building is still surrounded by taverns and public houses, many from Tudor times, including the Lord Raglan situated next door (originally known as *The Bush*, one of the oldest taverns in the City). Matters grew worse when Sir Francis Freeling died, and Colonel Maberly took over. Misunderstandings occurred, such as Anthony being accused of losing a letter accompanying some money. In indignation he struck the table, accidentally splashing the contents of a large bottle of ink over the Colonel's face and shirt.

Anthony's office at the back of the building overlooked Foster Lane, still housing Goldsmiths' Hall and St Olave's Court, and Old Jewry, where Jewish and Protestant places of worship originally sat either side of a narrow alleyway. Here Anthony not only saw the moneylenders who feature prominently in his Palliser novels but he also succumbed and experienced their visits and '*Do be punctual ...*' methods of recovering money. Incredibly, there were originally thirteen churches in total on Foster Lane, which combined into *St Vedast*, as late as 1956.

Tom wrote of enjoying watching the mail coaches leaving St Martin's le Grand at 8 p.m. and described it '*as one of the sights of London*':

One went there on the anniversary of the king's birthday, when all the guards had their scarlet coats new, and the horses' heads were all decked with flowers. And truly the yard around the Post Office offered on such an occasion a prettier sight than all the travelling arrangements of the present day could supply.

This busy square-mile financial district has people scurrying to and fro much as they would have done in 1834, and the street names reflect their original functions: Cheapside, Ironmongers Street, Poultry, Milk Lane, Bread Street etc., and St Paul's Churchyard leading to Paternoster Row and the coffee houses feature in many novels, including by the Brontës and Dickens. Anthony used his knowledge of stamps and their features in *John Caldigate* when Bagwax, sleuthing on John Caldigate's behalf in reference to an alleged former marriage in Australia, used his magnifying glass effectively:

Now the argument with Bagwax was this – that if he found in the Sydney post-marks of 7th May, and in those of 13th May, the same deviations or bruises in the die, those deviations must have existed also on the days between these two dates – and as the impression before him was quite perfect, without any deviation, did it not follow that it must have been obtained in some manner outside the ordinary course of business?

The Lord Raglan tavern, rebuilt 1852, incorporating parts of Roman wall, still next door to St Martin's le Grand

An Overview of the Post Office, Anthony's Eventual Successful Career and the Introduction of Post Boxes

Anthony (now a young man and hereafter called 'Trollope') eventually enjoyed a very successful career in the Post Office, travelling the world setting up postal systems, whilst simultaneously being a popular novelist.

According to Julian Stray at the Postal Museum Archives (BPMA), the concept of an efficient worldwide postal service which had begun in 1512 as a private service for Henry VIII was extended by Charles I in 1635 into a public service, hence the name 'Royal' Mail. In 1661 Henry Bishop, Postmaster General, introduced the world's first postmark, and in 1782 theatre owner John Palmer's introduction of a coach to move actors between theatres inspired the use of mail coaches. By 1793 letter-carriers wore a uniform of red coat and black hat, and guards (equipped with blunderbusses c.1820) rode on the outside of the coaches.

The recipient paid the postal charge according to the distance travelled, which by 1837 (not long after Trollope joined the service) could cost the equivalent of twelve loaves of bread, an impossible amount for most people. Senders therefore frequently used a prearranged code on the outside of envelopes allowing recipients to quickly interpret the message before refusing to accept delivery.

Accordingly, Sir Rowland Hill (Trollope's future boss) introduced radical reforms: postage would be paid by the sender with charges based on weight, and a letter weighing up to half an ounce (15g) would cost one standard penny. A public competition was held, and accordingly an adhesive stamp overlaid by the date and place of posting, proposed by James Chalmers from Dundee, was adopted, to which Rowland Hill added the 15-year-old Queen Victoria's head, as being both 'Royal' and difficult to forge. This design was used until her death. A Penny Black, as it was called, was the world's first stamp in 1840 but by 1841 changed to the Penny Red. This allowed black ink to overlay the red stamp, being thus easier to read than red ink over the former black stamp.

In 1853, Trollope suggested trialling roadside posting boxes in the Channel Islands, an idea already adopted in France, stating, *'all that is wanted is a safe receptacle for letters, which shall be cleared on the morning*

An Overview of the Post Office, Anthony's Eventual Successful Career and the Introduction of Post Boxes

... and at such times as may be requisite'. Many shapes, sizes, colours and inscriptions have been introduced over the years, in particular with the succession of each monarch. These are still used today, and Trollope saw at least six different designs before he died, ranging from free-standing to wall-mounted, round or hexagonal: an ornate green/gold box produced after a competition even had a compass on the top, but regrettably no aperture in which to place the letters! Early dark-green boxes were changed to red when it was realized they were more visible when sited near greenery. In 1859 Charles Dickens lobbied for a wall-mounted box outside his home, and by 1878 individuals and businesses could have a private box for an annual fee. As an explosion of literacy enabled more people to write, spawning a whole new industry of writing materials, this caused the postal system to grow to over a billion letters posted every year by 1875.

As Trollope did not retire until 1867, he would have witnessed many other changes in the service. Exhibitions at the Debden Post Office Archives and the Post Office Museum in London demonstrate that by the mid-1850s, when he was about 40 years old, London was divided into ten areas with relevant codes, local post offices and sorting offices, and two years before his death bicycles and tricycles with storage drums in front were trialled which continued to be used until recently. In 1838, as the new rail network expanded, a specially adapted mail coach was introduced where letters could be sorted en route to their destinations (discontinued only in 2004). As part of Trollope's job expanded to meeting and arranging contracts with railway companies, he developed a sympathy for towns which were bypassed by the railways or main roads, such as Stamford (see above) and Perivale in *The Belton Estate* (1865):

> ... the incipient growth of grass through some of the stones which formed the margin of the road would have been altogether unendurable ... That street had formed part of the main line of road from Salisbury to Taunton and coaches, wagons, and posting-carriages had been frequent on it; but now, alas! it was deserted. Even the omnibuses from the railway-station never came there unless they were ordered ...

He would also have witnessed the Pneumatic Despatch Company creating an underground railway in 1863 where packages were propelled by air pressure at up to 35 mph in iron tubes below ground. Alas, this delivery system was very dangerous as gas built up, and horses' hooves clattering across gratings in the road above could create sparks to ignite the gas. Unsurprisingly the staff below became so nervous that an Act of Parliament was necessary to force them to work with the tubes. Frequent

Selection of historical designs for post boxes

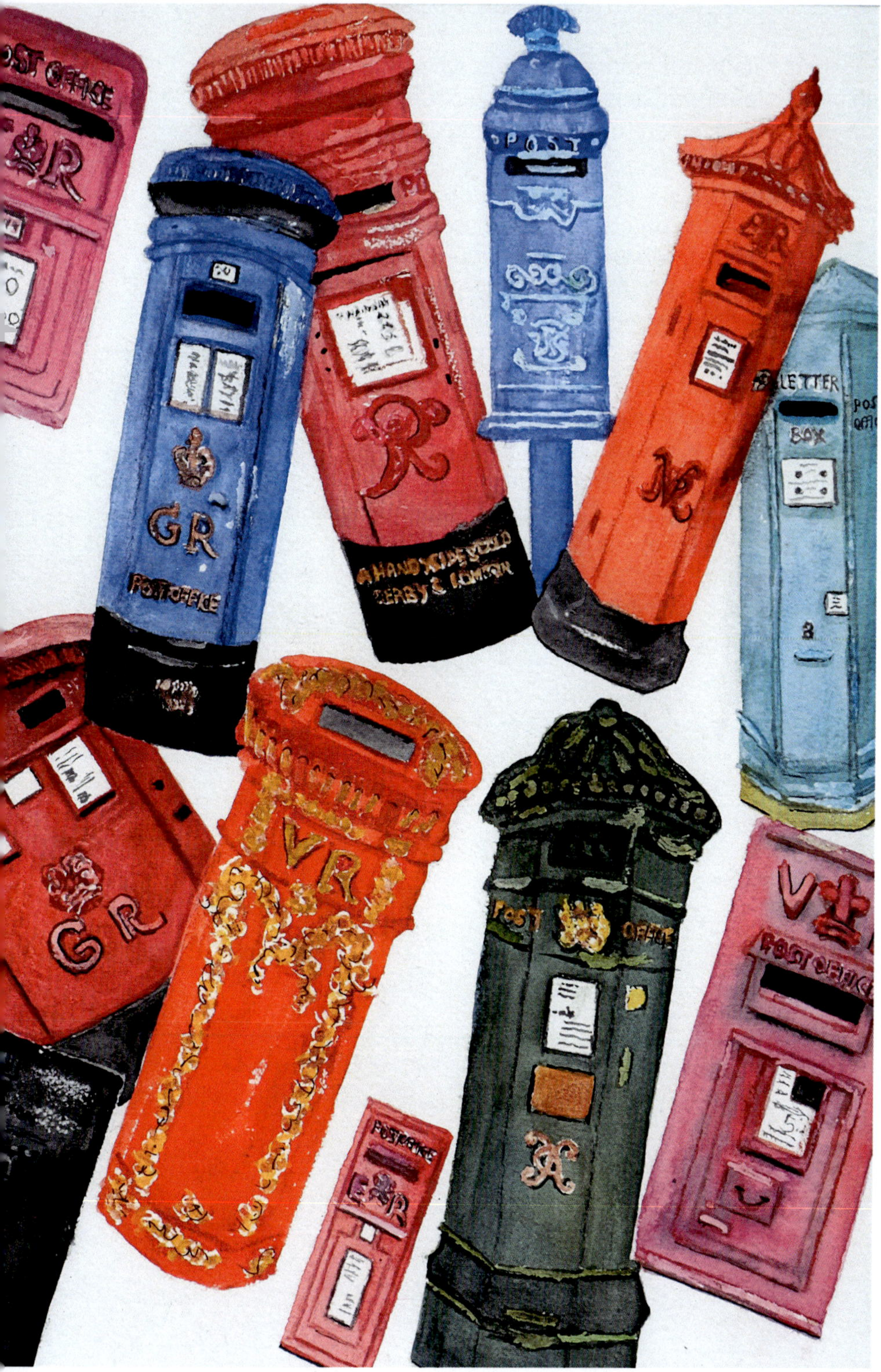
POST OFFICE
GR
POST
LETTER
BOX
VR

explosions killed both men and horses. On one occasion, flames shot 30ft high over Holborn, causing the collapse of the original St Martin's le Grand in 1874: its replacement on the same site is recalled by Tom:

> ... when the huge edifice in Saint Martin's le Grand was built ... the ridicule and the outcry that was raised at the size of the building, so enormously larger, it was supposed, than could possibly be needed! But it has now long since been found altogether insufficient for the needs of the service.

The collection at the BPMA also encompasses telephone kiosks and Anthony would have known about the advent of telegraphy when he wrote the short story 'The Telegraph Girl' for *Good Words* in 1877.

Trollope worked for the Post Office for thirty-three years at a time of innovation and extension, in which he was instrumental; it also provided inspiration for much of his writing. Not only did he progress in the Post Office to record and set up postal systems around the world, but he also married happily, had children and hobbies, and became a most successful and prolific novelist.

Lodgings in London

Northumberland Street, Marylebone (now Luxborough Street)

Once again Trollope's *Autobiography* gives a gloomy account of both his early days at the Post Office and loneliness in his lodgings at no. 22 Northumberland Street, Marylebone, probably about half an hour's walk away from both Harrow and his workplace in St Martin's le Grand. The house was owned by a tailor and the tailor's mother, another detail which Trollope absorbed for future use, as both tailors and bootmakers were staples of later novels.

Although the lodgings were very cheap (£90 p.a. rising to £140 p.a. after seven years), Trollope managed to be in debt for most of the time and had to be bailed out by his mother. The University of Westminster now takes up the whole of that side of the street, but the view of the large two-storey workhouse housing up to a thousand inmates, and the adjacent burial ground in what is now Paddington Gardens, is still what he would have seen from his window: '... *on to the back door of which establishment my room looked out – a most dreary abode*'. This was not a happy sight for a 19-year-old setting out upon his career, whilst mourning his lost older brother and father. It was also an unhealthy area, with rat-infested sewers and deadly fevers.

His journeys to work would have been more exciting than the lonely muddy lanes he took to school, but they would have been more perilous. He could have taken one of the new horse-drawn omnibuses which travelled to Bank, around half a mile away from St Martin's le Grand, but they carried only twelve people or so, were expensive, queues were targeted by pickpockets, and there were many accidents. If, as seems likely, he walked to work instead, the pavements were often shared with animals going to market, and in any case the roads would have contained piles of horse dung, which in hot weather would turn to dust and blow around, and in wet weather turn to sludge and splash around.

In spite of his gloomy reminiscences and protestations that his schooldays had been friendless, he now had some jolly times not only with his brother (who briefly lodged with him before taking up a teaching post in Birmingham) but also old school friends from Harrow and Sunbury, such as a nephew of his old tutor Harry Drury, with his brothers Herman and

Workhouse and graveyard as viewed by Trollope from his room at Northumberland Street

Charles (who became the historian and Dean of Ely) and lifelong friend John Merivale. He did not mention them in his *Autobiography*, or that together they formed a club called the Tramp Society with the objective of roaming on foot around nearby counties such as Buckinghamshire and Hertfordshire, and even as far away as Southampton. They did not spend above 5 shillings per day and were noisy and troublesome to residents. They also frequented pubs and eating houses around town (they had to fend for their own food); they would have seen the areas of Belgravia and Pimlico and the squares of Gordon, Tavistock, and Eaton, which master-builder Thomas Cubitt was transforming at that time and became the haunts of many of Trollope's characters. They would also have noticed the terrible slums at St Giles and Seven Dials with prostitutes as young as 13 or 14 years old and would know that even able-bodied men took care walking at night. Most men carried life preservers and violence was frequent, again to be recounted later by Trollope. Additionally, he complained that he did not meet suitable young ladies at salons, hinting that perhaps he only met girls of the *'lower orders'* in the pubs around town.

Monken Hadley

Soon Fanny returned to England with Cecilia and Emily, to a rented house called Grandon at Monken Hadley, near Barnet in Hertfordshire. Trollope could now visit and stay for whole weekends, travelling by coach which left twice daily from The Old Bell Inn in Holborn (a four-hour return trip). However, once again the family was followed by tragedy: while Cecilia was away visiting an aunt and Tom was teaching in Birmingham, Fanny wrote:

> *I am very greatly alarmed about my Emily. She has lost strength rapidly, she eats nothing, her cough is decidedly worse than it has ever been. My anxiety is dreadful and the more so because I dare not show it.*

In *Trollopiana* no. 93 (2012), London Guide Paul Baker describes how on 12th February 1836 Trollope's youngest sister, Emily, also died, only one year after their father and two years after Henry. Trollope wrote to Tom, on his mother's behalf:

> *It is all over! Poor Emily breathed her last this morning. She died without any pain, and without a struggle. Her little strength had been gradually declining, and her breath left her without the slightest convulsion, or making any change in her features or face. Were it not for the ashy colour, I should think she was sleeping. I never saw anything more beautifully placid and composed. It is*

much better that it is now, than that her life should have been prolonged only to undergo the agonies which Henry suffered. Cecilia was at Pinner when it happened, and she has not heard of it yet. I shall go for her tomorrow.

Emily's was the first family funeral attended by Trollope, who had been only nine when his brother Arthur died, and in London when Henry and his father died in Bruges. She is buried in St Mary the Virgin Church just 100 yards away from the house. The inscription on her tomb reads: '*Sacred to the memory of Emily Trollope the youngest daughter of Thomas Anthony and Frances Trollope who died on the 12th February 1836 aged 18 years*' (Paul Baker pointed out that this is not quite correct as she was actually one month short of 18 years).

After the family settled down again, with Cecilia and Tom back at home, Fanny wrote *The Vicar of Wrexhill*. Not only did she work with her usual routine of starting at 5 a.m. and working for four hours before the rest of the house woke up, but she again became sociable and made new friends. Trollope continued to visit on many weekends, and wrote: '… *I remember well how gay she made the place with little dinners, little dances, and little picnics, while she herself was at work every morning long before others had left their beds*'.

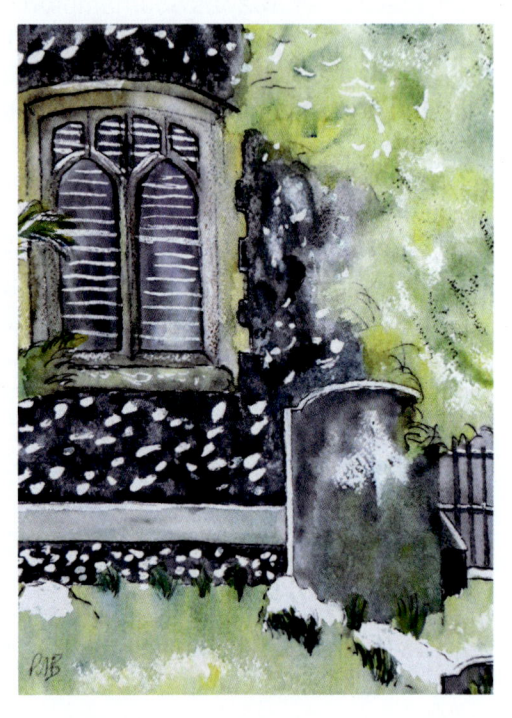

Emily's tomb at St Mary the Virgin Church

They all enjoyed a Christmas party in 1837 with friends made in Germany and Baron Charles Hugel from Vienna, and Trollope added his old friends from Harrow (again unmentioned by him). They played popular parlour games such as *bouts rimés* where one takes the last rhyming word of each line from a famous poem and uses it to write an entirely new poem, at which Anthony was said to be very good.

The Reverend John Richard Thackeray soon became rector of the church, accompanied by his wife and family. Trollope particularly liked Marianne and Georgina, who were both in his age group, shown by a letter from Fanny in 1837 suggesting he would not visit one particular Saturday as the Thackeray family would be away, implying he would not use up his time or money on the coach journey. Coincidentally, the rector was a cousin of William Makepeace Thackeray, later Trollope's friend and colleague, and about whom he wrote *Thackeray* in 1879 as part of the series 'English Men of Letters', published by Macmillan & Co. In 1838 Trollope took his Post Office friend John Tilley to Monken Hadley with him; he and Cecilia fell in love and married a year later. When she too died eleven years later in 1849, Anthony wrote: *'God bless you, my dear John ... I sometimes feel that I led you into more sorrow than happiness in taking you to Hadley'*.

While based in Barnet Fanny continued to travel, spending a year in Austria where she met Prince Metternich, the Austrian diplomat/statesman. She subsequently wrote both the travel book *Vienna and the Austrians* and the novel *The Romance of Vienna*. On her return, she recorded *'her pleasure at finding the roses in bloom, and in the peace and quiet of the place'*.

Later, while walking in the garden, Tom and Fanny had a long talk and, as Tom had been unhappy teaching, decided that he would give it up and devote himself *'to becoming her companion and squire'* (travel companion and factotum).

Looking back forty years later, Trollope indicated how much he had enjoyed visiting Monken Hadley (despite losing his sister Emily of whom he had been very fond), by writing *The Bertrams* (published 1859). Although it was written whilst he was on Post Office business travelling through Egypt and Gibraltar, much of the story is set in Hadley which, in another example of his prodigious memory, he still remembered in minute detail:

> *Hitherto George had always passed some of his vacations at Hadley. The amusements there were not of a very exciting nature; but London was close and even at Hadley there were pretty girls with whom he could walk and flirt, and the means of keeping a horse.*
>
> (Chapter 5)

In Chapter 28 Solicitor General Sir Henry Harcourt and Caroline Waddington go for a walk around her grandfather's house:

> *And so they started on their walk. It was the first that they had ever taken together. What Sir Henry may have done before in that line, this history says not ... There is – or perhaps we should say was, for time, and railways, and straggling new suburban villas, may have now destroyed it all; but there is, or was, a pretty woodland lane, running from the back of Hadley Church, through*

> the last remnants of what was once Enfield Chase. How many lovers' feet have crushed the leaves that used to lie in autumn along that pretty lane? See how he opens the gate that stands by the churchyard paling? Does it stand there yet, I wonder[?] Well, well, we will say it does. And then there was a short pause, and they got on the green grass which runs away into the chase in front of the parsonage windows. I wonder if the wickets are ever standing there now on the summer afternoons!

Trollope also remembered the sadness and the happiness in Hadley Church:

> And then the bells were rung, the Hadley bells, the merry marriage bells ... I know full well the tone with which they toll when the soul is ushered to its last long rest. I have stood in that green churchyard when earth has been paid to earth, ashes to ashes, dust to dust – the ashes and the dust that were loved so well ... But now the scene was of another sort. How merrily they rang, those joyous marriage-bells! Out rung the Hadley bells, the happy marriage bells.
>
> And the merry bells went on ringing as they trooped back to the old manor house. They went in gay carriages though the distance was but some 100 yards. But brides and bridegrooms cannot walk on their wedding day in all their gala garments though it be but a few hundred yards.

According to Paul Baker, the woodland lane, the kissing gate and the parsonage are still there, cricket is still played, and it is also 100 yards between the church and Grandon, the fictional home of old George Bertram; the priest who '*smiles and grasps their hands as he gives them his parting friendly blessing*' is probably based on J R Thackeray. Another funeral, in contrast to the happiness of the wedding ceremony, is that of old Mr Bertram:

> ... he could hardly realize it to himself ... he was going to put under the ground <u>almost his nearest relative</u> ... And then there was a scuffling heard on the stairs – a subdued decent undertakers' scuffling – ... Feet scuffled down the stairs outside the dining-room door, and along the passage. And then the door was opened, and in low, decent undertaker's voice, red-nosed, sombre, well-fed Mr Mortmain told them that they were ready.

Obviously a very poignant memory of his sister Emily's death.

The novel is set in *'the year 18-'* (a typical Victorian description), and, as Paul Baker also pointed out, presumably before the railway station opened in nearby Barnet. It would also have taken longer than a quarter of an hour to walk from there, but writing from the distance of time and from abroad Trollope presumed a station had already opened when he wrote: *'2pm had been named for reading of the Will, as the train arrived at 1.45'*.

Paul Baker also pointed out that there were three pubs in the village of Hadley at the time the family were there, and several in nearby Barnet, which coincidentally Dickens frequented and included in his journalism and novels, particularly *Oliver Twist*. Paul Baker pointed out the remarkable coincidence that both W M Thackeray and Dickens frequented the area in the 1830s; and that in the future their paths would cross many times, although there is no record that Trollope and Dickens ever met at that time.

Tom and Fanny then installed themselves at 20 York Street, Portman Square, off Marylebone Road, near Trollope, still living in Northumberland Street.

Grandon, Monken Hadley

Trollope's Illness in Northumberland Street

Perhaps Trollope was more deeply affected by the accumulated deaths in the family than he showed, and perhaps especially by the death of Emily, his youngest sister; perhaps he was also affected by the knowledge that his friend John Tilley had now moved to take up a Post Office position in the Lake District, taking his sister Cecilia with him. Perhaps also he surmised that his mother and Tom would eventually move away again, and he imagined future loneliness. His work was also uninteresting; he again felt depressed, and possibly worried he was becoming like his father, or even that he too would succumb to the family disease. He said that even at that age he often cursed the hour he had been born: *'I acknowledge the weakness of a great desire to be loved – of a strong wish to be popular, with my associates. No child, no boy, no lad, no young man, had ever been less so'*.

C P Snow described his physique as being like his personality: more complex than it seemed. Although a lumbering young man he had small hands and feet and danced very well. His physique and temperament were made to endure. He was probably about 5' 10', not tall to us, but would have been considered so in the 19th century, with brown hair which turned white early, very dark blue eyes, almost black, and spectacles, with a penetrating observant gaze. Most heroines in his novels similarly enjoyed brown hair, and also usually dimples: from her portrait his mother probably also had brown hair although it is not known if either she or Trollope's sisters had dimples. Like many depressed people, he was full of high spirits in public, but eventually his physical and mental malaise combined to make him seriously ill: he was in debt, hounded by moneylenders and the mother of a girl who believed he had betrayed her daughter (narrated in *The Three Clerks* below). It is also thought that he projected many of these earlier feelings onto the luckless Johnny Eames in *The Small House at Allington* (1864), and a similar 'hobbledehoy' described in *Ayala's Angel* as *'one of those overgrown lads who come late to their manhood'*, but often followed by favourite sayings to justify delayed maturity, such as *'the fruit which ripens slowest is the sweetest'* – i.e. ultimately a better man than the 'young Apollo' or 'curled darling'.

Once again, we learn more detail of his affairs through his brother and particularly his mother, who wrote:

> ... *I abandoned my plans to go north to the christening of my first grandchild, and took temporary lodgings at 3 Wyndham Street [even nearer to Northumberland Street] so I could nurse him. His illness took the form of asthma with severe weakness and wasting, combined with a deep depression. The doctors I consulted could*

> find neither reason nor cure. I told my friend Rosina Bulwer in Paris; He is frightfully reduced in size and strength; sure I am that could you see him, you would not find even a distant resemblance to the being who, exactly three months ago, left us in all the pride of youth, health and strength. Day by day I lose hope. And so, I am quite sure, do his physicians; we have had three consultations, but nothing prescribed relieves him, nor has any light been thrown on the nature of his complaint .... Because of my debts I could not take time off from my writing, but managed to write two books, while nursing Anthony during the day. The books were written as a warning of both the pleasures and pitfalls for young authors in the London literary set. They were written with Anthony in mind for I knew he wanted to be a writer.

Trollope confessed to her that his only hope for a future was to become like her, a writer of novels, like other members of the family. His mother reminded him he had left school earlier than planned and advised him to:

> Make good the dropped stitches of your education before you take upon yourself to teach or amuse others in print. We Trollopes are far too much given to pen and ink as it is, without your turning scribbler when you might do something better. Harrow and Winchester will stand you in good stead at the Post Office; make St Martins-le-Grand the instrument that will open the oyster of the world.

During the three months of his mother's devotion and care while she continued her writing regime, he was able to observe how she organized her day and built her novels around observed characters and situations. He could also read and discuss her books. Again, she advised him:

> Remember, the time for reading is now. Reading you must have, not so much because of what it will tell you, as because it will teach you to observe, and supply you with mental pegs on which to hang what you will pick up about traits and motives of your fellow creatures.

He slowly recovered and by the end of July he was well enough to go back to his job and his mother made the postponed visit north to see her first granddaughter. However, he was still unsettled, had debts and had quarrelled with the Secretary-Colonel, and had also a *'full conviction that life was taking him downwards to the lowest pits'*.

He also continued his self-education by reading Horace and leading poets, and improving his French and Latin (although he once threw a volume of Johnson's *Lives of the Poets* out of the window '*because he spoke sneeringly of Lycidas*'); and his mother wrote that in early 1840 he got leave from his job and was able to join her in Paris for a holiday, again unmentioned by Anthony in his *Autobiography*, but his mother wrote:

> *It was a promise of long standing to Anthony, whose official duties had prevented his sharing our travelling delights, and he was permitted to be with us for a few weeks – a couple of months we hoped – which would give him, perhaps the only opportunity of seeing la belle ville.*

All Trollope's worries ended when he chose to further his career in Ireland.

Ireland

Everything changed for Trollope when, on 15th September 1841, aged 26, the deaths, debts and boredom of his early years vanished, and a new life began in Ireland. When an opportunity arose for him to escape St Martin's le Grand and his London lodgings, he borrowed £200 from a cousin, the family lawyer, and volunteered as one of the newly appointed surveyor's clerks for the Post Office in Ireland:

> *When I told my friends that I was going on this mission ... they shook their heads, but said nothing to dissuade me. I think it must have been evident to all who were my friends that my life in London was not a success ... my mother and elder brother ... did not even know my intention in time to protest against it ... our family lawyer ... lent me the money, and looked upon me with pitying eyes, shaking his head. 'After all you were right to go'. he said to me when I paid him the money a few years afterwards.*

Although his previous humble Post Office duties had been to copy letters, and although he knew nothing of Ireland other than that it *'was a land flowing with fun and whisky'*, he suddenly found himself to be a deputy-inspector of country post offices *'and that among other things to be inspected would be the postmasters' accounts! But as no other person asked a question as to my fitness for this work, it seemed unnecessary for me to do so'*. His new chief said he would judge him solely by his merits, and so Trollope began his travels throughout the country: to Cork, Donnybrook and Belfast, in addition to the areas listed below.

Ireland was the catalyst for many changes in his life: not only did he advance in his career, but he gained inspiration for writing novels, became a Freemason, met his wife, had two sons, and acquired his lifelong passion for hunting. Several novels were set wholly in Ireland, including his first (initially not well received) and his last (the latter unfinished at his death and published posthumously by his son): *The Macdermots of Ballycloran* (1847), *The Kellys and the O'Kellys* (1848), *Castle Richmond* (1860), *An Eye for an Eye* (1879) and *The Landleaguers* (1883). He also wrote *Famine Letters* (1849–50) and the short stories 'The O'Conors of Castle Conor, County Mayo' (1860), and 'Father Giles of Ballymoy' (1866).

Banagher

He was first sent to Banagher on the Shannon, ready to make inspection tours into Connaught and *'over a strip of country eastwards, which would enable me occasionally to run up to Dublin'*. On his first arrival, and following dinner at the local hotel, he reflected over some whisky punch how it had come to be that the inspection of accounts was to be the *'destiny of me who had never learned the multiplication table, or done a sum in Long division!'*

Banagher is a small town with one long main street at right-angles to the River Shannon, and Trollope stayed for a couple of years at 24 Main Street in a modest single-storey house with a very large peat-storage shed for heating. Charlotte Brontë and the reverend Arthur Bell Nicholls spent their honeymoon in the village, staying with Arthur's relatives, and are buried in the nearby churchyard of St Paul's. When members of the Trollope Society visited the house in 2006, the then owner told us she had been mistress of Banagher Post Office for thirty years. The Royal Shannon Hotel where Trollope would have spent his first night is strategically placed near the old crossing of the river, where he must have watched the new bridge being built during his stay (1841–3) connecting the counties of Galway and Offaly, known then as 'the King's County'.

It was in Banagher that Trollope was introduced to both hunting and Freemasonry – two pursuits which changed his life and provided inspiration for many of his novels. Hunting became *'one of the great joys of* [his] *life'*, which he enjoyed several days a week each season until he was old, stout and short sighted. His superior, the Surveyor, Mr Drought, ran a pack of hounds (even while unable to hunt himself), and encouraged Trollope to buy a hunter which he stabled at a house called Kennets next to the Post Office. He hired a stableman called Barney who became a faithful and loyal servant for many years. Trollope was also proposed for membership of the Freemasonry Lodge of Banagher (no.36) founded in 1758 by Brother J Bird and Brother Harrington.

Drumsna

In autumn 1843, Trollope went *'to the quiet little village of Drumsna on the mail coach road to Sligo ... where the postmaster* [William Allen] *had come to some sorrow about his money* [a discrepancy of a few pence]; *and my friend John Merivale was staying with me for a day or two'*. When Trollope and Merivale took a walk over rough terrain to a desolate and dilapidated mansion they found Headford House, about a mile from the village. This ruin of roofless ivy-covered walls and exposed fireplaces and beams is still there today, and villagers can recall their parents remembering the occupants upon whom the characters in the book were based. Trollope continued:

... we turned up through a deserted gateway, along a weedy, grass-grown avenue, till we came to the modern ruins of a country house. It was one of the most melancholy spots I ever visited ... Oh, what a picture of misery of useless expenditure, unfinished pretence, and premature decay! ... The knocker was still on the door – a large modern lion-headed knocker; but half the door was gone; on creeping to the door-sill I found about six feet of the floor of the hall had gone – stolen for firewood. But the joists of the flooring were there, and the whitewash of the walls showed that but a few, a very few years back, the house had been inhabited.

Headford House became the inspiration for that first paragraph of Trollope's first book, *The Macdermots of Ballycloran*, and the residents of Drumsna have extended enormous hospitality and unshakeable links to members of the Trollope Society, resulting in Mary McAleese, then President of Ireland, officially opening a new 'Trollope Trail' to the clearly marked spot for future devotees of Trollope to follow.

The *'little inn'* mentioned in *The Mcdermots of Ballycloran* (now Taylor's Bar) also features hilariously in the (semi-autobiographical) short story 'Father Giles of Ballymoy'. After a weary journey to Drumsna awaiting his friend Merivale, Trollope had arrived at the only inn late in the afternoon, and his resultant experience led to the character Archibald Green climbing an almost perpendicular flight of stairs – half stairs, half ladder – to a small room which had two beds, a table, a chair and a basin-stand but no lock or bolt on the door. Being tired he fell into a restless sleep. Suddenly he heard a stealthy footstep and, frightened and only half awake, leapt from his bed, seized the intruder, and found himself grappling with a man clad, like himself, only in his shirt, whom he held so tightly by the throat that he could not speak. In the ensuing struggle the intruder stumbled and fell down the stairs. Archibald (or perhaps Trollope?) was almost lynched for this act as the said 'intruder' turned out to be the local priest going to sleep in the next bed! Sharing rooms and even beds was quite common in hotels at that time.

A few yards away the original water pump, no longer operational, stands on the corner in a central position and would have provided the water supply in Trollope's day.

Carrick-on-Shannon

Also in County Leitrim, three and a half miles from Drumsna, is the little town of Carrick-on-Shannon where Trollope would have seen evidence of the great potato famine and the huge copper 'soup pots' for the mass of

Taylor's Bar, Drumsna

people without food. His sympathy is evident in *Castle Richmond* with his poignant descriptions of the loss of food, money and ultimately life, with starving children and dead babies lying with their prostrate mother:

> *They who were in the south of Ireland during the winter of 1846–47 will not readily forget the agony of that period. For many, many years preceding and up to that time, the increasing swarms of the country had been fed upon the potato, and upon the potato only; and now all at once the potato failed them, and the greater part of eight million human beings were left without food.*

The Courthouse features in not only *The Macdermots* but also the unfinished *The Landleaguers*: the Irish National Land League had begun in County Leitrim in late 1880 with the aim of helping poor tenant farmers to abolish 'landlordism', buy their own land, and thus work for themselves. Its inception helped to calm things down during evictions and forced sales of goods and crops. Carrick was the scene of many rallies.

The Courthouse building nowadays has a modern canopy over the door and houses a smart shop and café, but the on left-hand side, beside the chimney, one can still see the small doorway and tunnel where prisoners such as Thady in *The Macdermots of Ballycloran* would have been brought up from the dungeons.

The Courthouse, Carrick-on-Shannon

At the other end of the main street is the workhouse with its famine ward and a tasteful Remembrance Garden where one can see the tremendously large cooking pots used by soup kitchens. Dr Yvonne Siddle of Chester University points out in *The Literary Encyclopedia* (2013) that Trollope's series of letters to the *Examiner* (1849–50) support the British government's belief that the famine was preordained by God in order to stop irresponsible landowners profiting from the subdivision of land, thus encouraging the overplanting of potato crops. However, by 1859–60 when he wrote *Castle Richmond*, Trollope included a memorably heartfelt description of the plight of a dying woman lying in a hovel beside her starving children:

> *But as his eyes became used to the light he saw her eyes gleaming brightly through the gloom. They were very large and bright as they turned round upon him while he moved – large and bright, but with a dull, unwholesome brightness – a brightness that had in it none of the light of life ...*
>
> *And then he looked at her more closely. She had on her some rag of clothing which barely sufficed to cover her nakedness, and the baby which she held in her arms was covered in some sort; but he could see, as he came to stand close over her, that these garments were but loose rags which were hardly fastened round her body ...*
>
> *In those days there was a form of face which came upon the sufferers when their state of misery was far advanced, and which was a sure sign that their last stage of misery was nearly run. The mouth would fall and seem to hang, the lips at the two ends of the mouth would be dragged down, and the lower parts of the cheeks would fall as though they had been dragged and pulled. There were no signs of acute agony when this phasis of countenance was to be seen, none of the horrid symptoms of gnawing hunger by which one generally supposed that famine is accompanied. The look is one of apathy, desolation and death ... For a while Herbert stood still, looking around him, for the woman was so motionless and uncommunicative that he hardly knew how to talk to her ... he could see through the gloom that there was a bundle of straw lying in the dark corner beyond the hearth, and that the straw was huddled up ... he could see that the body of a child was lying there, stripped of every vestige of clothing ... it was not yet stone cold ... had been about four years old, while that still living in her arms might perhaps be half that age. 'Was she your own?' asked Herbert ... 'Deed, yes!' said the woman. 'She was my own, own little Kitty.' But there was no tear*

in her eye or gurgling sob audible from her throat. 'And when did she die?' he asked. 'Deed, thin, and I don't just know – not exactly.'

Kingstown, now Dun Laoghaire

In the summer of 1842 Trollope's future success and happiness was further cemented when he met Rose Heseltine who was holidaying with her family in Kingstown (now known as Dun Laoghaire). They married two years later in 1844 and had two sons, Henry Merivale and Frederick James Anthony, born in 1846 and 1847.

Rose was honest, practical and affectionate. Trollope's work is always praised for his depth and understanding of the female psyche, but it was most likely Rose who provided this insight into a woman's mind, and information on dress and fashion, and was also probably a model for some of his characters. As a boisterous hunting, clubbing man he would not have been able to depict his female characters so realistically without her help. She also copied his manuscripts and checked his proofs, and later steadfastly accompanied him on lengthy and arduous trips not only throughout Europe but also to America (1861) and Australia (1871). Later they informally adopted her niece, Florence Bland (Bice), who gradually took over some of the duties of an amanuensis, and it was Bice's friend Ada Strickland who went on to marry Henry.

Newly restored Victorian bandstand located between the two piers at Dun Laoghaire

At last Trollope's fortunes were completely changed. He was no longer a hobbledehoy but a successful postal surveyor, travelling around the country on horseback checking accounts and setting up new postal routes and systems; he had begun his ultimate ambition of writing novels, acquired lasting hobbies and interests, and had now founded a family.

However, as is typical in his *Autobiography*, he gave very sketchy information about the details of his private life. His life story laments his hardships and indignities but gives scant comment on the people he loved and who supported him, and the wide circle of relatives who befriended him. When recounting his marriage, he merely stated: 'Perhaps I ought to name that happy day as the commencement of my better life', and again, later on: 'My marriage was like the marriage of other people, and of no special interest to anyone except my wife and me'.

The Cliffs of Moher

As Trollope said: '*The Cliffs of Moher in County Clare, on the western coast of Ireland, are not as well known to tourists as they should be. ... they are beautifully coloured, streaked with yellow veins, and with great masses of dark red rock ...*' but they are also spectacularly fearsome and dramatic, towering high with roaring sea below and strong winds above, and they are where Mrs O'Hara in *An Eye for an Eye* faced the handsome young Fred Neville, Earl of Scroope:

> She had not brought him there that she might frighten him with that danger, or that she might avenge herself by the power which it gave her. But now the idea flashed across her maddened mind. 'Miscreant!' she said. And she bore him back to the very edge of the precipice.
>
> 'You'll have me over the cliff,' he exclaimed, hardly even yet putting out his strength against her.
>
> 'And so I will, by the help of God ...'. And as she spoke she pressed him backwards towards his fall. He had the power enough ... to crouch beneath her grasp on to the loose crumbling soil of the margin of the rocks. ... on a sudden, she spurned him with her foot on the breast ... and the poor wretch tumbled forth alone into eternity. That was the end of Frederick Neville, Earl of Scroope, and the end, too, of all that poor girl's hopes in this world.

Mrs O'Hara had been opposed to Fred Neville's courtship of her daughter Kate, fearing his bad intentions – he had, in fact, been young, unwise and naïve. In a poignant mirror image of Phineas Finn in the later book of that name who honourably went back to Ireland to marry his childhood sweetheart, Fred Neville had honourably gone back to the O'Hara family to at least explain his family situation and the fact that he could not marry her honourably.

Trollope wrote *An Eye for an Eye* in less than a month from 13th September to 10th October 1870 (although it was not published until 1879) when he was married with a family and had returned to the area for Post Office business and probably recalled the fact that he had lived with Rose about six miles way.

Mallow

There is some controversy over exactly where Trollope and Rose lived – oral tradition believes they lived in a three-storey Georgian house at the corner of Emmet Street in what is now called 139 Bank Place next to the Catholic church. His mother visited in 1849, and also that year they took into their home Edith Diana Mary Tilley, one of John Tilley's five daughters by Cecilia, after her mother's death. Mallow is in the heart of hunting country; the Castlecor Chase is believed to date from 1745, and became the Duhallow Hunt Club in 1800, boasting a very fine new uniform of scarlet coat and Duhallow Hunt button. Trollope would have heard and assimilated many amusing and frightening stories and tales of typical hunting characters from those hunting expeditions.

Clonmel

Trollope's two sons, Henry Merivale and Frederik James Anthony, were born after the couple moved to a first-floor apartment in a house off Main Street (the present O'Connell Street) in Clonmel, where they stayed for three and a half years. Both boys were baptized in Old St Mary's Church. Although he did not perform the baptisms himself, a Reverend Bury Palliser was connected to the church and the Trollopes would have known him. This historic name had been prevalent in the area since the 1700s, and was reminiscent of the carving in the Harrow schoolroom. This name, combined with Trollope's ability to retain information and inspiration for many years, probably led to the creation of one of his most famous characters, the gentle and conscientious Plantagenet Palliser, Duke of Omnium in *The Prime Minister* (1876) and *The Duke's Children* (1880). In Clonmel, Trollope was received as a 'gentleman' and entertained by lawyers, doctors, prosperous merchants, garrison officers and families, with invitations to dinners, balls and hunts. '*It was altogether a very jolly life that I led in Ireland*'. Significantly, he listed his occupation on the baptismal register for Henry as 'gentleman' and as 'Post Office Inspector' for Frederick.

Clonmel was a rich source of inspiration for names and characters, such as the mayor and coaching entrepreneur, Charles Bianconi. His successful

Irish novels, left to right: *The Kellys and the O'Kellys*, *Castle Richmond*, *An Eye for an Eye*, *The Landleaguers* (Folio Society editions); *The Macdermots of Ballycloran* (The Bodley Head)

ANTHONY TROLLOPE

THE LANDLEAGUERS

FOLIO SOCIETY

THE MACDERMOTS OF BALLYCLORAN
ANTHONY TROLLOPE

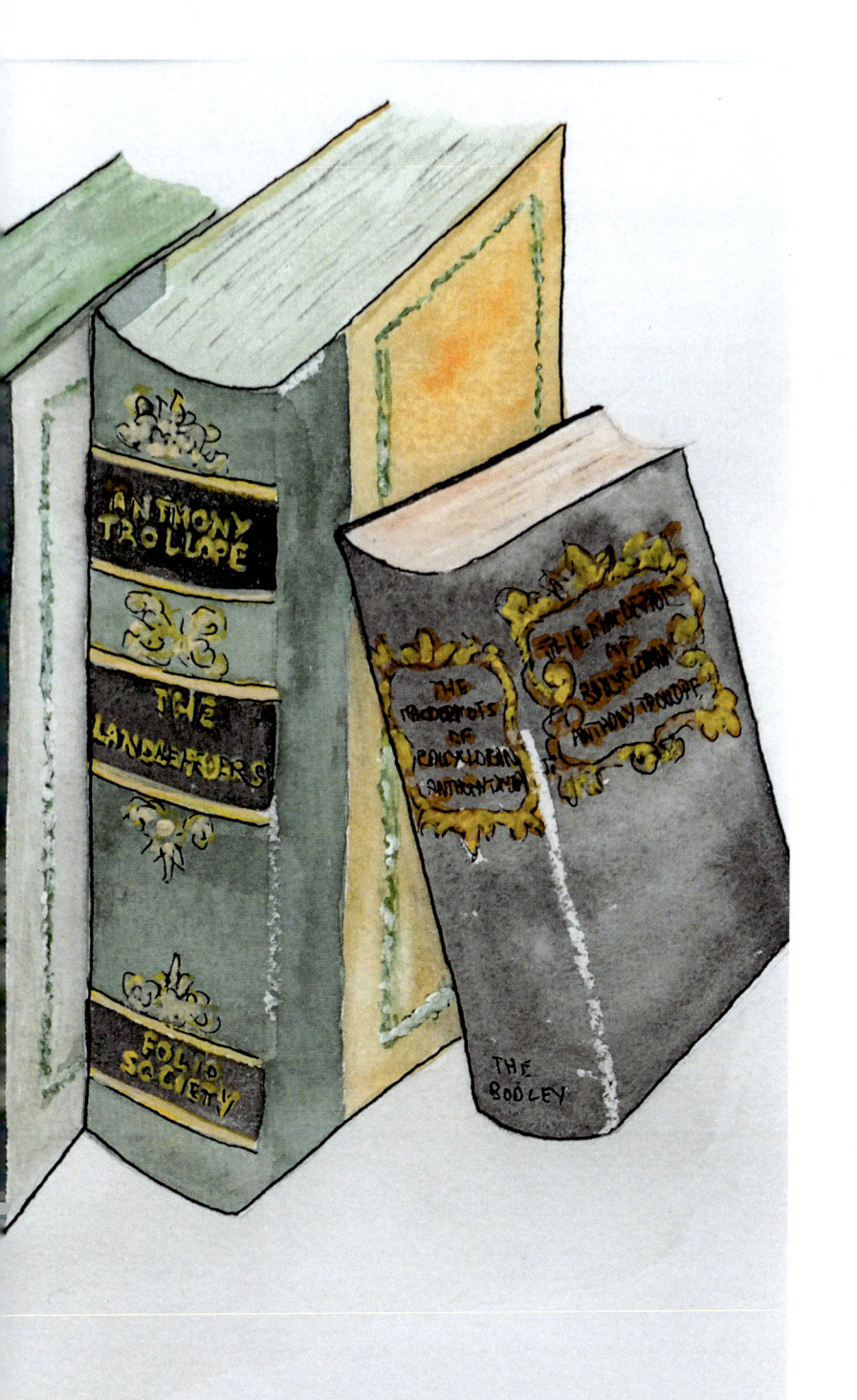

THE MACDERMOTS OF BALLYCLORAN
ANTHONY TROLLOPE

THE BODLEY

coach system carried mail: the 'Bians' were four-wheeled carts drawn by three or four horses carrying both mail and passengers. By 1843 Bianconi had over 1,300 horses, 100 vehicles and an estate of 1,000 acres at Longfield House near Clonmel. He provided insights into the complex social and economic relationships of Ireland, all possible information streams to feed into the character of Melmotte in *The Way We Live Now* (1875). In a report to the Post Office in 1857, Trollope mentioned Mrs Bianconi with admiration and respect, and later his son Henry wrote a biography of Mr Bianconi, published in 1878. Local connections of the DeBurgo and Fitzgerald families, also within the manor of Clonmel, connect with one of Trollope's main heroines: Lady Glencora Palliser mourned the fact that she had been forced to marry Plantagenet instead of the love of her life, the handsome, aristocratic but penniless rake called Burgo Fitzgerald.

The time spent in Ireland, meeting Rose, having children and taking up hobbies, changed Anthony Trollope into a happy man, and in 1852 he wrote to his mother: *'I can't fancy anyone being much happier than I am, or having less in the world to complain of. It often strikes me how wonderfully well I have fallen on my feet'* (Letter I, 30, from *The Letters of Anthony Trollope*, edited by Bradford Allen Booth, Oxford University Press, 1951, hereinafter referred to as Booth, *Letters*).

Rotherham

Rotherham today is a large industrial city, but with evidence of a Roman past and Tudor prosperity. When Trollope and Rose married there in 1844, the area would have been similar to that depicted in a painting of 1840 by Christopher Thomson (1799–1871), showing a rural idyll of grassy banks around a wide river and a prominent spire in the distance. Still today the Minster, formerly All Saints Church, stands high and proud in the centre, adjacent to a narrow street originally accommodating nine public houses. Three of these beamed and pargetted coaching-houses are still operative: the Black Horse Inn, Pack Horse Inn and Three Cranes Inn, with their rickety sloping upper floors and stabling. On the corner of this street is the listed bank premises where Rose's father, Edward Heseltine, was the manager. When we visited, the bank was owned by RBS but about to revert to Williams & Glyn. Prior to that it had been the Sheffield and Rotherham Joint Stock Banking Company Limited, founded in 1792 by the Walker brothers (famous local steelmakers), Vincent Eyre (agent of the Duke of Norfolk and principal landowner), and William Stanley, owner of nearby Cliffe Castle, Grade II* Listed. Cliffe Castle is now a museum housing many fine paintings of the area by, among others, William Cowen, one of the eight founders of the Royal Institute of Painters in Watercolour.

The Heseltine family were prominent in what was a prosperous area, with many other wealthy landowners and iron-work owners; the then Prince and Princess of Wales visited nearby Cliffe Castle. The Heseltine family lived in what looks to be a very large mainly two-storey apartment curving around the corner into Wellgate Street, above the bank. A large sign carved over the doorway reads 'OLD BANK 1792' and a blue plaque on the wall reads:

> The Royal Bank of Scotland
> *Rose Heseltine (1822–1917)*
> The wife of Anthony Trollope
> *lived here in 1844*
> before their marriage in Rotherham Minster

Edward Heseltine was also a director of the Sheffield and Rotherham Railway Company and one of the town's leading citizens until discrepancies were found in the accounts and the family fled to France. He was not thought to have personally gained in any way but was probably too generous in awarding unsecured loans to his clients at a time of the 1840s Depression. This Depression culminated in the Panic of 1847, a British banking crisis associated with the end of the 1840s railway industry boom and leading to the failure of many smaller banks. The town's official website states that one of the people to whom Mr Heseltine had granted unsecured loans was, in fact, the disgraced railway magnate Mr Hudson, believed to be one of the inspirations for Melmotte in *The Way We Live Now* (1875).

On leaving Rotherham station it is necessary to go over a bridge, featured in many paintings, into which is built The Chapel of our Lady on the Bridge, used by travellers to pray for a safe journey, or give thanks for a safe arrival in Rotherham. Trollope would have also known that for many years it had been an almshouse, until at the turn of the 19th century it became a prison. Managing an almshouse is the central theme of the much-loved *The Warden*.

The town was distinctly '*opposed to the new religion*' (Methodism) and objected strongly to Whitefield and Wesley addressing the people, generally treating them with contempt and sometimes violence; as already mentioned, such religious competition being a feature of many of Trollope's novels.

Although living in Ireland, Anthony and Rose married in the imposing Grade I Listed All Saints, Rotherham Minster. The building, set atop steps in a big square adjacent to the bank, is the third church on the site since before AD 937 and is described by Pevsner as '*one of the largest and stateliest of the churches in Yorkshire*'. At the time of their marriage another pub, the Ring O'Bells, was built into the side of the Minster, and a ditty written by Stan Crowther, former mayor and MP, marks its demise:

> The good old Ring O Bells had stood from 1823
> And a cosier little boozer boys
> We never more shall see
> The gents was rather primitive
> It was just a wall outside –
> But when they pulled the Ringers down
> We all sat down and cried.

Rose was reputed to be small and distinctly pretty, and when she and Trollope became prosperous, was noted for being beautifully dressed. Trollope's mother, Fanny, was said to have been snobbish about her

Old Bank, Rotherham

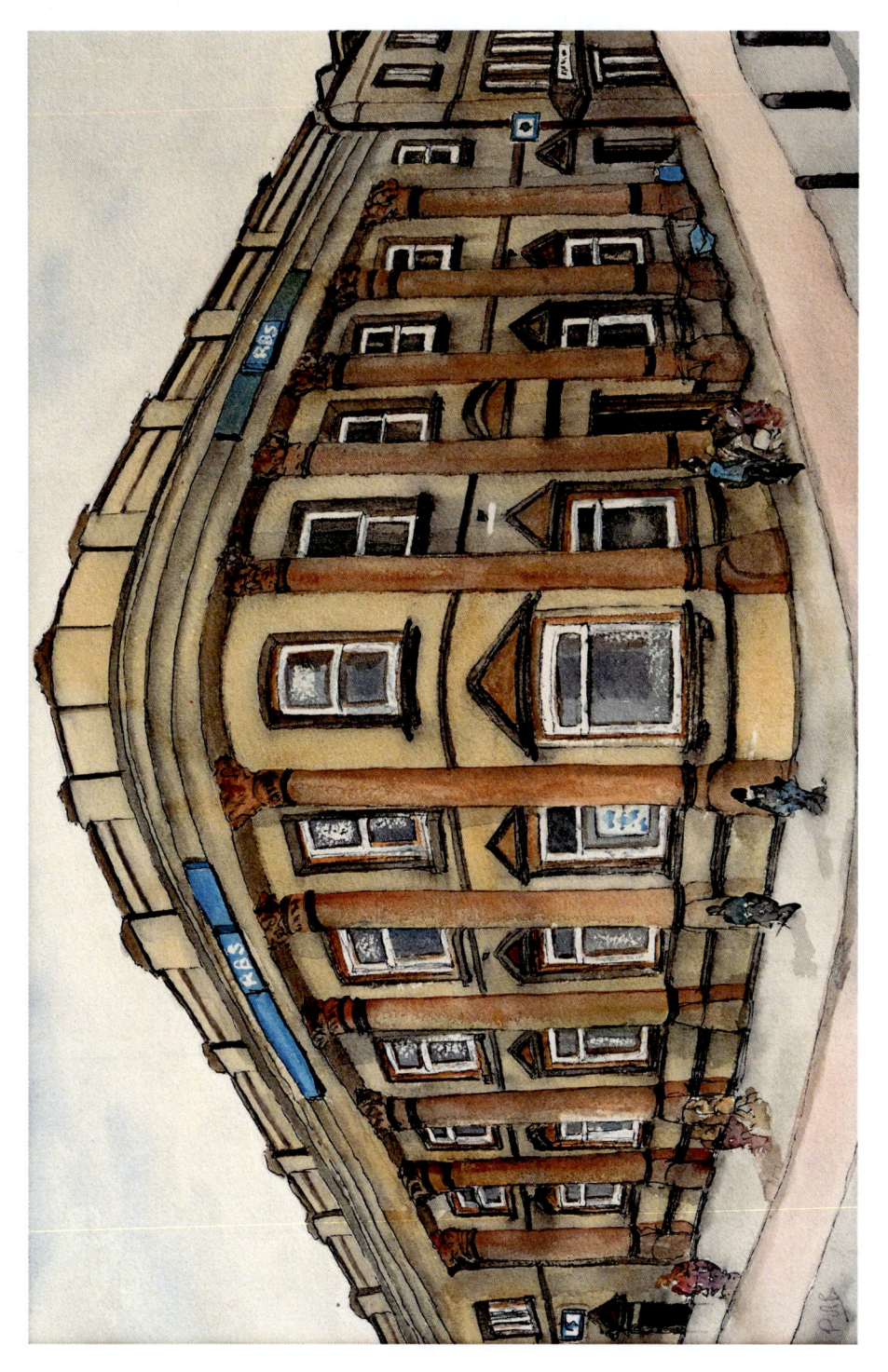

'*lower-middle-class*' origins and about her not having brought money into the marriage (money always being a consideration in the family and in Trollope's books) but I think this improbable considering Fanny's own background. Rose was probably the inspiration behind Trollope's strong-minded heroines such as Lucy Robarts, Mary Thorne and Lady Mabel Grex who are all witty, high spirited, strong willed and often so much cleverer than their men. Rose and Trollope's income was about £400 p.a. (£51,157 today), and Trollope pointed out that '*people thought we would be poor but since that day have never been without money in pocket and able to pay what owed.*' However, it was twelve years before he began receiving payment for his literary work.

Penrith

Meanwhile, Trollope's newly married sister, Cecilia, and her husband, John Tilley, moved to Penrith in Cumberland when he became resident Post Office Surveyor of the northern district. They lived in a pretty house situated between the town and the well-known Beacon on the hill to the north of it, at Beacon Lane, now known as Nicholson Lane. Shortly after, Tom and Fanny (in 1842, the year Trollope met Rose) also moved to the area. At first, they stayed with the Tilleys before purchasing land for £300 about a mile out of the town on the Langwathby Road, being:

> *All that lose or inclosure of land situate, lying and being on a place called Carleton Fell ... containing four acres one rood and nineteen perches ... late part of the commons and waste lands within the Honor of Penrith and Forest of Inglewood.*
>
> (Purchase deeds sourced by Guy Robinson)

The entrance to the site nowadays is a driveway with brick gateposts exactly at the point of a sharp bend on a fast-moving dual carriageway with no pavement. The drive curves away through shrubberies and trees (many planted by Tom) to the top of a hill where they built a substantial house, stables and outbuildings. Tom refers to it as a '*pretty paddock*' and devoted himself '*heart and body*' to building and beautifying the property. He also described it as '*... overlooking the ruins of Brougham Castle and the confluence of the Eden with the Lowther*'. As the building and upkeep were costly, Fanny continued writing hard.

At first Fanny and Tom were very pleased with the lake scenery and in letters mentioned frequent walks and drives within a wide radius around Penrith. Again, Fanny found and made a wide circle of friends such as Sir George (10th Baronet) and Lady Musgrave of Eden Hall (a large stately home and gardens now open to the public), and Lord Lonsdale with his daughter Lady Frederick Bentinck at Lowther Hall (now a ruin). They were also friendly with a Dr Nicholson and his daughter, also called Fanny.

Prior to his marriage to Rose (during the year they met), Trollope had spent a holiday with his brother Tom, exploring the area and taking long walks over many miles of countryside, climbing hills and exploring valleys in every direction from Carleton Hill. It was here that he and Rose came for their honeymoon. By all accounts Fanny and Rose got on well together and later Rose praised her mother-in-law. In another contrast to a failure of memory in his *Autobiography*, Trollope's recollections of these occasions served him well later when he recalled many of the sights and atmospheres of the area for his novels, such as Vavasor Hall in *Can You Forgive Her?* (1864–5); Humblethwaite Hall (north of Keswick, Skiddaw and Saddleback) in *Sir Harry Hotspur*; Lovel Grange (ten miles from Keswick) in *Lady Anna* (1874); Hautboy Castle on the banks of the Eamont in *Marion Fay*; 'The Mistletoe Bough' (wholly set in Thwaite Hall and again on the banks of the Eamont); and *The Bertrams* (two funny chapters relating to expeditions to see Lord Stapledean in Bowes on '... *the Eastern borders of Westmorland*'). According to Guy and Susan Robinson who knew the area very well, he describes the setting accurately by referring to real places and mountains and valleys. He was certainly fond of the area even if the gentle slopes of his imaginary Barsetshire were his ideal. Also, five miles north of Penrith is the village of Plumpton, where two churches vie for parishioners, St John the Evangelist and The Cottage Wood Methodists, which in 1709 was known as Backstreet Chapel. Was the name 'Plumpton' useful for Anthony, and could the competitive nature of the churches have provided yet another contribution to his budding inspiration for *The Vicar of Bullhampton*? As we have seen, he stored up information and situations for many years before making use of them.

Knowing of course that his mother had by this time many published novels, Trollope took *The Macdermots of Ballycloran* to Penrith to show her and ask advice on publication. Although his mother had written several years previously when nursing him at Northumberland Street that he had

Plaque at the entrance to the driveway of Carleton, Penrith

confided to her a wish to be a novelist, he nevertheless wrote modestly in his *Autobiography* of a different reaction to his having written a first novel:

> *I could see in the faces and hear in the voices of those of my friends who were around me at the house in Cumberland – my mother my sister, my brother-in-law and, I think, my brother – that they had not expected me to come out as one of the family authors. There were three or four in the field before me, and it seemed to be almost absurd that another should wish to add himself to the number ... I could see that this attempt of mine was felt to be an unfortunate aggravation of the disease ... I was sure that the book would fail, and it did fail most absolutely. I never heard of a person reading it in those days.*

He also states that she did not attempt to read *The Macdermots*, although she managed to arrange publication two years later, by Thomas Cautley Newby, 72 Mortimer Street, Cavendish Square, who had previously published Emily Brontë's *Wuthering Heights*. Trollope wrote: 'Expected nothing and got nothing'. This first book actually received good reviews but only 400 copies were produced, and, as it coincided with the Irish famine, it was depressing for the public. It was also marketed as being written by his mother, Fanny. For his second novel, *The Kellys and the O'Kellys* in 1848, he changed his publisher to a Mr Colbourn in Great Marlborough Street, but again had no recognition of any kind, until reviews in *The Times*, the *Spectator* and the *Athenaeum* resulted in a total sale of 375 copies, giving the publisher a loss of £63.10s 1d, and causing Mr Colbourn to point out that Irish novels were not popular. Nevertheless, he promised to look at *La Vendée*, the historical novel, which was now ready.

After only 'one winter and half a summer', in 1849 Fanny and Tom concluded that '*the sun yokes his horses too far from Penrith town*': put simply, the climate was too cold and Fanny was used to travelling abroad frequently, and, as Cecilia wrote: '*... the pleasant persons were widely scattered over a considerable tract of country. The plums in the social pudding were too few and far between both in space and time*'. Consequently, after staying briefly in London and Exeter, they moved permanently to Florence until Fanny's death in 1863 aged 76, suffering from dementia. She had written 114 volumes, beginning at the age of 50. Sadly, not long afterwards Cecilia died leaving orphaned children, after which John Tilley remarried.

The original plaque on the wall by the gateway correctly stated that Trollope 'stayed' there, but the owner of the house at one time complained to the Penrith Historical Sub-Committee and requested alterations. Subsequently the plaque now erroneously reads 'lived' here!

Rose Trollope

It has sometimes been hinted that Fanny Trollope had not only been neglectful of Trollope but had also been disparaging about Rose, but according to memoirs by novelist Frances Eleanor Trollope, Tom's second wife, Fanny was utterly devoted to both of them. When Anthony and Rose went to Penrith to meet the family, Rose herself praised her mother-in-law:

> Nothing could have been kinder or more affectionate than the way she received kind, good and loving, then and ever afterwards. No one who saw her at this date could suppose she was in her sixty-fourth year, so full was she of energy. There was no one more eager to suggest, and carry out the suggestions, as to mountain excursions, picnics, and so forth. And she was always the life and soul of the party with her cheerful conversation and her wit. She rose very early and made her own tea, the fire having been prepared overnight – (on one occasion I remember her bringing me a cup of tea to my room, because she thought I had caught cold during a wet walk in the mountains) – then sat at her writing-table until the allotted task of so many pages was completed; and was usually on the lawn before the family breakfast-bell rang, having filled her basket with cuttings from the rose bushes for the table and drawing-room decorations ...

Later, when Fanny stayed with Rose and Anthony in Cork, Ireland, in July 1848, they both recounted a happy and jolly time, with Fanny writing 'Anthony and his excellent little wife are as happy as possible'.

Meanwhile Rose wrote:

> We took her to Killarney, with which she was enchanted. Lord Kenmare's park especially delighted her. She walked through the gap of Dunlo as easily as if she had been twenty-nine instead of sixty-nine! And she was delighted with young Spellan, the bugler. In the evening we had old Spellan the piper introduced with his bagpipes into our sitting-room – at first to her dismay. But soon tears were rolling down her cheeks from the pathos of his music.

> *One day we put her on one of Bianconi's cars running to Glengariff, after much protest on her part against the ramshackle-looking machine. Presently, however, after a few jerks, and a dozen 'Niver fear, her honour!' from Mick the driver she almost persuaded herself that she would rather travel through Ireland in that way than any other!*

After she had stayed about a week Fanny espied Barney, the old Irish groom, breaking up stones under her window, and Rose, mischievously, related Barney's reaction to being given a tip: '*Sure, her honour gave the ould man a shilling every day for a month*' – adding that very soon the amount in Barney's telling grew into half a crown. Rose went on: '*When told of the delightful advance of her one sixpence to half-a-crown a day, she laughed, and said, "Ah, that shows on what slight threads hangs the report of our good deeds – and our evil ones!"*'. After returning home Fanny wrote and praised the delicious salmon, gooseberries and brown bread that they had eaten.

Rose also detailed her next visit to Florence in April 1853:

> *The next time I saw my dear old mother-in-law ... She took me about everywhere, and explained everything to me. And she made me happy by a present of an Italian silk dress. She also gave me a Roman mosaic brooch, which had been a present to her from Princess Metternich during her stay in Vienna. It is a perfect gem.*

Before her death, Rose handed it on to her daughter-in-law Ada, who passed it on to her daughter Muriel, who described it '*as a cherub with iridescent wings, drawing a pearly nautilus shell as a minute chariot on a black ground. It almost reminds one of Queen Mab's chariot in A Midsummer Night's Dream. The gold surrounding it is likewise lovely.*' Rose also described her mother-in-law thus: '*I thought her the most charming old lady who ever existed. There was nothing conventional about her and yet she was perfectly free from the vice of affectation ... I do not think she had a mean thought in her composition*', the implication being that her husband, Anthony, also held the same feelings.

Rose is often described as having '*exquisitely tiny feet*' (like Fanny), being well-dressed and, unusually for the time, hatless, but with a rose in her hair. The illustration on the next page is of a sleigh used by Lady Chesterfield around Nunburnholme Estate, near Pocklington, Yorkshire, and is of a type used by many wealthy Yorkshire landowners at the time, examples of which are displayed in a museum at Hull. It is remarkably similar to one shown in a photograph of Rose believed to have been taken abroad, although we do of course know the family connection with Yorkshire.

Sleigh as displayed in the Museum of Life in Hull, Yorkshire

Salisbury and Winchester
(*The Warden* and Barchester Novels)

Although Trollope had not received much money or acclaim for his Irish novels or the historical *La Vendée*, another seismic change occurred when he visited Salisbury in 1852. He declared in his *Autobiography* that he *'stood for an hour on the little bridge in Salisbury and made out to my own satisfaction the spot on which Hiram's Hospital should stand'*. Inspired by the view of Salisbury Cathedral, he conceived the imaginary area of Barchester, with a similar cathedral, cathedral close, prebendaries (honorary canons), archdeacons with their rivalries and dilemmas, and constant battles between the traditionalists and the evangelists. He immortalized the phlegmatic Archdeacon Grantly, the henpecked Bishop Proudie, his domineering but comedic wife Mrs Proudie, and his curate, the oily Obadiah Slope. The latter was probably modelled on the Reverend Cunningham from Harrow, and the Reverend Mr Crawley, with his learned stubbornness, was probably influenced by his own father. The novels also feature the well-connected Canon Stanhope, prebendary of the cathedral who, after living in idleness in Italy for years leaving his three parishes in the care of his curate, returned to England. This is reminiscent of Trollope's grandfather Milton, who lived out of his parish, although certainly not idle, but it was known that many clergymen did live idle lives abroad and were a much-discussed topic in the 1840s and '50s. Canon Stanhope returned with his mysterious and intriguing daughter Madame Neroni, predictably a magnet for young suitors of the parish. It was in the wheels of her chaise longue that the long train of Mrs Proudie's gown humiliatingly and hilariously became trapped, causing it to tear away in front of her guests at a reception! *The Warden* was the first of several novels connected to Barchester, including *Barchester Towers*, *Framley Parsonage*, *Orley Farm* and *The Last Chronicle of Barset*.

The Warden was conceived in 1851, begun in 1853 while Trollope was on Post Office business in Tenbury, and finally published in 1855. It is set in an almshouse named Hiram's Hospital. The warden of the title is Mr Septimus Harding, a kind and gentle elderly man, who is also rector of St Cuthbert and St Ewold churches and Provost of the cathedral. He genuinely loves the occupants, his work, his daughters, his residence, and playing his cello to the bedesmen and women, but becomes racked by doubt and his own conscience after a crusade by local surgeon and reformer John Bold (who is also in love with Harding's daughter Eleanor) highlights the immorality of Harding's income. This crusade is adopted by Tom Towers, a pushy young London journalist of *The Jupiter*. In a subtly ironic overlay: the music played by Mr Harding is probably *Home Sweet Home* composed by Henry Bishop and re-issued in 1852.

Barchester novels: top to bottom: *Dr Thorne* (The Bodley Head), *The Warden* (Oxford University Press), *Barchester Towers* (The Bodley Head), *The Last Chronicle of Barset* (Zodiac Press), *The Small House at Allington* (The Folio Society)

As Trollope stood on the 17th-century Harnham Bridge, Salisbury's St Nicholas Hospital would have been in view, but it is generally accepted that the main model for Hiram's Hospital is the St Cross Hospital of Winchester, not far from Salisbury, which had been accused of mismanagement by a Henry Holloway and became public knowledge in 1853, coincidentally the year after Trollope began his novel. The original hospital housed 134 old men, but Hiram's of *The Warden* houses 12 old men and 12 old women. However, other almshouses may also have fed into his imagination: the Seth Ward almshouse in Buntingford near his paternal relatives, founded by the Bishop of Exeter and Salisbury, the almshouse in Rotherham, and Browne's Hospital in Broad Street, Stamford near Casewick, which suffered a similar controversy to Hiram's Hospital.

Trollope probably retained a fondness for the St Cross Hospital of Winchester from his schooldays, and his brother Tom described '*the charming little village of St Cross*', where in the holidays the schoolboys went badger-baiting and mouse-digging nearby. Tom also mentions a warden from their school named Huntingford, Bishop of Hereford, considered by boys to be '*somewhat mystic, awe-inspiring*' and the ultimate threat for unruly behaviour. As usual Trollope probably incorporated previous observations from several areas, in this case Hereford, Ely and Winchester cathedrals and the Cathedral Close of Norwich.

There were many other reasons for the novel's topicality including recent scandals in cathedrals and cathedral schools as well as almshouses. There was general public disfavour, gossip in the gutter press and hostile questions in Parliament. The Poor Law Amendment Act of 1834, influenced by social theorists such as Jeremy Bentham and Thomas Malthus, gave power to new Poor Law Commissioners to form almshouses, workhouses or 'bedeshouses' – so-called as giving alms derived from the beads of a rosary, but only for the able-bodied poor and 'malingerers' were discouraged. The Act was designed to bring down the cost of 'the benefit system'.

According to Professor Dame Gillian Beer FBA, Professor Emerita of English at Cambridge University, the 1850s were uncertain times: theories such as Darwinism had provided a 'reality' which led to a public backlash of 'fantasy' or 'a way out', expressed as a need for escapism in novels, an expectation *The Warden* would have fulfilled.

Peter Blacklock, a resident of Salisbury, writing in *Trollopiana* no. 96 (2013), believes that Trollope's descriptions of Archdeacon Grantly's Plumstead Rectory match the large, four-square house next to Bishopstone Church about five miles away, as it has a dull, heavy air set in gardens and gravel drive; similarly, his descriptions of the Bishop's Palace are authentic. After the Reformation, bishops were able to marry, often having large families together with large numbers of staff filling the palaces. Grounds were frequently turned into extensive gardens: Bishop Wordsworth, nephew of the poet and son of the Bishop of Lincoln, and, like Trollope, an old boy of Winchester, employed ten indoor servants, three gardeners, two coachmen, a groom and a gatekeeper. As a Post Office Surveyor, Trollope would have called at such big houses and householders in any given area to discuss collections and deliveries of letters and arrange routes for letter-carriers. As the Bishop of Salisbury was regarded as a prince of the Church, and as such a superior being, it was unlikely that Trollope, then an unknown person, would have spoken to him personally, but as his descriptions of the interior, and particularly Mrs Proudie's Drawing Room, are so accurate, it is possible that he was shown around by a member of staff. Victorian literature records that it was quite common for visitors to be shown around big houses by a housekeeper or upper servant after the butler had accepted a tip!

The Very Reverend Keith Jones points out that Archdeacon Grantly was very much like Trollope himself, or at the very least a companionable man of the sort that he would have met in the clubs in London. When Trollope wrote *Clergymen of the Church of England*, he showed that between himself and archdeacons there was indeed an affinity:

> ... above all things, an Archdeacon should be a man of the world ... The man who won't drink his glass of wine, and talk of his college, and put off for a few happy hours the sacred stiffnesses of the profession and become simply an English gentleman, he is the clergyman whom in his heart the Archdeacon does not love.

The Reverend Jones also points out that Lord Palmerston, who became Prime Minister in February 1855, was uninterested in church life and therefore disapproved of the clergy promoting the church as an institution, preferring them to stick to religious matters without troubling him. Consequently, he found Evangelicals more congenial, but Trollope's genius lifted the work above the issues of his own day: the politics of mid-Victorian church and state are long forgotten but Bishop and Mrs Proudie and Archdeacon Grantly are still alive.

St Cross/Hiram's Hospital, Winchester

Somerset House

Following his success with *The Warden* (1855), *Barchester Towers* (1857) and *Doctor Thorne* (1858), that same year Trollope published the largely autobiographical *The Three Clerks* (1858). One of the clerks, the hero Charley Tudor ('*a gay-hearted, thoughtless, rollicking young man*') whose admission to the Internal Navigation Office at Somerset House is based on Trollope's own experiences of joining the Post Office at St Martin's le Grand in 1823, fits Trollope's own description.

Charley was similarly asked to copy some lines from the *Times* newspaper with an old quill pen, '*and at once made a series of blots and false spellings*'. When asked if he was proficient in arithmetic he felt he had '*no more idea of the rule of three than of Conic Sections*'. As in his own life, later at home Charley made a '*beautiful transcript of four or five pages of Gibbon*' under the surveillance of his elder brother, but the following morning no one '*condescended even to look at my beautiful penmanship*'. Again echoing Trollope's career, when Charley later achieved promotion, he was dissatisfied with the reception from his superior colleagues and consoled himself by calculating how long it would be before he was in their shoes.

Trollope used his character of Sir Gregory Hardlines to mock his superior Sir Charles Edward Trevelyan's introduction of the new public Post Office examinations to be taken by all prospective employees, in contrast to Trollope's (and Charley's) haphazard selection process. Trollope disapproved of the examinations, feeling that applicants could be crammed beforehand and thus not show fully their education, and he wrote '*I doubt whether more harm has not been done than good*'. He did, however, concede it was good to end the system of patronage, as MPs had often felt compelled to distribute clerkships amongst voters, with consequent embarrassing refusals and time-consuming correspondence. Knowing his *Autobiography* would be unread until after his death, Trollope dared to say the unprintable, namely that some positions needed to be filled by '*gentlemen*', a term often used in his novels. No one could define it, but everyone knew what it meant. Particular cases of '*ungentlemanly*' behaviour were Theodore Burton in *The Claverings* (1867) wiping his shoes with his handkerchief, and Samuel Rubb in *Miss Mackenzie* wearing bright yellow gloves – ugh! Trollope once told an audience that the novelist's duty was to teach ladies to be ladies, and men to be gentlemen. However, when Lady Mary Palliser tells her father, the Duke of Omnium, that the man she wishes to marry is a gentleman the Duke demurs: *'the word is too vague to carry with it any meaning'* (The Duke's Children, 1880).

Although Somerset House at that time housed the Royal Society, the Society of Antiquaries and the Royal Academy (where the first portrait of Trollope in the 1850s probably hung before the gallery's move to Burlington House in 1867), his fictional department of the Internal Navigation Office was aptly named: such a department must surely have become necessary at that time. The Canal Museum at Kings Cross, London, shows how miles of canals criss-crossed the country in the 19th century, with horse-drawn barges carrying cargo – coal, food, goods – from one end to another. Such canals, and their frequent locks in hilly areas (such as the Five Rise Locks, a misnomer as there are actually seven in a row, in Bingley, Yorkshire) are still an amazing feat of engineering and would have needed constant repair and supervision; tow-paths also needed to be kept clear for horses tugging along at one and a half mph.

When writing *The Three Clerks* Trollope would not have known that Mary Anne Evans, who wrote under the name of George Eliot and later became a friend and colleague, would walk on the terrace overlooking the Thames at the back of the offices on Sunday afternoons with Herbert Spencer.

In *The Three Clerks*, Charley was a hobbledehoy, deeply in debt, like Trollope, and had to go to the office by a circuitous route to avoid Mr M'Ruen, a Jewish money lender, to whom he owed money he could not pay, and whose injunction *'do be punctual'* occurs frequently in many novels, reflecting Trollope's own experience. Charley endures embarrassment when the mother of a barmaid he had almost promised to marry appeared in the office complaining loudly; but he eventually married the right girl and settled down. In his own memoirs, Trollope's brother Tom told the tale (used in *The Three Clerks*) of an anonymous *'old friend, school-fellow'* who had had dealings with a moneylender, *'in some hole-and-corner shady manner so that the man had induced him to put his name to two blank bills'* thereby making them legally payable by someone who would have been unable to pay if the borrower had defaulted. After consulting various people, they (Trollope?) were recommended to a certain police officer who guessed the name of the people concerned and advised them to go to the bank of Lloyd & Co for advice. But when he saw the:

> *... ludicrously chap-fallen and contrite appearance of 'poor friend', 'generally a choleric and sufficiently self-asserting man'* [sounding again like Trollope himself!], *he told them an 'Hanecdote', i.e. that 'such a man as the lender might be drinking in a certain pub that evening, and leaving about midnight with bills in pocket-*

book in breast-pocket of coat. One young gent tripped him up while the other collared the bills, all done in about two minutes. Odd coincidence your man frequents the same Saturday night there, as regular as clockwork – which advice they took with a fellow Wykehamist. Bills for four figures each.

All three clerks regularly visit the Woodward family, who live in Hampton with a garden going down to the Thames, eventually marrying all three daughters, almost as a forerunner of *Ralph the Heir*. Trollope would have known about the Bishop's Palace at Fulham from family travels (see above) and that in the 19th century the resident bishops and their wives wished to share the extensive land and gardens with the community, hosting large parties and church pageants. When describing Mrs Woodward begging Charley to be '*steady*' and not to get into trouble, he was perhaps remembering Mrs Clayton Freeling who, on hearing that he himself was liable to be dismissed from the office (for lateness, untidiness, possibly drunkenness), '*with tears in her eyes, besought me to think of my mother*'; his own illness in 1843 may have been transposed onto Kate Woodward, after being warned off Charley by her mother. '*The passage in which Kate Woodward, thinking that she will die, tries to take leave of the lad she loves, still brings tears to my eyes when I read it. I had not the heart to kill her. I never could do that*'.

His brother Tom quotes a letter to his wife from Mrs Browning:

I return The Three Clerks *with our true thanks and appreciation. We both quite agree with you in considering it the best of the three clever novels before the public. My husband, who can seldom get a novel to hold him, has been held by all three, and by this the strongest. Also, it has qualities which the others gave no sign of. For instance, I was wrung to tears by the third volume [instalments]. What a thoroughly man's book it is! I much admire it, only wishing away with a vehemence which proves the veracity of my general admiration, the contributions to the Daily Delight – may I dare to say it.*

Waltham Cross

Although the family were happy in Ireland, with Trollope's writing career now flourishing it seemed desirable to move back to England, with publishers nearby to enable discussions on subjects, terms, editions, and later editorships of magazines. He would also be nearer to wider family members and a different source of inspirations. He therefore petitioned the Post Office for a transfer to the Eastern District of England, and took up a post surveying Essex, Suffolk, Norfolk, Cambridgeshire, Huntingdonshire and the greater part of Hertfordshire in late 1859–71.

Accordingly, in 1859 Trollope and Rose leased Waltham House in Waltham Cross, about twelve miles from London, where they stayed for twelve years and eventually bought outright, and in 1863 were joined by Florence Bland (Bice), Rose's niece. It was one of two large Georgian houses behind gates. Waltham House faced Harold House at the end of a main street consisting of several public houses, one of which still has a gantry across the middle of the road in the manner of the Wild West. Apart from Harold House and a few original buildings in that part of the main street, the remainder of Waltham Cross is now one of the few places associated with Trollope which has changed beyond all recognition, with depressing 1930/60s buildings in a shopping precinct. According to C P Snow, Trollope lived here like an East Anglian squire; he *'had a soft spot for squires, much more than for aristocrats or the up and coming rich'*.

Down Park Lane/Berkeley Street almost opposite where Waltham House had been situated, I met an elderly lady whose late husband had lived in the area all his life and spoke of an Oyler's Farm once situated at the end of the lane having an unusual thatched refrigerator barn, considered to be at least 200 years old. This farm would probably have been visible from Trollope's house, and locals would certainly have walked there for milk and cream for their strawberries as did Rachel in *Rachel Ray* (1863). Could the name 'Oyler's Farm' also have influenced his choice of name for *Orley Farm* (1862)? Another farm in that direction was Theobalds Park Farm, with its footpath known locally as the Twopenny Tube, connecting with Bullscross Ride.

On the road to Waltham Abbey, about five miles away, is the 17th-century Royal Gunpowder Mills described in the 1860s by Colonel George Rains as the *'best existing steam-powered mills in any country'* and therefore important at a time when many people kept guns for their own protection, and shooting parties, being a popular aristocratic pastime, occur frequently in Trollope's novels. Waltham Abbey itself remains unchanged and would have provided some inspirations. Parts of the Abbey are ruined and one particular crumble of bricks in a dark leafy corner reminds me of Glencora's folly where she walks in the cold night air, catches pneumonia and dies, leaving her husband to cope with their children's problems of suitable marriages and gambling debts in *The Duke's Children* (begun in 1876 and serialized in *All the Year Round* 1879–80). Built amongst the ruins of the Abbey is the church of Holy Cross and St Lawrence and a pub, beside the marketplace and a main street of shops. One could easily imagine Glencora whispering to the bootmaker and butcher, and the residents adoring Lord Silverbridge. The bootmaker's shop is a reminder of Jones the Bootmakers and Lady de Courcy's new-fangled '*cork soles*'.

In this then semi-rural area, the Trollopes kept three cows and pigs, grew cabbages, asparagus, peas, strawberries and outdoor peaches, and made their own butter, and life was good. The house was said to be not always watertight, and Anne Thackeray wrote in her journal of 1865 that '... *It was a sweet old prim chill house wrapped in snow*' (*Anthony Trollope* by Hugh Walpole, Macmillan & Co, 1928). However, it was quite large with extra space for servants (including the faithful Barney who accompanied them from Ireland) and for washing and drying clothes by hand, such as long heavy skirts and petticoats, and of course for cooking basic foods such as bread from scratch. The domesticity must have suited Trollope: a sociable evening was described by W. Lucas Collins who wrote:

> *... in the warm summer evenings, the party would adjourn after dinner to the lawn, where wines and fruits were laid out under the fine old cedar tree and many a good story was told while the tobacco smoke went curling up into the soft twilight.*

Collins also wrote to John Blackwood on 31st May 1870 saying:

> *The Trollopes came on Thursday and left on Saturday. We like them very much, him especially, he was very pleasant to talk to, and at the same time so perfectly unassuming. What I like best in Mrs T is her honest and hearty appreciation of her husband.*

(Booth, *Letters*, I, 496)

Trollope himself wrote to George Henry Lewes saying: '*As to myself personally, I have daily to wonder at the continued run of domestic & worldly happiness which has been granted me; to wonder at it as well as to be thankful for it.'* Sir Frederick and Lady Pollock stayed at the house in 1866 and mentioned large rooms, a good staircase, *'a handsome stiff garden of the Queen Anne style, with a square pond at one end of it and a smooth grass lawn at the other'*, plus two outer wings, one for the stables and one converted into an office for Trollope's Post Office use.

Trollope was able to continue his passion for hunting, and during the season he could arrive at the Post Office at about 11.20 a.m. (permitted for high civil servants until about 1939) but there were still many stresses at work. Relations with his immediate superior, Sir Rowland Hill (originator of the Penny Post), were mutually abrasive, although fortunately his brother-in-law John Tilley, by now higher up the chain, was able to smooth over any problems. In spite of his boisterous and bluff character, Trollope was conscientious and believed not only in providing a good service to the public, but also that postal workers should have some free time, especially on Sundays. He also believed they needed to be adequately paid and not worried about job security, and he was prepared to support this over Rowland Hill's head. When Rowland Hill left owing to ill health and Trollope was bypassed for promotion, he was at first bitter but came to realize that the increased salary he would have received would not have compensated him for the loss of his literary earnings, and that he would not have enjoyed the extra stress:

> [I] ... *suffered very much bitterness on that score in reference to the Post Office; and I had suffered not only on my own personal behalf, but also and more bitterly when I could not procure to be done the things which I thought ought to be done for the benefit of others.*

After two years' deliberation he eventually resigned in 1867 aged 52, fully aware that at this age he would forfeit his pension. A glowing letter from John Tilley dated 9th October 1867 reads:

> *You have for many years ranked among the most conspicuous servants ... which ... has reaped much benefit from the great abilities which you have been able to place at its disposal ... notwithstanding the many calls upon your time, you have never permitted your other avocations to interfere with your Post Office work, which has always been faithfully and indeed energetically performed ... the Duke of Montrose desired me to convey to you his own sense of the value of your services, and to state how alive he is to the loss which will be sustained by the Department in which you have long been an ornament, and where your place will with difficulty be supplied.*

Rear of Waltham House and garden

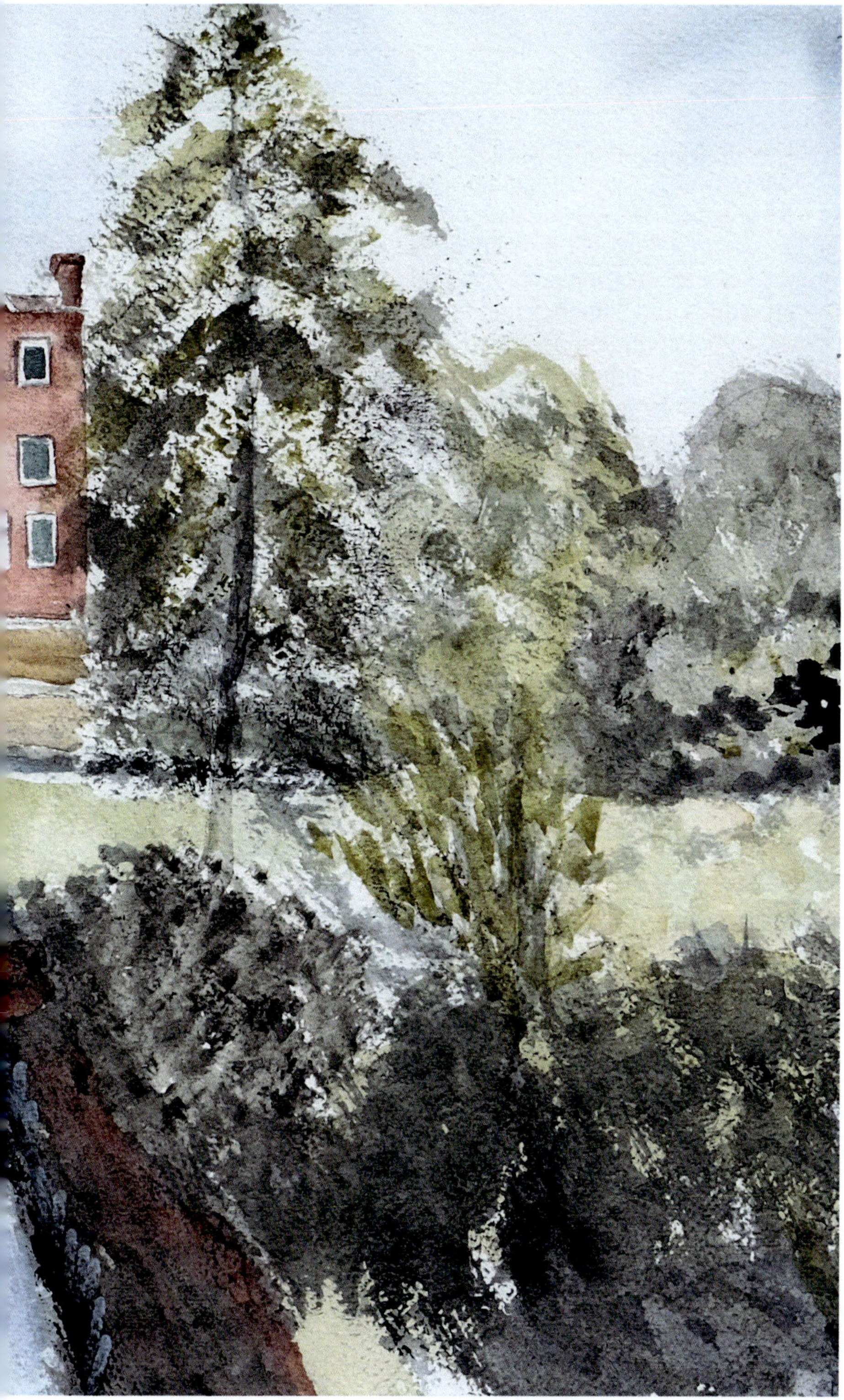

Freedom from the Post Office, election to gentlemen's clubs in London, members of the wider family, grand dinner parties and new hunting areas all provided new subjects, inspirations and terrain for his novels, leading to a very fertile writing period with the publication of many of his most famous novels, totalling twenty-eight altogether, and including *Castle Richmond*, *Framley Parsonage*, *The Vicar of Bullhampton*, *Orley Farm*, *Rachel Ray*, *The Small House at Allington*, *Can You Forgive Her?*, *Miss Mackenzie*, *The Last Chronicle of Barset*, *The Claverings* and *Phineas Finn*. He also wrote several short stories and Sketches and Commentaries. Additionally, some, such as *Sir Harry Hotspur*, *Ralph the Heir* and *The Golden Lion of Granpere*, were written whilst in Waltham Cross, but not published until later. During this time, he also published *Nina Balatka* anonymously as an experiment, but critics soon recognized his style. He also became a member of the General Committee of the Royal Literary Fund, began contributing to the *Pall Mall Gazette* and joined in the founding of the *Fortnightly Review*.

Hunting

Trollope repeatedly intended to give up this particular hobby but *'As, ... the money came in, I very quickly fell back into my old habits'*. He said he loved it with an affection which he could not *'fathom or understand... No man has laboured at it as I have done, or hunted under such drawbacks as to distances, money, natural disadvantages.'* Sometimes during the winter season he would hunt two or three days a week, not including the travel time there and back. He owned four hunting horses (even five when his sons were at home), which Barney looked after, an important function. Horses, being essential for transport as well as hunting, have small stomachs and need to eat little and often. Their diet consists of chaff or hay which Barney and the Trollopes made themselves at Waltham (long grass, dried and cut up), mixed with 'chop' (oats and bran as a laxative). Horses also need the right quantity of peas and beans to prevent them becoming over-excitable and dangerous, plus cod liver oil and salt. Big horses can drink as much as five buckets of water per day, drawn from the well. On hunting days, Barney sometimes rode the horses in advance to Trollope's intended destination or sometimes, as railways were now opening, they could be transported by train (and sometimes get mixed up as when Frank in *The Duke's Children* accidentally took the wrong horse *'off the rail'* when travelling to the hunt). Trollope would sometimes even travel all night outside a mail-coach. A rail station had opened between Waltham Cross and Waltham in 1840 for journeys into London, and by 1842 a terminus with four lines and a turntable opened at nearby Bishop's Stortford, with trains going at 36 mph to Norwich in Norfolk in 1845 and to Dunmow and Braintree in Essex in 1869. When Anthony rode around on Post Office business it was often necessary for two supplementary horses to follow him, probably costing about £2,300 p.a. in today's money. To him, hunting was a quintessentially British activity, which united the best and the bravest from different social classes, such as Lord Rufford hunting with Lawrence Twentyman in *The American Senator* (1877).

Riding horseback from Waltham Cross passing through Waltham Abbey, it is 15.7 miles along minor country roads, and 12–13 miles cutting through fields, to the picturesque villages of Matching Tye and Matching Green, both of which are remarkably unchanged, the former being little more than a hamlet dominated by The Fox public house where to this day the Essex Hunt (founded 1785) have their Boxing Day Meet. They obviously now drag a scent after fox hunting with dogs in England was banned in 2005. The nearby village of Matching Green consists of thatched Tudor and 18th-century cottages dotted around the edges of a large green, with one very large house which could have spawned ideas for 'Matching', the more comfortable home of the Palliser family. On some routes he would have passed through the village of Clavering, and in 1867 *The Claverings* was published.

Trollope also hunted in the opposite direction, in the Fitzwilliam Hunt in Cambridgeshire, and the Quorn, Belvoir and Pytchley hunts around the village of Melton Mowbray in Leicestershire. This village (known as Melton) is no longer full of hunting necessities, but the countryside around is almost intact, with coverts (ideally small gorse and blackthorn copses of between two and twenty acres) still carefully preserved and owned by hunts themselves. Melton's county emblem is still a fox, although now standing erect and alert instead of running, and the county's motto remains 'For'ard, for'ard Leicestershire'. The area is still famous for its pork pies, invented as a convenient and easy-to-carry food for huntsmen. After the Wreake canal opened in 1794, providing Melton with increased supplies, it became a magnet for foxhunters throughout Europe and beyond. Hunting 'boxes' (or 'lodges') were built for wealthy foxhunters to take for the season, as well as exclusive 'hunt clubs' where a handful of hunting men could live communally, such as the Buckinghamshire '*Moonbeam*' in *Ralph the Heir*, or the '*Tally-ho Lodge*' in *The Duke's Children*. From around 1800 there was a huge influx of money into Melton, with large numbers of top-class horses and hard-riding men needing a commensurate number of farriers, livery stables, forage suppliers, saddlers, loriners, bootmakers and so on. It became a place everyone went to – if they could afford it.

Another area for hunting was from Casewick, when around once a year Trollope stayed with his cousin Sir John Trollope (later the first Lord Kesteven). The journey there usually took him about eleven days, when he and his hunters (sometimes six) stayed at different friends' country houses along the way, such as at Stilton; and with the mother of Cuthbert Bede in Orton where he was described as '... [cutting] *a comical figure when arrayed in a somewhat soiled pink coat, cord breeches, and shiny mahogany top-boots ... rough-mannered, but good-hearted and genuine*'. He often amused the children of these establishments by pretending to talk to his socks or boots, and ruffling his hair. There was general surprise at his rising at five in the morning to write (earning £20 as he said) after staying up smoking and talking until nearly 11 o'clock the night before, and still fresh for his onward journey to Casewick. He also often stayed with the Reverend W Lucas Collins at Lowick (where, on a holiday once with Rose, he took advantage of being snowed in for three weeks by writing *Dr Wortle's School*). Characteristically he communicated his plight in correspondence:

> *That I, who have belittled so many clergymen, should ever come to live in a parsonage! There will be a heaping of hot coals. You may be sure that I will endeavour to behave myself accordingly, so that no scandal shall fall upon the parish. If the bishop should come that way, I will treat him as well as e'er a parson in the diocese. Shall I be required to preach, as belonging to the rectory? I shall be quite disposed to give everyone my blessing ... Ought I to affect dark garments? Say the word, and I will supply myself with a high waistcoat. Will it be right to be quite genial with the curate, or ought I to patronise a little? If there be dissenters, shall I frown on them, or smile blandly? If a tithe pig be brought, shall I eat him? If they take to address me as 'the Rural Anthony', will it be all right?*

Trollope frequently lost his glasses whilst hunting which fortunately were usually rescued by companions, and he once suffered an accident when he was almost kicked in the head after falling on his back near the horse's hooves. His companions took him to a nearby priory to recuperate,

Typical hunting meet

a situation probably used later as a way of furthering a love affair between Felix Graham and Madeline Stavely in *Orley Farm*. Hunting was an all-consuming passion for Lord Chiltern, of *Phineas Finn*, who used all his energy inspecting coverts and managing his hounds, and for some women too, such as Chiltern's niece Adelaide Palliser, possibly based on Aunt Meetkerke at Julians (see above).

There were many other people for whom it was a vital activity, and Friedrich Engels wrote to Karl Marx in 1857: *'That sort of thing always keeps me in a state of devilish excitement for several days; it is the greatest physical pleasure I know. I saw only two out of the whole field.'*

Trollope's great energy and stamina in the saddle were also useful whilst travelling for the Post Office. An anecdote describes his riding forty miles or so in great heat in the West Indies to get letters delivered and save the Post Office money. On becoming saddle-sore he was said to have sat in a basin full of brandy, and announced that he was totally recovered the following morning.

London Clubs

London clubs were a rich source of material for Trollope. On non-hunting days, while still at the Post Office and after beginning the day with his writing routine, he would work straight through until about 5 p.m. and then visit one of his clubs to socialize, smoke, drink, discuss politics, and play whist and bridge. It was possible first to have a cup of tea – an innovation at this time as hitherto it had only been drunk first thing in the morning, or as a nightcap after dinner. The clubs were for men only (some still are) and they would have been defined by 'gentlemen' of particular ideologies: members of the Athenaeum were elected according to their achievements; the Reform Club welcomed rebels against the Tory ideologies of the Carlton Club; and the National Liberal Club was frequented by gentlemen with more liberal ideas. All the clubs are still housed in large, grand buildings around Pall Mall, except the Garrick, where Trollope became a member in 1864. This was a club for artistic members and being thus considered lower in the social scale, was located in King Street, a slum area, before moving to its present site in Garrick Street, Covent Garden.

Members of the Garrick Club included actors of note such as Johan Zoffany, Thomas Lawrence, David Garrick, John Gielgud and Henry Irving, whom Anthony helped to join, and also writers such as his friend William Makepeace Thackeray, rival Charles Dickens and The Hon Frederick Walpole. Another friend was Henry Nelson O'Neil, the leading Victorian painter of historical and genre scenes, particularly of the Indian Mutiny, who in 1869 painted a group oil portrait of forty-three members: the bearded Trollope, in wire-rimmed spectacles and evening dress, is fourth from the left in the top row. John Everett Millais (who later became his illustrator) is also portrayed on the right, holding a billiard cue and looking straight at the viewer. Today the club houses a large and significant collection of British theatrical art. In 1858 there was a 'Great Squabble' in the club between Thackeray and Dickens, which may have fuelled Trollope's antipathy towards Dickens: he had previously portrayed him as Mr Popular Sentiment in *The Warden* and as '...*very ignorant and thick-skinned*'.

Trollope revelled in his memberships, writing that he had:

> ... *long been aware of a certain weakness in my own character, which I may call a craving for love. ... In schooldays no small*

part of my misery came from the envy with which I regarded the popularity of popular boys. And afterwards in the Post Office had few friends ... the Garrick Club was the first assemblage of men at which I felt myself to be popular.

Sometimes he entertained people in the club: according to Richard Mullen in the *Penguin Companion to Trollope* (1996), he arranged for a haunch of venison, given to him in Sussex, to be served at the Garrick, and on the 1st November 1882 he gave dinner there to Robert Browning. Two years after joining the Garrick, Trollope's good friend Thackeray died, and he was consequently invited to fill his place on the committee.

Trollope also belonged to the Athenaeum (as did Thackeray and the Hon Frederick Walpole), and would have benefited from their extensive libraries and art collections. Many of his young male characters spent many hours in their clubs, particularly the fictitious Bear Garden (probably based on the Savage Club, a club within a club at the National Liberal Club which, like the Garrick, to this day does not admit women). He also belonged to the Cosmopolitan Club, or 'Cos', which met two evenings a week in a painter's studio off Berkeley Square; its object, said J L Motley *'seems to be to collect noted people and smoke very bad cigars'* (*The Correspondence of John Lothrop Motley*, ed. George William Curtis (1899) as stated in the Gutenberg Press). And Sir Francis (Frank) Burnand described it as both *'a very exclusive literary, artistic and parliamentary club'*, and *'a superior sort of free-and-easy, where pipes could be smoked'*. Trollope recalled a mixed group there, among them several politicians, who *'whisper[ed] the secrets of Parliament with free tongues'*. It is thought that Trollope used this as the basis of *'the Universe'* and *'the club where the best-informed political gossip is heard'* in *Phineas Redux*, where members met every Sunday and Wednesday evenings for the greater part of the year. The name was supposed to be a joke, as it was limited to ninety-nine members, and *'Its attractions were not numerous, consisting chiefly of tobacco and tea'* (*Phineas Redux*). After having eaten dinner in clubs, gentlemen would often go into the smoking room, particularly if they wanted to avoid a private conversation, such as the dubious Count Pateroff in *The Claverings*, and later some would lose a lot of money playing cards – or else clandestinely win! Whilst writing in the Athenaeum library, alongside Matthew Arnold, Thackeray and Bishop 'Soapy Sam' Wilberforce one day, Trollope *'overheard two clergymen sitting either side of the fire each with a magazine, abusing and reading some part of a novel of mine'*. Their main complaint was the fact that he reintroduced the same characters so often (a feature we now particularly appreciate): one mentioned the Archdeacon, and the other the old Duke *'whom he has talked about till everybody is tired of him'*. But it was

Whist table at the Athenaeum

when they mentioned Mrs Proudie that Trollope jumped up impetuously, saying he would '*go home and kill her before the week is over*'. Later he admitted that he was sorry to kill off one of his best-known characters, but her demise allowed us to see that she was not just '*a bully, a tyrant, and a very vulgar woman*', but that she was a more rounded character and over-conscientious and anxious to save the souls around her.

Near the Athenaeum, on the site of the Carlton Club, there had originally been two inns, the Star on one side of the road and the Garter on the other. Trollope would have heard the stories that in 1774 '*The noblemen and gentlemen of the Jockey Club*' had met in the Star to revise the laws of cricket (*The Fixed Period*, 1882, features many cricketing rules) and that in 1765 Lord Byron, great-uncle of the poet, and his neighbour Mr Chaworth, took part in a famous duel, when Mr Chaworth was killed. Trollope featured a duel between Phineas Finn and Lord Chiltern, who is not only the son of his patron and sister of pining Laura, but his love rival for Violet Effingham; he also depicted violence in the murder of Mr Bonteen on the steps of his club, for which Phineas is wrongly blamed in *Phineas Redux* (1873). Luckily, he is saved by Madame Max, whom he eventually marries. There is also another love rival fight, this time against the railings in Charles Street at 2 a.m., when Harry Annesley attacks Mountjoy in *Mr Scarborough's Family* (published posthumously in 1883).

Trollope was not a member of the Reform Club (unlike his character Phineas Finn), but his friend Thackeray was a lifelong member from 1841 and Trollope would almost certainly have visited 'the strangers' room' as his guest. It is thought to have been named in honour of the Great Reform Act of 1832 which aimed to rid Parliament of 'rotten boroughs' and give representation to the growing cities of the Industrial Revolution. Even if Trollope had not visited the Reform, he would have known the reputation of the revered chef, Alexis Benoit Soyer, who donated money to the poor by selling recipes, including to Mr Crosse and Mr Blackwell. Trollope also would have known that during the Irish potato famine, Soyer took leave of absence to cater for over 8,000 people in Dublin, with his newly invented soup boiler, which held 40–50 gallons to feed 200–300 people at a time, such as the ones now displayed in Carrick-on-Shannon, as mentioned earlier. He also encouraged 'charitably inclined ladies' to make soups for the poor, subscribed towards a soup kitchen in Leicester Square, and later organized food for troops during the Crimean War.

After leaving the Reform Club in 1850 over a disagreement, Mr Soyer organized grandiose banquets all over the country and Thackeray said he had the friendliest feelings and genuine admiration for him. Knowing Trollope's talent for storing up every morsel of information for use in later novels, perhaps this knowledge contributed to his ideas of grand banquets in *The Way We Live Now* (1875).

Beverley

Trollope had always expressed the belief that *'to sit in the British Parliament should be the highest object of ambition to every educated Englishman'* and *'that to serve one's country without pay is the grandest work that a man can do'* (MPs are paid today of course). His Uncle Henry had once asked him about his hopes for a future life, and on hearing that he would like to be a Member of Parliament, commented sarcastically that as far as he knew not very many Post Office Clerks became MPs. However, Trollope clung to the ambition. He would presumably have preferred to stand in Essex where he was well known and might even have succeeded, but as that was not possible, against all advice, he stood in 1868 for Beverley. Dickens wrote to Tom saying the decision was *'inscrutable'* while Trollope himself later wrote that it was the *'most wretched fortnight of my manhood'*. Tellingly, one year later Lord Chiltern in *Phineas Finn* (1869) said *'Parliament is meanest trade going'*.

Trollope's much-loved friend Charles Buxton proffered advice:

> ... you won't get in. I don't suppose you really expect it. But there is a fine career open to you. You will spend £1,000 [£120,000 today], and lose the election. Then you will petition, and spend another £1,000. You will throw out the elected members. There will be a commission, and the borough will be disfranchised. For a beginner such as you are, that will be as a great success.

He was 53 years old, enjoying success in the Post Office and success as a novelist, performing Freemasonry duties and hunting two or three days a week in season, and even questioned his own wisdom, writing in his *Autobiography*:

> I was thus aware that I could do no good by going into Parliament, that the time for it, if there could have been a time, had gone by. But still I had an almost insane desire to sit there, and be able to assure myself that my Uncle's scorn had not been deserved.

He also knew that he was unsuitable for Parliament as he was not a good public speaker; he lacked patience for the detail of practical politics and still, uncomprehending why (like his enthusiasm for hunting), he nevertheless persisted in standing in 1868 as a political candidate for the town of Beverley, a byword for corruption, near Hull, in the East Riding of Yorkshire.

Four candidates stood in the election: two Conservatives and two Liberals. Trollope presented himself as an advanced, but still conservative, Liberal with a tendency towards equality, being willing to help the many ascend the ladder. All the dire warnings and predictions came to pass and are recalled by Sir Thomas Underwood who stood as a Conservative in '*Percycross*' or Percy St Cross, in *Ralph the Heir* (1871). Other elections take place in *The Way We Live Now* (1875) and *The Duke's Children* (1880).

Beverley is still a beautiful, unspoilt medieval city, with tiny lanes and alleyways and street names such as Hengate, Sun Hill Road, Dog and Duck Lane, Laundress Lane, and North Bar Within (inside the City gate) and North Bar Without (outside the gate). At one end of the main thoroughfare is the Wednesday Market, dominated by the Minster, and at the other, the Saturday Market, dominated by St Mary's Church, an equally imposing

Bandstand at Beverley, near Hull, Yorkshire

structure. When Trollope spent two weeks canvassing he found the east wind to be very cruel (also my experience)!

He is said to have spoken at both the Mechanics and the Temperance Halls (no longer there), and from a balcony above a tailor's shop in the market square. The only balcony I saw was on a very grand building (now a bank) overlooking the Saturday Market, a much bigger and more imposing area than the Wednesday Market, complete with a central bandstand, and was therefore the area I chose to paint.

Unlike my recollections, Trollope found it be an *'uninteresting town'*, as he tramped around the lanes and byways *'canvassing every voter, exposed to the rain, up to the knees in slush, and at night had to speak somewhere, or worse, listen to others'*. Once again *'... felt to be a pariah, and voters cared nothing for my doctrines and could not even be made to understand that I should have any'*.

I finished my stay in Beverley by *'ending up in the Beverley Arms for tea'*, as Philip Larkin and Maeve Brennan had usually done after pedalling there at weekends.

There is not enough room here for me to print Trollope's address 'To the Freemen and other Electors of the Borough of Beverley'; the 'Canvassing Notice to Electors of Beverley'; 'Letter to Lord Herries after Defeat' or any of the full articles in the *Beverley Recorder*, but they are freely available in the Beverley Archives. However, the following poems in the press sum up the proceedings:

Electoral Tip for Beverley

Ho! Rhubarb, magnesia, ho! Bismuth and jalap!
Ho! Jenkins and Robinson Walker and Brown;
'Tis said that our friend Anthony Trollope
Would like to be Member for Beverley town.
Oh! I do not elect him, 'twould be such a pity.

For really with work he is getting quite thin;
Just fancy him stuck on a Draining Committee,
Or bored like his own Phineas Finn!

Say no to him sweetly without any fighting,
And leave not the Tories you have, in the lurch:
Friend Anthony Trollope is wanted for writing
And not, sirs, for wronging poor Pat and the Church!
So all ye good Yorkshiremen, cunning as Reynard,
And able, they say, to bite living or dead,
Cheer Maxwell and Trollope, but put Mr Kennard
Up on the poll second with Edwards as head!

>Will-o-the-Wisp
> The Conservative *Beverley Guardian*

ELECTORS OF BEVERLEY
BE NOT DECEIVED

'Sir Henry Edwards and Lord Hotham voted with the Tory Government to take one member from us. Facts are stubborn things. The names of those who vote in the House of Commons are preserved.'

Sir Henry Edwards sat on the government wall,
Sir Henry Edwards obeyed the government call;
Sir Henry Edwards will have a great fall,
And all Sir Henry's shufflings, and all his Men,
Can't lift Sir Henry on the wall again.

ELECTORS! Vote for
MAXWELL AND TROLLOPE

Pamphlet

Electors! Men of Beverley,
Whom the Tories now Tax well,
Vote like wise and good men
For Trollope and MAXWELL

They are the men of Progress,
Who give fair play to all;
And will see our ancient Borough
Does not go to the wall.

They're not like the Tories,
Who dare not own their name;
They are the Liberals in Principle,
And in Practice the same.

Electors! Men of Beverley,
For the honour of our Town
Let not the Colonel dare again
To say we are his own.
He, in his place in Parliament,
Did advocate for years
The spending of your money
For his mounted Volunteers.
Some of you remember
When the Yeomanry Cavalry
Did, in the Town of Manchester,
Commit horrid butchery.
Poor, defenceless women,
To the Butchers fell a prey;
The charge was led by a Tory Lord,
Whose name was Castlereagh.
So know, my gallant Colonel,
And my gallant Captain, too;
For the thinking men of Beverley
Your principles won't do.

Then vote for noble Maxwell,
And learned Trollope too;
They are the Men for Beverley,
They're Reformers good and true.
I, William Padget,
Who, in Liberty glory,
Am not such a fool, yet,
As to Vote for a Tory.
Liberal *Beverley Recorder*

Politics and the Houses of Parliament

Trollope's interest in politics may have begun in 1834 when, aged 19, he and Tom joined huge crowds to watch as first the House of Lords and then the House of Commons raged with fire. Only the Jewel Tower, the Undercroft Chapel, the Cloisters and Chapter House of St Stephen's, and Westminster Hall were saved, largely owing to a change in the direction of wind during the night and the skill of the fire service. The fire of course led to the new design by Augustus Pugin and the rebuilding by Charles Barry – a feat which was twenty-five years late and three times over budget. Obviously, a design and rebuilding project of this importance and magnitude would have been at the forefront of public awareness and discussion for many years. Trollope's later years in Ireland would also have alerted him to political decisions regarding Irish famine, Home Rule and the Catholic Emancipation Act of 1829, as well as the Corn Laws which were not repealed until 1846. Additionally, the Great Stink of 1858 provided another big topic for public awareness and discussion.

He was to write in his pamphlet at Beverley (see above) that:

> *The Protestant Church as it now stands established in Ireland means the ascendancy of the rich over the poor, of the great over the little, of the high over the low. It has none of those attributes which should grace a church. It does not open its bosom to the poor. It lacks charity. It assumes the virtues of the Pharisee. It is hated instead of loved by the people. That the Irish Protestant Church will speedily be disendowed and disestablished no intelligent politician in England or Ireland now doubts.*

He was referring to Ireland in the 1840s where selfish landlords, many of them absentee, imported huge quantities of grain while the peasant population, who depended on the potato, died of hunger; the Westminster government was scandalously late in reacting, believing that the famine was a Malthusian 'solution' to the 'problem' of a large anti-English, Roman Catholic population. *An Essay on the Principle of Population* (1798) by scholar and economist Reverend Thomas Malthus had taught that population growth is potentially exponential, but the growth of the food supply is linear.

Houses of Parliament

Trollope's first political novel, *Phineas Finn*, was published in 1869, a year after his failed attempt for election in Beverley; it is not directly political but focuses on the lives, worries, loves and achievements of people who moved in political circles. The main character, Phineas Finn, is a young and bright Irishman, who believes that getting into the House of Commons is the most worthwhile of all ambitions, and is '*a sound Liberal, not to support a party but to do the best I can for the country*', while his friend Barrington Erle simply wishes to support his leader. Phineas goes through political turbulence, personal unhappiness and violence and a trial at the Old Bailey (Trollope's account of which is influenced by his own experience of barristers), but eventually finds happiness in *Phineas Redux* (1873).

The Prime Minister (1876) and *The Duke's Children* (1880) evoke a whole network of characters, linked by Plantagenet Palliser, his wife Glencora and their children Lord Gerald and Lord Silverbridge (and the latter's fiancée Isabel Boncassen), and Lady Mary and her fiancé Frank Tregear. Certain of the characters also appear in *Can You Forgive Her?* (1864-5) and *The Eustace Diamonds* (1872).

Railway Stations and Speculation

The subjects of railways, guano and speculation were also topical in the mid to late 1800s: Euston Station was originally built in 1837 but expanded from two platforms to fifteen in 1849, and similarly Paddington Station, built in the 1830s, was expanded in the 1850s by the addition of a new Great Hall designed by Isambard Kingdom Brunel in the manor of Crystal Palace.

By 1873 when Trollope wrote *The Prime Minister* (published 1876), 24,000 miles of track had been laid with a web of connections, and many other novelists such as Thomas Hardy, Dickens, Mrs Henry Wood, Wilkie Collins and George Eliot also began to feature them in their fiction. Trollope himself wrote extensively with a portable desk whilst travelling, so it would seem natural to feature railways also. He mentioned WH Smith & Sons at Paddington Station, founded in 1848 by William Smith, 3rd Viscount Hambledon, to sell cheap 'Special railway' editions of novels for reading on trains. Novel reading and rail travel became closely connected. Adolphus Crosbie ends up *'prostrate among the newspapers'* in the WH Smith bookstall after being assaulted by Johnny Eames for abandoning Lily Dale in *The Small House at Allington* (1864). Paddington Station is the Great Western Railway terminus, with a branch line going on to the fictional Barchester. Characters such as Miss Mackenzie meet Mr Rubb before taking a cab together to her brother Tom's house in Gower Street (see above) and Sophie Gordeloup passes through in *The Claverings*. Marie Melmotte (*The Way We Live Now*) and her maid go to Liverpool early one morning and '[a]*t the station they got some very bad tea and almost uneatable food*'. Bad food is also mentioned in *The Eustace Diamonds* (1872).

It was at Paddington Station that Miss Francesca Altifiorli, descended from the Fiascos and the Disgrazias, arrived early in the hope of meeting Sir Francis Geraldine in *Kept in the Dark* (1882): '*It is the privilege of unmarried ladies when they travel alone to spend a good deal of time at stations. But as she walked up and down the platform, she had an opportunity for settling her thoughts.*' Later she '*enjoyed the pressing of Sir Francis' hand*'.

In contrast, the ostler at the Courcy Inn in *Dr Thorne* (1858) bemoans the good old days when mail coaches stopped at the inn, bringing business and prosperity to the town which the railways had bypassed (see Perivale and Stamford above).

Speculation – railway speculation – is the subject of *The Way We Live Now* (1875) where Melmotte, the ultimate speculator, urges investors to buy shares in the South Central Pacific and Mexican Railway, introduced by a sharp American called Hamilton K. Fisker. Nominally the company exists to build the transcontinental railway, but everyone knows its real function is share speculation. Melmotte gives the impression of wealth by holding huge and splendid banquets (perhaps a reference to Alexis Soyer above) for aristocrats and royalty, leading of course to disaster. The main influence of course was probably the same Mr Hudson who used some money lent by Trollope's own father-in-law, bank manager Edward Heseltine. Known as the 'Railway King', he basically financed his projects of building railways, such as the 1847 journey from York to Hull (at 70 mph), with magnificent stations, by a Ponzi scheme. Before his disgrace he also acted as chairman of many companies, becoming MP for Sunderland and three times a mayor.

Both speculation and guano are the subjects of *The Prime Minister* (1876) with a dramatically violent scene taking place at '*Tenway Junction*' after Ferdinand Lopez loses his speculative (and borrowed) investment in guano. Guano (fertiliser from bat and seabird droppings) had become popular, used in Cambridge college gardens for example, and whilst hunting on the Essex/Suffolk border Trollope may have heard of the dealer Thomas Patrick Hitchcock (1813–84), subject of a recent exhibition in the Little Hall Museum, Lavenham, Suffolk, abutting Essex. He sold guano to farmers throughout the area after sourcing it from a Peruvian entrepreneur called Francisco de Quiroz who, like Lopez, in turn drew on capital from various English firms. The price went up and up, but new sources and popularity of demand led to prices dropping from £18 per ton to £12–13, leading to his and Lopez's losses.

Dramatically, Lopez takes the omnibus and underground train from Gower Street to Euston Station, eats a mutton chop and tea for breakfast, and buys a first-class return ticket to '*Tenway Junction*', six or seven miles from London, on the first week in March. This was probably based on Willesden Junction which, to a Victorian used to walking and horse-riding as a means of transport, would have seemed to be very large and noisy with trains bustling furiously past in all directions: '*Not a minute passes without a train going here or there, some rushing by without noticing Tenway in the least crashing through like flashes of substantial lightning, and others stopping, disgorging and taking up passengers by the hundreds*'. Despite being watched and followed by a suspicious worker, Lopez calmly walks up and down until:

> *... the morning express down from Euston to Inverness was seen coming round the curve at a thousand miles an hour ... with*

quick, but still with gentle and apparently unhurried steps, he walked down before the flying engine – and in a moment had been knocked into bloody atoms.

From the 1830s to the 1850s trains could travel at 30 mph, but by 1850 could go as fast as 70 mph which would have appeared as extraordinarily fast compared to a horse. The Vintage Carriages Trust Railway Museum

Heritage train

in Ingrow, a mile outside the village of Haworth in West Yorkshire, houses several heritage trains, many of which were used for filming, including the one used in the televised adaptation of *The Way We Live Now*. The carriages, of course, are third, second and first class, and one can sample at first hand that even first class would have been claustrophobic and uncomfortable, especially if fellow passengers were ladies wearing large crinoline skirts. However, the use of trains enabled Trollope to write whilst travelling, using a portable writing desk in a way he was not able to do on horseback.

WH Smith, Paddington Station

According to Professor Rohan McWilliam of Anglia Ruskin University in Cambridge, all types of people and classes in the Victorian era were constantly on the move, around the country and abroad. *The Railway Station*, painted in 1862 by William Frith RA, shows a manically crowded London station bustling with people, children, animals, luggage and porters.

The Palliser Novels

As we have repeatedly seen, Trollope took inspiration from people he knew, his surroundings, the areas he hunted in or visited on business, and social visits he made, and clearly remembered details from the distant past. He also drew inspiration from subjects which would have been discussed among his friends and at the clubs. When he began the Palliser series whilst living at Waltham Cross with *Can You Forgive Her?* (1864-5), followed by *The Prime Minister* (1876) and *The Duke's Children* (1880), it was at a time when many large houses were being built or enlarged nationwide and in his own neighbourhood. Although classified as political novels, the Palliser series also contains love stories and diversions, one large diversion being Gatherum Castle, where Lady Glencora entertains throughout the summer.

Gatherum Castle is the outrageously splendid family seat of the Dukes of Omnium, where Lady Glencora organizes a constant stream of guests coming and going throughout the summer Parliamentary recess. Politicians, relatives and people of society, frequently with thirty or more guests for dinner, come together to play quintain, archery or whist. Lady Glencora feels it to be her duty to entertain on this scale to help her shy Prime Minister husband, but he loathes this show of ostentation. In truth the family are much more comfortable off-season in their (slightly) more modest home of Matching.

There are many influences which could have inspired Trollope for his choice of both names and places, particularly Gatherum and Matching: he must have remembered the large houses from his childhood, such as the stately Julians at Rushden or more rural and peaceful Casewick, which could have been enlarged and enhanced in grandeur for novelistic purposes, or used as inspiration for the more modest Matching residence. We have seen that he passed through the villages of Matching, Clavering and Ongar whilst hunting in Essex, possibly utilizing their names (Lord Ongar and the unconnected Lady Julia Ongar and *The Claverings* (1867)), a name also later adopted by Trollope's son Fred for his residence in Australia. Trollope would also have known that Queen Victoria had engaged Thomas Cubitt in 1857 to enlarge Buckingham Palace and build the main façade for her new permanent residence, and that Prince Albert had built Osborne House in the Isle of Wight as a 'family house' in 1845-51. He would also have remembered Stratfield Saye, the large, grand residence and estate of the revered Duke of Wellington a mile away from his grandparents' home in Heckfield – his grandfather may even have ministered to him, or been invited to 'the big house' – and he would have known also the fact that the Duke much preferred his 'smaller' and more comfortable residence of Apsley House built just behind Buckingham Palace. The Trollope family would have passed by Apsley House when visiting Heckfield from London by stagecoach, as it was situated beside the Toll Gate through which it was necessary to pass. It was well known that the monastic Duke not only preferred Apsley House but also preferred a simple way of life and his own very small single camp bed which he took with him wherever he stayed; an appropriate model for Palliser preferring a simple way of life.

Another possible inspiration is closer to Trollope's home in Waltham Cross. On a journey to the Essex Hunt through Waltham Abbey there is still a clear view to the large house and estate of Copped Hall perched high on top of a hill. Dating from about 1150, the estate includes a 60-acre park, 100 acres of arable land, and 20 acres of meadow. It was once owned by the Abbot of Waltham; Henry VIII visited several times, and in 1548 the young Edward VI granted Copped Hall to Mary Tudor. By the time of Anthony and Rose's move to Waltham Cross in 1859 the owner was Henry John Conyers, Deputy Lieutenant of Essex, Master of the North Essex and Epping Hunt (reputed to have spent over £100,000 in hunting), and a Tory Candidate who filled his speeches with 'Tally-Ho'. It was said that his treatment of foxes on the property, where the Duke of Richmond shot with him, was as indefensible as his language on the hunting field.

When Trollope wrote *Can You Forgive Her?* he would surely have been aware of the estate and its occupants. The garden was described as 'a magnificent Victorian jigsaw' of beds, borders, statues, two temples or follies, kitchen garden, two lawns, plus Bowling Lawn (lined with lime trees), colonnade, Pan Garden, Rose Garden, Bothy and Western Shrubbery, Rock Garden, racquet court, parterre, and a yew-lined walk known as 'King Henry's Walk', said to be looking 'like a cathedral', where Henry VIII paced up and down whilst waiting to hear a gun signalling the beheading of Ann Boleyn. In 1594 *A Midsummer Night's Dream* had been performed in the long gallery of the east wing. The extensive cellars and dairy, kitchens, drying rooms and game larder led to the stable block. Later, in 1870, two new wings and a large conservatory were added.

At Gatherum Castle:

> ... thousands of pounds were being spent in a very conspicuous way. Invitations to the place even for a couple of days – for twenty-four hours – had been begged for abjectly. It was understood everywhere that the Prime Minister was bidding for greatness and popularity. Of course the trumpets were blown very loudly

... Perhaps of all the persons, much or little concerned, the one who heard the least of the trumpets – or rather who was the last to hear them – was the Duke himself. He could not fail to see something in the newspapers, but what he did see did not attract him so frequently or so strongly as it did others.

The Prime Minister, 1876

'I think I shall go down with you at once to Gatherum' [the Duke said. But:] *She did not want him to come at once to Gatherum. A great deal of money was being spent, and the absolute spending was not yet quite perfected. There might still be possibility of interference. The tents were not all pitched. The lamps were not all yet hung in the conservatories. Wagons would still be coming in and workmen still be going out. He would think less of what had been done if he could be kept from seeing it while it was being done. And the greater crowd which would be gathered there by the end of the first week would carry off the vastness of the preparation.*

The conscientious Plantagenet Palliser is a reluctant Prime Minister in a tied government. He feels inadequate, but his friend and constant guest the Duke of St Bungay assures him that his real task is to sit tight and hold the country together. His friends find him too reserved, even Phineas Finn, married to Madame Max, holder of a special place in the Palliser family because of her attentions towards the old Duke: when she asked Phineas if he would leave the Duke he said he liked the money and the authority: '*But in serving the Duke I find a lack of the sympathy which one should have with one's chief – he is too bored to speak and when he needs to he ... writes a minute for Warburton who then writes to Morton – and then on to* [me].'

Trollope said of *The Prime Minister*: '*I look upon this string of characters as the best work of my life*'. It was written at a time of social reforms and technological change, often brought about by dishonourable men. There were discussions of Home Rule in Ireland: '*Not – any more than I would allow a son to ruin himself because he asked me. But I would endeavour to teach them ... that their taxes would be heavier, their property less secure ... their chances of national success more remote than ever*' (p. 115).

And referring to Plantagenet Palliser, the Prime Minister: '*it was understood everywhere that the Prime Minister was bidding for greatness and popularity*'. He was '*endeavouring to define for himself, not a future politician but the best policy of the last month or two*' and '*The Duke, always right in his purpose but generally wrong in his practice, had stayed at home working all morning thereby scandalizing the strict, and had gone to church, alone in the afternoon, thereby offending the social'*.

After the hunting owner John Conyers, above, died, George Wythes of Bickley Hall in Kent bought the estate in 1861. He was a self-made businessman, who foresaw the importance of affordable transport and moved from building canals into railways, going on to build the Eastern Counties, South Western and Brighton lines. He also worked in Europe, South America and the USA, and his son George Edward Wythes became a director of the London, Brighton and South Coast Railway. Both these characters also sound familiar to Trollope's readers, and are possible background material for *The Way We Live Now*. Although this novel was written later whilst Trollope lived in Bloomsbury, he nevertheless returned to hunting in the Essex area, and would have once again been reminded of local characters.

Copped Hall is not open to the public, but I was fortunate in being able to join a small group on an Open Day tour of the house and grounds organized by Alan Cox, the architect who has made its restoration his life's work. Either of the temples in the grounds could have provided inspiration for Glencora visiting a folly '*in cold moonlight*' thinking of her first love, Burgo Fitzgerald, from where she caught a chill and died. However, the temples at Copped Hall are pleasant and inviting, whereas the remains of an earlier mentioned ruined 'folly' beside a dark tree-shrouded river at Waltham Abbey are distinctly gloomy, beside the Abbey graveyard: '[At Matching] *amidst the ruins of the old Priory, there is a parish burying-ground, and there, in accordance with her own wish, almost within sight of her own bedroom-window, she was buried*' (*The Duke's Children*). Perhaps Copped Hall and Waltham Abbey could both have combined to provide inspiration. A love scene between Lady Glencora's son Silverbridge and Isabel Boncassen also takes place in ruins later in *The Duke's Children* after Glencora has died. Another possible inspiration, in part or in combination with the above speculations, is that as Trollope would have socialized with fellow novelist the Hon Frederick Walpole at the Garrick and Athenaeum Clubs (see above) he would have heard about the latter's renovations of Rainthorpe Hall in Norfolk, and specifically have heard about his sister, Lady Dorothy Nevill, who caused a scandal in 1847 when she was found in a greenhouse with notorious rake George Smythe MP.

If Trollope had not visited this most prominent house for either business or pleasure, he would surely have heard its history and that of the occupants. He would also have been aware of the Duke of Wellington's and the Royal Family's residences. Many factors in the area at the time of his writing could have provided ideas, coupled with memories of Julians and Casewick, not only for the hospitable Gatherum Castle and the more rural and peaceful Matching, but also perhaps for the characters of Lord Chiltern and Adelaide Palliser, and for Melmotte in *The Way We Live Now* (1875).

Ruined folly at Waltham Abbey

Copped Hall with folly

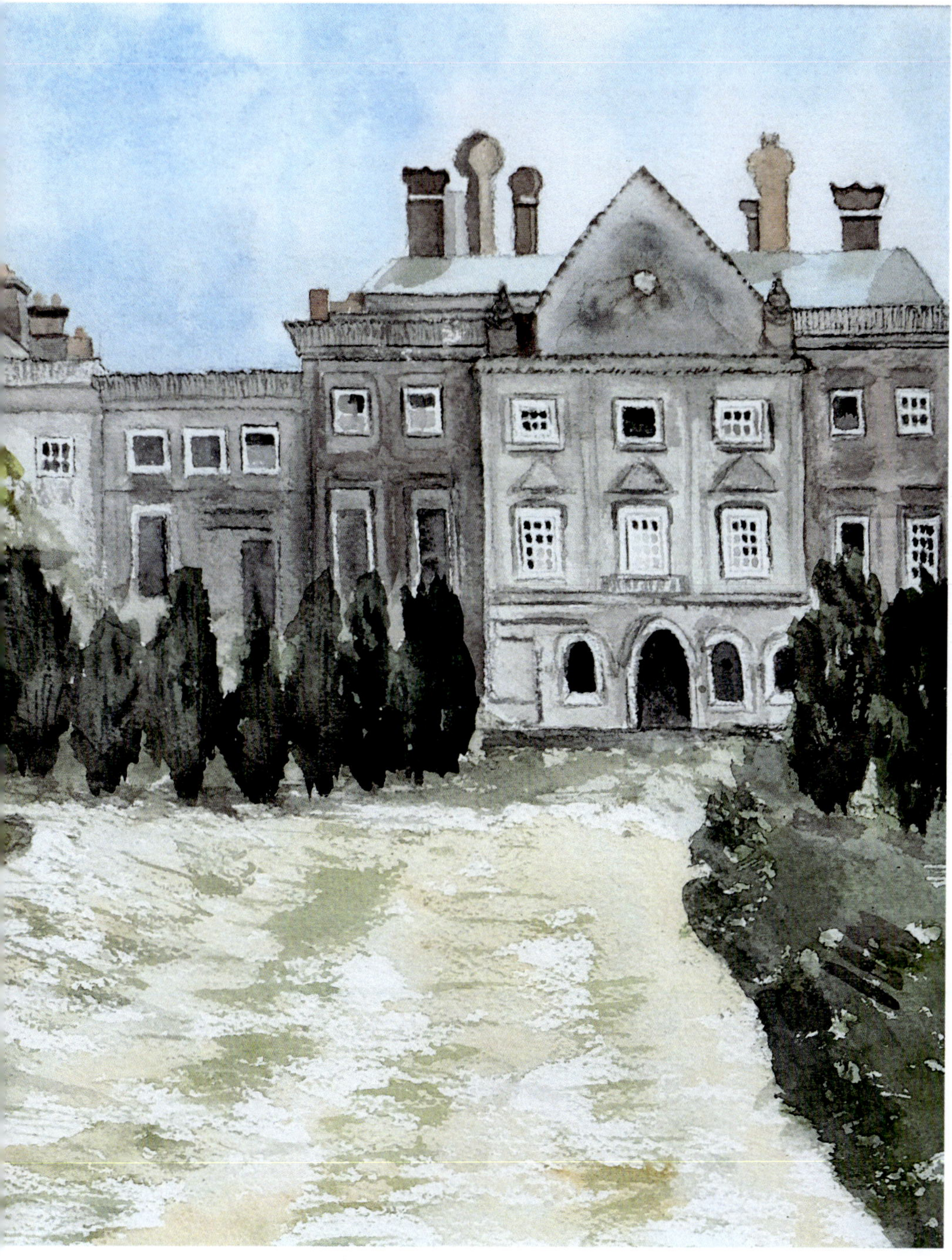

Recurring Themes

Oxford and Cambridge

Many of Trollope's clerical characters had been Fellows of Oxford or Cambridge, and automatically entered the church. There may have been a reference to his father in *The Vicar of Bullhampton*, where Gregory Marrable spent his whole time amongst books: '... *revising and editing a very long and altogether unreadable old English chronicle in rhyme for publication by one of those learned societies which are rife in London*'.

Lord Gerald Palliser in *The Duke's Children* was a student at Cambridge, from where he went to London to meet Lord Silverbridge and dubious friends in order to accompany them to Newmarket. He was able to catch the Norwich to London train at Cambridge, stopping at Bishop's Stortford, just as it does now. Many students also bunked off to go straight to Newmarket from Cambridge on a direct line. Horses were a constant topic of conversation in Cambridge, not only for racing and hunting, as students needing to hire one from Mr Hobson could choose whichever mount they wished – but always finished up with 'Hobson's Choice'.

Although a reliable source of fresh drinking water was not available everywhere, it was available in Cambridge from 1855 (from Hobson's Conduit), but students and schoolboys in Trollope's novels continued to drink watered down beer (called 'small beer', or mild ale) as well as stronger beverages, meaning that both students and staff were constantly drunk. Both Gerald and his brother Lord Silverbridge led campaigns for the health-giving properties of tea as an alternative to ale. Cambridge colleges, like other great households, brewed their own beer.

At an exhibition in Sidney Sussex College in Cambridge I saw many historical examples of students being drunk: '*drinking in Alehouses 3 to 4 days together, & corrupting other young schollers, and striking att the Cook & tripping by his heeles in the lower part of the Hall*' and '*for goyng upon Sunday last to Trumpington, and there beying from 9 a clock ... till 3 a clock and ... till the next morning*' and '*at the Dolphin where he distempered himself by excessive drinking & came not into the Coll. Till 12 of the Clock at night, to the disturbance of the same*'.

Trollope knew the dangers of falling in love with landladies' daughters, a theme in *The Three Clerks*. A St John's College handbook advised students 'not to get too familiar with your landlady's daughter as she is probably more clever than you', i.e. in 'encouraging' the student to marry her! It went on to say that *'With other men's landlady's daughters you may be less particular, but even then take care ... we know that it is only natural that a man should require ladies' society and that if he cannot meet ladies of his own station in life he is driven into less desirable circles'.*

John Caldigate, set in Cambridgeshire and Australia, chronicles John Caldigate's hardships whilst panning for gold in the Australian Gold Rush, and after a romance begun on board ship and his reputed 'marriage' to Euphemia Smith, he returns home and marries the very respectable Hester Bolton from Puritan Grange in Cambridgeshire. Searching for gold was a popular activity for aristocratic gentlemen of little funds, and topically a small amount of gold was even found in Wales at this time in Clogue St David's Mine at Bontddu in north Wales. Known as Welsh Gold, to this day it is used by members of the Royal Family.

Horse Racing and Newmarket

Betting on horses and going to the races at Newmarket were favourite pastimes for many rich young men in Trollope's novels. Cheating and losing vast amounts of money were also common in real life. An exhibition at the Jockey Club in Newmarket showed a John Gull who lost 40,000 guineas (almost £6 million today) in an afternoon, and some gamblers even lost whole country estates. There was the 'Great Turf Scandal' of 1844 when Running Rein won the Derby with claims of substitution, nobbling and false bets. Therefore, when Major Tifto tampers with Lord Silverbridge's horse the night before the big St Leger race in *The Duke's Children* (1880), readers would have recognized the situation:

> *It was on the Tuesday evening that the chief mischief was done* [at Doncaster Club] *Before the night was over bets had been booked to the amount stated, and the Duke's son, who had promised that he would never plunge, stood to lose about seventy thousand pounds upon the face.*

Then the terrible deed ...

> *It was soon known to Lord Silverbridge as a fact that in very truth the horse could not run. Then sick with headache, with a stomach suffering unutterable things, he had, as he dressed himself, to think of his seventy thousand pounds* [roughly £8 million today]. *Of course the money would be forthcoming. But how would his father look at him? How would it be between him and his father now?*

And then:

> After such a misfortune how would he be able to break that other matter to the Duke, and say that he had changed his mind about his marriage – that he was going to abandon Lady Mabel Grex and give his hand and a future duchess's coronet to an American girl whose grandfather had been a porter?'

Thus Silverbridge is subdued and learns his lesson.

The younger son, Lord Gerald, also acquires bad habits and wants to join his brother and friends at dinner at the Bear Garden; however, after many escapades Trinity College forbids young men leave to go – but the hapless Gerald decides otherwise! He knows there is a train leaving Cambridge at an early hour which would get him to London in time for the dinner and a return train home to Cambridge *'before the college gates were shut'*. Needless to say, the dinner is very jolly, and very long, and Lord Gerald delays, thinking he can catch the 'special' which will not leave until half past nine because *'a lot of fellows ... are dining about everywhere, and they would never get to the station by the hour fixed'*. But when they arrive at Liverpool Street, of course the train has left. Knowing that Gerald will be 'sent down', Lord Silverbridge says *'After what happened to me it will almost break the governor's heart'*.

Aristocracy

Trollope's definition of an aristocrat was someone with a knowledge of the classics – as in Aristotle's *aristokratia* meaning 'rule by the best'. His aristocratic characters are the Duke of Omnium, squires and gentry, well-born and wealthy people, and those who raise themselves such as Henry Lovelace, Dean of Brotherton, who '[got] *rid of the last porcine taint'* in *Is He Popenjoy?* (1878). He also refers to the *'upper 10,000 of this our English world'* in *Can You Forgive Her?* and his political novels revolve around the ducal family of the Pallisers, with the benefits and disadvantages of hereditary aristocracy. During the Crimean War (1853–6) both Thackeray and Dickens criticized an aristocratic government, but Trollope wrote in the *New Zealander* that 'the main duty of all aristos, and we may say their only duty is to govern'.

He highlighted the fragility of financial life at the time, such as in his own family who, however, conquered their difficulties with hard work and writing abilities. He depicted genteel poverty, with mothers striving or in many cases 'capturing' suitable young men to marry their daughters – or fathers urging sons to marry wealthy heiresses and widows. As stated above, the main employment for men of his class was the ministry, military, university or, particularly, what he referred to as *'the noble art of politics'*. The only other real alternative was writing, and the earlier-mentioned Professor Rohan McWilliam says that there was an explosion of authors in the 19th century, e.g. Dickens, Wilkie Collins, Thackeray, George Eliot, James Payne, Thomas Hardy, Bulwer-Lytton, Margaret Oliphant, Rhoda Broughton – not all of whom are remembered today. Many young men were forced to earn money either gambling or borrowing on their inheritances (in some cases the value of a whole estate) from the moneylenders, or live on 'tips' from pretending to befriend richer acquaintances (Sophie Gordeloup in *The Claverings*). Young people falling in love of their own accord often debate if, when married, they would be able to eat more than potatoes, or even 'potato peelings', perhaps a memory of his Irish days. He also wrote:

> ... I do not scruple to say that I prefer the society of distinguished people, and that even the distinction of wealth confers many advantages ... and will honour the owners [self-made men] the more because of the difficulties they have overcome; but the fact remains that the society of the well-born and of the wealthy will as a rule be worth seeking. I say this now, because these are the rules by which I have lived, and these are the causes which have instigated me to work.

Freemasonry

On 21st May 1842, only a few months after his arrival in Ireland in 1841, Trollope was proposed for membership of the Lodge of Banagher No.306, founded by Brother J Bird and Brother Harrington. He was eventually raised to the degree of Master Mason, gaining a vellum certificate of membership along with a masonic apron. His autograph signature appears in the attendance book on 5th August 1844, and he later attended other lodges as he moved around. His brother Tom must also have been a Freemason at some point because his initialled masonic gloves and wallet are in existence, indicating that he probably visited England regularly.

Freemasonry is one of the world's oldest secular fraternal societies, dating from 1717 when a group of like-minded men got together in a London coffee house and devised a non-sectarian, egalitarian club in which 'men of integrity' could fraternise, whilst avoiding the issues of religion and politics. The idea possibly grew out of the Trades Guilds as a way for uneducated apprentices, like stonemasons, to show their competence or status, by way of a qualification. Hence the Guiding Metaphor comprises the square, compass and apron, taken from the trade of stonemasons. Freemasons acquire its precepts by a series of ritual dramas following ancient forms using stonemasons' customs and tools as allegorical guides; the only secrets being the traditional modes of recognition. In the 19th century Freemasons met in function rooms above taverns; unsurprisingly refreshment became an important part of the proceedings, spawning an industry of glass, porcelain and pottery vessels decorated with masonic symbols. While Trollope does not mention the subject of freemasonry directly, his male characters often meet in taverns and hold what might loosely be termed informal committee meetings. Many characters also quote Freemasonry symbols such as 'all square' or 'on the square': Vignolles in *Mr Scarborough's Family* (1883) cheats at cards to get money but feels he is *'on the square'* because he always pays up (unlike some other characters).

Emblem of Freemasonry

The function of Freemasonry is to uphold moral values with non-political charitable work, in a quiet, discreet, but not secret manner. It transcends and encompasses all religions and promotes fortitude and prudence. A Brother is taught that his prime duty is to God, the laws of his country, his family, showing brotherly love, relief and truth, and dedication to building a better life. Now in the 21st century all the lodges are built in the same manner, with a Throne for the Grand Master, one for the Middle Master and one for the Junior Master. Nowadays there are also lady Freemasons although the two lodges do not mix. The black-and-white square-chequered floor covering is a reminder of the human chequered existence; one enters in a state of darkness that ends in enlightenment: we hear, see and are silent. There are lodges in England and Ireland, India and Japan, but not Scotland or Northern Ireland. One must already be a Freemason in order to join the Knights Templar. In England the Grand Lodge is at Freemasons'

Hall in Holborn, near the British Museum, and next door to the tavern where meetings would originally have been held.

There are believed to be approximately six million Freemasons in the world today, including royalty, statesmen, judges, police, military top brass, lawyers and bishops. Many military and artistic men ranging from the Duke of Wellington, Lord Kitchener, Oscar Wilde, Arthur Conan Doyle, Rudyard Kipling, actor Sir Henry Irving, Gilbert & Sullivan, Thomas Telford and Harry Selfridge have been masons.

Violence

Police feature in many novels in one way or another, either in a kindly, fatherly role, rescuing wayward drunken young gentlemen after an evening's revelry, or solving a crime such as the mystery of Lady Eustace's missing diamonds (once fraudulently and once genuinely). A professional force of policemen (known as 'peelers' or 'bobbies') had been set up in 1829 by Robert Peel, then Home Secretary, but people were still wary of crime and felt the need to protect themselves: most young men carried 'life preservers' and/or pistols. In 1862 an Anti-Garrotting Cravat was registered, in response to an MP's robbery by garrotting, i.e. being throttled from behind with a cord, or an iron bar as happened to Mr Kennedy in *Phineas Finn* (1869), on the corner of Brook Street and Park Street. An article in the *Telegraph* newspaper (6th Oct 2014), stated that an invention craze to combat such violence had begun after laws allowing ideas to be copyrighted quickly and cheaply were introduced in 1843.

Prostitution was also prevalent in London in the 19th century and openly discussed in the press and Parliament when the introduction of the Contagious Diseases Act, designed to protect the armed forces from venereal infection, was introduced in Parliament. Green Park was said to be full of prostitutes and a contemporary wrote '*It is my business every evening to cross the Green Park, being the nearest way to Piccadilly from Westminster. I am constantly annoyed by prostitutes who frequent the paths as soon as it becomes dusk.*' Trollope too hinted at prostitution with Carrie Brattle in *The Vicar of Bullhampton*.

Violence and prostitution feature in *The Prime Minister* (1876) when Everett Wharton ignored the advice of friends not to walk through St James's Park at night and was robbed and assaulted by a man and two women. He was ironically saved by Ferdinand Lopez defending him with cudgels and his stout hat.

> *On Thursday night (being very foggy) there was an unusual number, and no sooner did a person appear than he was assailed by them, and if he used a little violence, so as to escape, he was instantly set upon by numbers, and frightfully ill-treated if not robbed.*

Phineas in *Phineas Finn* fought a duel with Lord Chiltern over Violet Effingham (having speedily forgotten his love for Lady Laura!). Duels were illegal in this country and so they went abroad to fight. In *Phineas Redux* (1873) he was doubly unlucky, being shot at by Mr Kennedy in a seedy hotel room in Judd Street, as he was jealous of Phineas' attentions to his wife, Lady Laura; and then being accused of clubbing to death Mr Bonteen after they had both had an argument in their Mayfair Club, and for which he endured being put on trial at the Old Bailey. He would have been jailed had it not been for Madame Max's researches abroad and subsequent testimony. George Vavasor in *Can You Forgive Her?* (1864–5) had killed a burglar in his youth leaving him with a 'cicatrice' on his own face, which reddened angrily when irate (a symbol of his abusive character). He also broke his loving sister Kate's arm and, even worse, abandoned her exposed to the elements in the Fells near Penrith. Cousin Henry in the book of that name hurled himself at the throat of the attorney in the polite and narrow confines of a book room. There are also suicides: in addition to Lopez at '*Tenway Junction*', Melmotte in *The Way We Live Now* took prussic acid with his brandy nightcap and Sir Henry Harcourt, after losing his money and his wife, shot himself in the splendour of his Eaton Square house.

Young Men Brawling outside a Gentleman's Club by Gwen Raverat (taken from *The Bedside Barchester* compiled by Lance O'Tingay, pub. Faber & Faber).

Women too could be violent, such as Mrs O'Hara pushing the Earl of Scroope to a horrible death on the rocks beneath the Cliffs of Moher in *An Eye for an Eye* for consorting with her daughter; Lady Anna's mother (*Lady Anna*) unsuccessfully trying to kill her daughter's suitor (a tailor and thus '*unsuitable*') having first considered whether or not to shoot her own daughter. Mrs Hurtle (a beautiful, feisty American) in *The Way We Live Now* (1875) is violent with a history of duelling with her husband and shooting another man, and there is almost a gunfight in *Dr Wortle*, over a woman.

There are scruples, however, as Dockwrath in *Orley Farm* (1862) has a lucky reprieve when young Peregrine says: '*I suppose he is not a man you can kick?*' and Lucius replies: '*I'm afraid not – he's over 40 years old and has dozens of children.*'

Hats, Beards, Boots and Shoes/Observations

Victorian etiquette demanded that hats be worn outside at all times: ladies wore bonnets, even to walk in the garden shrubbery, and gentlemen wore or carried their hats not only outside, but also sometimes inside when it was draughty, such as in clubs. Hats were worn in Parliament from the 16th to the early 20th centuries (when women joined as members) whilst sitting in chamber, but taken off when speaking, although they could be left on when making a point of order. Mr Monk gave kind words to Phineas when making his Maiden Speech of not more than three minutes and said: '*forget privilege of wearing ... hat*'. Hats were also worn by soldiers in messes, especially if they did not wish to speak during breakfast, and in a bank – when in credit! However, gentlemen always took them off in the presence of ladies!

Hats, therefore, were prevalent in Trollope's novels, often leading to unintended amusement when reading from our present-day perspective: Phineas Finn, after being shot at by Mr Kennedy, manages to escape down the staircase to be consoled by Mrs Macpherson's glass of brandy (for which he was charged 6d) but then to his horror, discovers he has left his hat behind – with the crazed gunman! He was in a serious predicament until:

> *Phineas was now in great doubt as to what duty was required of him. His first difficulty consisted in this, that his hat was still in Mr Kennedy's room, and that Mrs Macpherson altogether refused to go and fetch it. At last the door of the room above was opened, and our hero's hat was sent rolling down the stairs.*

When Lopez seeks a policeman after rescuing Wharton from being attacked in Green Park he finds that '*To the policeman's mind it was most distressing that a bloody-faced man without a hat, with a companion almost too weak to walk, should not be conveyed to a police-station*'.

A sadder, more dramatic occasion is when Lord Hampstead visits Marion Fay, in the book of that name (Ch. LIX) in what he knows will be the last time. As she lay dying, she tells him to leave her, saying:

> 'Call upon your courage to bear it'. 'I cannot bear it', he said, rising suddenly from his chair, and hurrying out of the room. He went out of the room and from the house, on to the little terrace which ran in front of the sea. But his escape was of no use to him; he could not leave her. He had come out without his hat, and he could not stand there in the sun to be stared at. 'I am a coward', he said, going back to her and resuming his chair ...

Similarly, when Phineas and the Duke sit on a seat during a walk, the Duke '*had thrown off his hat*' in his enthusiasm but later, upon realizing the consequences of this act, his '*face changed on a sudden and the Duke with an awkward motion snatched up his hat*'.

In *Is He Popenjoy?* (1878), the Dean, before grabbing Brotherton, has to rid himself of his hat by '*pitching it along the floor*' ... he is '*... fifty years of age but no one had taken him for an old man*'; and conversely the incumbent curate in *Can You Forgive Her?*, whilst preaching his sermon, cannot keep his eyes off '*that wonderful bonnet and veil*' worn by the indomitable Mrs Greenow.

During the Napoleonic Wars it had been considered manly and healthy to sport a beard, the bigger and bushier the better, to provide protection from germs and give visibility, a fashion which continued until the turn of the century. Men also wore boots with small heels, for military purposes and safety in mounting horses, and continued to do so with dress boots for evening wear. This fashion for heels continued until the design of coaches improved and railways were developed, and flat-soled boots could safely be worn again. These were usually made to specific requirements. However, hunting boots with heels continued to be necessary, and bootmakers and breeches makers were particularly prominent in hunting areas, as well as London. Jones the Bootmaker was established in 1857 and Timpsons Shoes (which now has 260 shops) in 1865. Trollope included these familiar subjects: Ontario Moggs was a bootmaker and son of a bootmaker in Old Bond Street. He won the hand of Miss Polly Neefit, daughter of a breeches maker, and was a political opponent of Sir Thomas Underwood in the Percycross by-election based on Trollope's experiences in Beverley and recounted in *Ralph the Heir*.

Lady Glencora Palliser chatted to Sprout the bootmaker in the village of Silverbridge (see Waltham Abbey above) in *The Prime Minister*; maker of the '*cork soles*' worn by Lady Rosina de Courcy and recommended by her to the Duke. The Melton Mowbray Museum displays bootmakers such as Rowell & Sons (1837–1904) who supplied the local Quorn, Belvoir and Cottesmore huntsmen, 1st and 2nd whippers and assistants. Specialist boots were available such as for Mr Sherriffe of Wyndham Lodge who ordered shooting boots, while Mr Everard of Peterborough wanted boots with a full-founded toe and Lord Percy of Burton Hall in Loughborough boots with *'no loop strap, centre toes knuckle up'*, both so their *'raised knuckles did not get blistered'*. Rowell & Sons also made Jaeger wool socks and stockings, being essential inside boots as they: *'keep[s] skin between toes dry and prevents soft corns'*. Trollope would have been familiar with such details both from hunting and staying in the Melton area.

When unsettled and confused by so many visitors at Gatherum Castle, Plantagenet Palliser often went for a long walk in the park with Lady Rosina de Courcy, even in inclement weather, because she provided an antidote to the excessive expenditure and ostentatiousness in his own home: *'She is proud of her blood and yet not ashamed of her poverty'*. She enthuses over the new American invention of cork soles: *'I think I owe my life to cork soles,'* said Lady Rosina ... *'I find I can wear Sprout's boots the whole winter through and then have them resoled. I don't suppose you ever think of such things?'* or *'I am very particular about* [thick boots] *and cork soles'*. To Palliser it is a relief to simplify life to a question of boots – and of finding a bootmaker who can supply an honest product. Earlier Glencora had told her cousin that Plantagenet was particular about his shoes, mirroring Trollope, comparing his own writing abilities and methodical working practices to working with a shoemaker's disciplined industry, which he recommended as a model for other novelists to follow: *'Think about your business as a shoemaker thinks of his. Do your best, and then let your customers judge for themselves.'*

Glencora teased the normally silent and reluctant dinner-table conversationalist Plantagenet by saying that Rosina de Courcy would be joining them the following day and as she would be the only guest, he would therefore be forced to entertain her. He understood the joke but when he replied with a similar joke about getting cork soles himself from Mr Sprout, Glencora shuddered.

As has been previously mentioned, Trollope's heroines were usually brown haired, with dimples, possibly like his mother, the exception being his characters Laura and Chiltern with their red hair (see 'Art and Illustrations' below). It has been suggested to me by Jessica Finch of Camsight that a reason for this may have been possible colour blindness. In the same way it has been mentioned by Frederic Harrison (*Studies in Early Victorian Literature* (1895)) that he was also *'blind to the loveliness of nature'* in that unlike Scott, Thackeray, Dickens, Bulwer and George Eliot, he did not describe beautiful scenery but that like a fox hunter he skimmed metaphorically over the landscape.

The Palliser novels, left: *Phineas Redux* (The Folio Society),
Top to bottom: Can You Forgive Her? Vols 2 and 1 (The Bodley Head), *The Eustace Diamonds* (The Folio Society) *The Prime Minister* (The Folio Society)

The Duke's Children (The Folio Society Special Edition),
Right: Phineas Finn (The Folio Society)

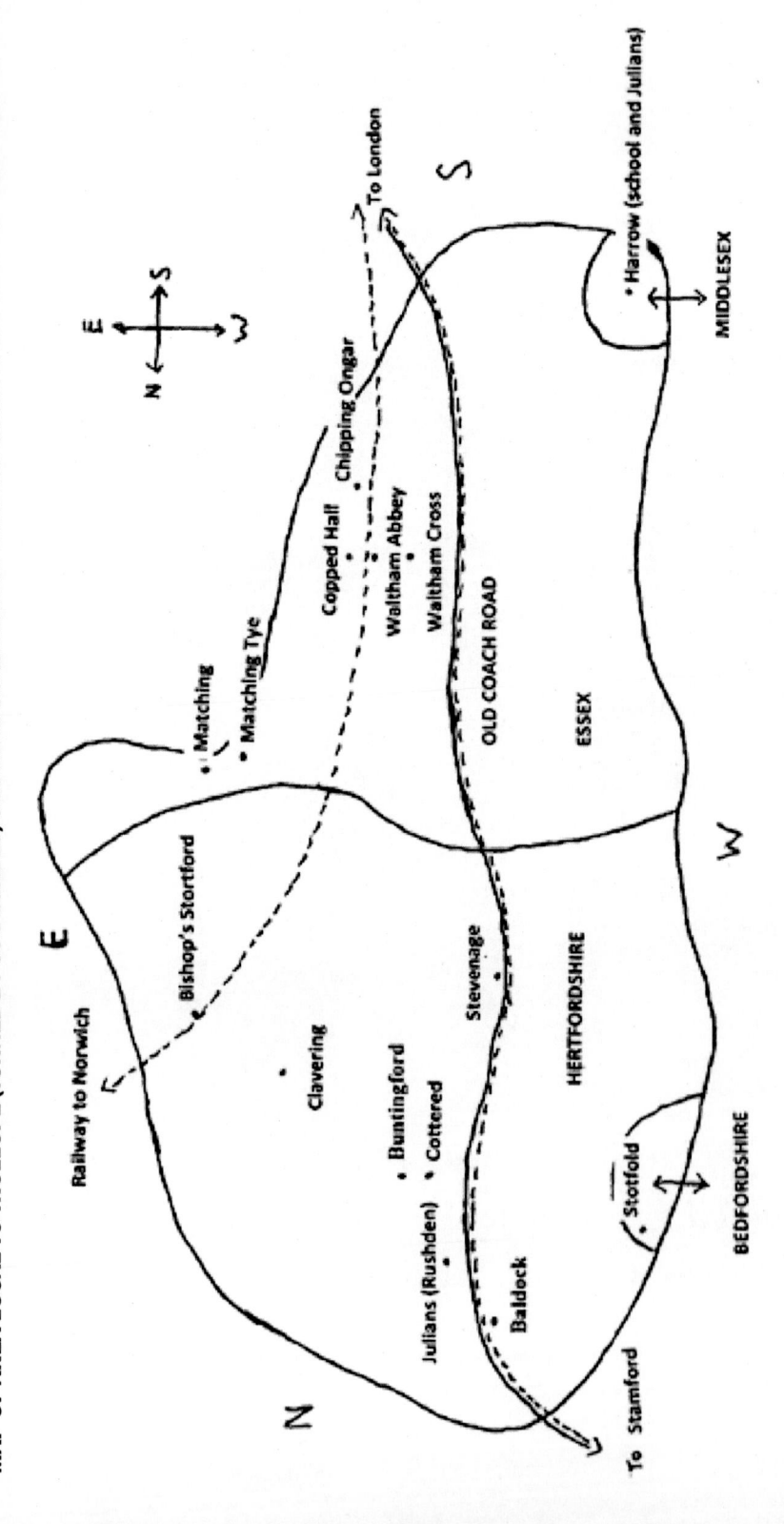

MAP OF AREA LOCAL TO TROLLOPE (TURNED BY 90 DEGREES) SHOWING CORRELATION WITH HIS OWN DEPICTION OF BARCHESTER BELOW

TROLLOPE'S BARSETSHIRE

REDRAWN FROM THE SKETCH-MAP MADE BY THE NOVELIST HIMSELF

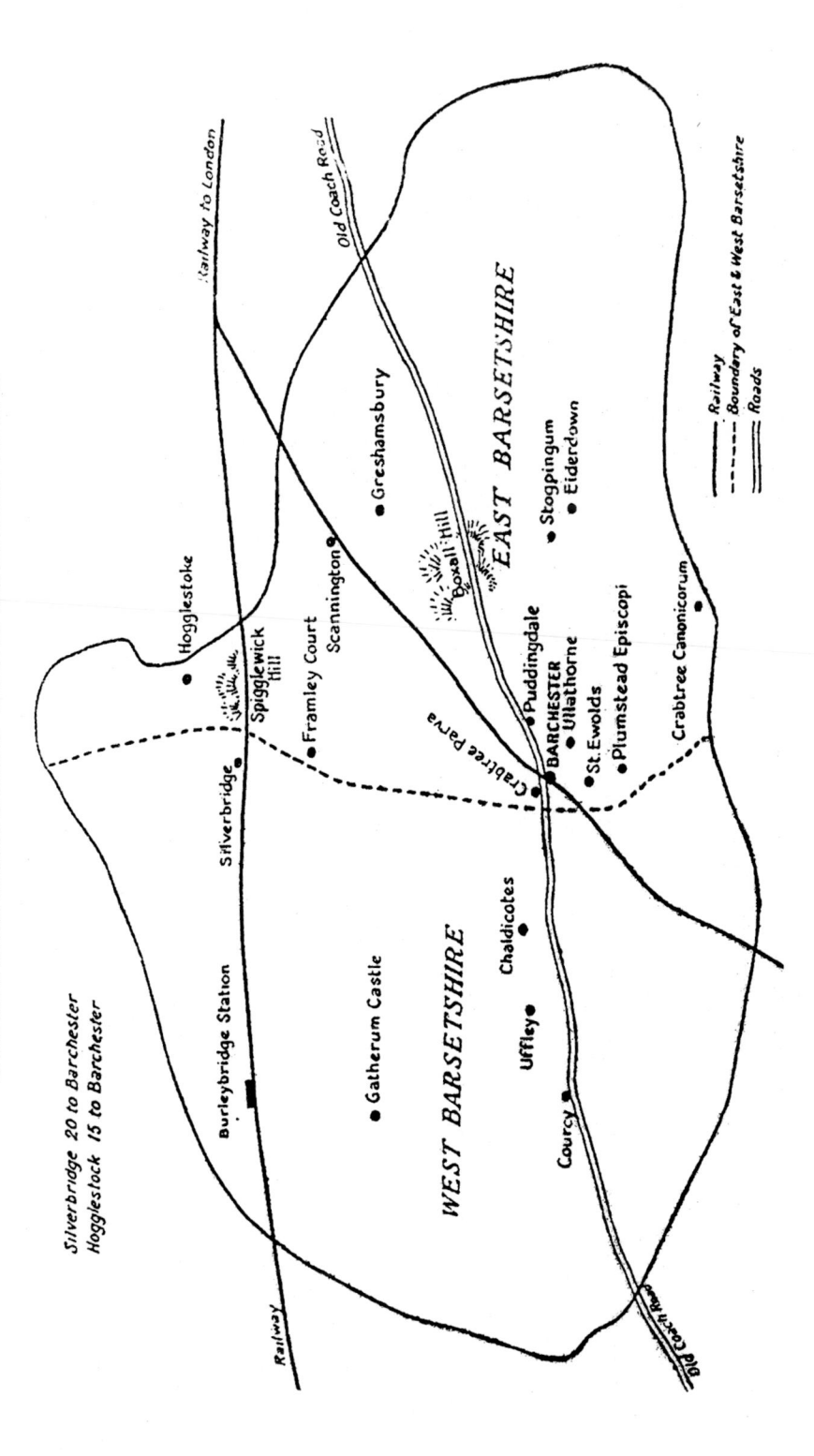

(Source: *Anthony Trollope* by James Pope Hennessy, Jonathan Cape, 1971.)

Strong Women

Trollope had several lady friends whom he met in society, through friends, relatives, and at publishers etc. and recorded:

> *I was never a learned man, nor even a philosopher. But I was a very clever person, and beautiful young women used to be fond of me. And I strove to be kind of heart, and open of hand, and noble in thought, despising mean things.*

Cecilia Meetkerke

A good friend and contemporary of Trollope's was Cecilia Meetkerke (1823–1903), ironically the wife of the son of the very Adolphus Meerkerke (1753–1840) whose marriage and children, it was said, prevented Trollope's father from gaining his inheritance. The fact that they were good friends disproves any animosity on his part. Her father was the Hon. Edward Gore, and her grandfather the 2nd Earl of Arran. She benefited from the many writing tips Trollope gave to her and subsequently enjoyed modest success in periodicals and as a writer for children. She wrote *The Guests of the Flowers; A Botanical Sketch for Children* (1880) and *The Guests at Home* (1881) not long before Trollope's death.

George Eliot

Trollope also enjoyed a close relationship with George Eliot (real name Marian Evans, partner and companion of G H Lewes) whom he had met at Fanny and Tom's villa in Florence. They perhaps provided inspiration for the unmarried Askertons in *Dr Wortle's School* (1881). Trollope and George Eliot sometimes exchanged notes about each other's work, and probably plot ideas and characterizations: for instance Eliot's characters often enjoyed looking at themselves in mirrors, such as in *Romola* (1862-3, first published in the *Cornhill* magazine), and Trollope's Miss Mackenzie enjoyed a long lingering look at herself. They both also wrote on clergymen of the Church of England. Both *The Mill on the Floss* and *The Vicar of Bullhampton* feature water-mills; he wrote the Palliser novels, and she wrote *Felix Holt*. George Eliot wrote *The Lifted Veil* in 1859 while Trollope published *Nina Balatka* in 1867: both novels being set in Prague involve the Jewish population and a synagogue, and also the bridge where Nina Balatka attempts to commit suicide. George Eliot wrote:

> *But, as I stood under the blackened, groined arches of that old synagogue, made dimly visible by the seven thin candles in the sacred lamp ... I felt a sudden overpowering impulse to go on at once to the bridge and put an end to the suspense I had been wishing to protract.*

She was not actually contemplating suicide as did Nina, but wishes to see a 'vision': '*There it was – the patch of rainbow light on the pavement transmitted through a lamp in the shape of a star*', whereas Nina, already on the bridge, contemplates falling:

> *In these moments her mind wandered in a maze of religious doubts and fears ... Could it be that God would punish her with everlasting torments because in her agony she was driven to this as her only mode of relief? Would there be no measuring of her sins against her sorrows and no account taken of the simplicity of her life? She looked up towards heaven, not praying in words, but with a prayer in her heart.*

Trollope found Eliot's work 'sometimes abstruse, sometimes almost dull, but always like an egg, full of meat' (Booth, Letters, II, 627). On her part she claimed that but for Trollope she could hardly have pursued the extensive study for *Middlemarch*. At her death he wrote: '*I did love her very dearly. That I admired her was a matter of course*' (Booth, Letters, II, 887).

Of George Henry Lewes he wrote:

> *There was never a man so pleasant as he with whom to sit and talk vague literary gossip over a cup of coffee and a cigar. That he was a great philosopher, a great biographer, a great critic, there is no doubt.*

Trollope was able to use his influence to help George Lewes' son Charles enter the Post Office by writing to the Duke of Argyll for a nomination and, when the job began to go wrong, was possibly reminded of his own hobbledehoy days, and again came forward to help. He also assisted in his becoming editor of the *Fortnightly Review* (May 1865).

George Eliot wrote many letters to friends in praise of Trollope, such as to Charles Bray (16 April 1862) '... *Anthony Trollope, on the other hand,* is a Church of England man, clinging to whatever is, on the whole, and without fine distinctions honest, lovely and of good report'*, and she wrote to Trollope himself:

> ... I am much struck in 'Rachel' [Rachel Ray (1863)] with the skill with which you have organized thoroughly natural everyday incidents into a strictly related, well-proportioned whole, natty and complete as a nut on its stem. Such construction is among those subtleties of art which can hardly be appreciated except by those who have striven after the same result with conscious failure. Rachel herself is a sweet maidenly figure, and her poor mother's spiritual confusions are excellently observed.
>
> But there is something else I care yet more about, which has impressed me very happily in all those writings of yours that I know – it is that people are breathing good bracing air in reading them – it is that they [the books] are filled with belief in goodness without the slightest tinge of maudlin. They are like pleasant public gardens, where people go for amusement and, whether they think of it or not, get health as well.

All the characters in Trollope's novels write frequent letters to their friends and relatives, particularly in their bedrooms after prayers in the evenings, and similarly George Eliot wrote to a friend:

> Yesterday Anthony dined with us and as he had never seen Carlyle he was glad to go down with us to tea at Chelsea. Carlyle had read and agreed with the West Indian book, and the two got on very well together; both Carlyle and Mrs Carlyle liking Anthony, and I suppose it was reciprocal, though I did not see him afterwards to hear what he thought. He had to run away to catch his train.

Interestingly, prior to the meeting Carlyle had written very disparagingly about Trollope's review of Ruskin's *Sesame and Lilies*.

Both Trollope and George Eliot were contributors to *Blackwood's Magazine*, but she was unable to keep her pseudonym and identity a secret for long. Consequently, a whirlwind of gossip followed not only about her being a woman (like the Brontë sisters), but a single woman living with a married man, and the couple were forced to flee back to Italy.

Kate Field

Lord Silverbridge, heir to the Palliser estate in *The Duke's Children* (1880), met and fell in love with Isabel Boncassen, an American lady. This was at a time when many impoverished young British lords sought wealthy brides from America to rescue their crumbling estates, although in Lord Silverbridge's case this was unnecessary as the family had untold wealth.

It is often believed she was based on Kate Field, whom Trollope met in 1860 at the Villino Trollope in Florence. Mary Katherine Keemie Field (1838–96) was beautiful and feisty, an actress and lecturer, daughter of the actor-playwright Joseph M Field, and best known for *Pen Photographs of Charles Dickens's Readings* (1871). She was said to have cultivated celebrities in England and Europe, including W S Landor and the Brownings, whom she also met in Florence. She described Trollope as '*an admirable specimen of a frank and loyal Englishman*'.

Trollope maintained a friendship with her for many years, mainly in correspondence, and Kate visited the family home at Waltham Cross, signifying a normal relationship. His letters to her were skittish and avuncular, but unsparing when it came to her literary efforts. There were frequent contributions from or concerning Rose, and indeed Rose wrote to Kate on her own behalf and sent manuscripts. At one point Trollope invited Wilkie Collins to meet her, who said '*Yes, I have heard of the American lady – she is adored by everybody, and I am all ready to follow the general example*' (Booth, Letters, II, 589). She wrote to her Aunt Corda in the autumn of 1860:

> *Anthony Trollope is a very delightful companion. I see a great deal of him. He has promised to send me a copy of the Arabian Nights (which I have never read) in which he intends to write 'Kate Field, from the Author', and to write me a four-page letter on condition that I answer it.*

When Trollope twice visited America, once on a postal mission and once on a literary mission, Rose had the opportunity to accompany him but preferred to sail home alone (see 'Australia' below), which she would not have done if she had been worried in any way. Many writers commented on his happiness at being involved in his own house and garden duties at the weekend such as '*charging round the garden*' with a roller. Several letters home written while on his travels testify to his happiness and homesickness, such as in 1861 when he wrote to George Lewes: '*As to myself personally, I have daily to wonder at the continued run of domestic & worldly happiness which has been granted me; to wonder at it as well as to be thankful for it*' (Booth, Letters, I, 145); and whilst in America in 1862 he spoke of the '*children & cows & horses and dogs and pigs – and all the stern necessities of an English home*' (Booth, Letters, I, 161). In South Africa in 1877, he wrote: '*Never so home-sick in my life*' (Booth, Letters, II, 740) and from Ireland in 1882 he enquired: '*How is the garden, and the cocks & hens, & especially the asparagus bed?*' (Booth, Letters, II,

966) all of which hardly seem to me to be the offhand letters of someone in the throes of an affair. Trollope saw Kate Field perhaps a dozen times (according to C P Snow) and her diary records normal social meetings such as '*Met Anthony Trollope. Same as ever. Trollope called in evening*' or '*Met Anthony Trollope again*' and '*Anthony Trollope called and went with us to the Capitol*' or '*Mr Trollope came and remained an hour or two. Asked me to write a story for his* St Pauls Magazine. *If I can it will be a feather in my cap. If I can't – well, we shall see*'. Her father worried about her being self-willed, and also that she provoked rapturous love in older women too, especially the Italian actress Ristori. The idea of Trollope having had a liaison with her arose after he wrote in his *Autobiography*:

> *There is a woman of whom not to speak in a work purporting to be a memoir of my own life would be to omit all allusion to one of the chief pleasures which has graced my later years. In the last fifteen years she has been, out of my family, my most chosen friend.*

– the words '*out of my family*' being explanatory and confirming to me a paternal relationship.

We do know he was many years older than her, had two sons but no daughter (although Bice acted as a surrogate daughter) and that he probably used Kate as inspiration for several characters in his novels: the above-mentioned young American woman Isabel Boncassen marrying into the Palliser aristocracy, and also the independent Ophelia in the short story 'Miss Ophelia Gledd'. More particularly he probably gained insights into unsuitable liaisons: the older Colonel Osborne in *He Knew He Was Right* (1869) visits the young Emily Trevelyan too frequently against her husband's wishes leading to a marriage break-up and a nervous breakdown, and the 'old' Mr Whittlestaff (in his forties) in *An Old Man's Love* (1884), unsuccessfully pursuing his young niece Mary Lawrie who inevitably prefers the young John Gordon.

Trollope corresponded with many strong women, and when he began to include them in his novels it was at a time when women generally were emerging from the decorous Victorian ideal of playing music and doing embroidery, whilst supervising their servants: Florence Nightingale was a contemporary of Trollope and by 1853 was running a women's hospital in London; Lady Caroline Jebb, American writer, socialite and friend of George Eliot, became famous; Lady Ida Darwin (whose husband was a fan of Trollope) fought for social and legislative reforms for mental health services; and women were beginning to be allowed into Oxford and Cambridge colleges.

As I have said earlier, it is strange that Trollope omitted direct mention of people and places obviously dear to him, possibly from fear of losing them, and instead frequently portrayed them in various disguises. Admittedly, it is strange then to include a couple of pages on Kate Field in his *Autobiography* alongside the emotional chronicles of complaints and hardships, but perhaps the very fact that he could write dispassionately about her showed that she was not as dear to him as his family were. As discussed, he was almost certainly depressed when he wrote his memoir, subsequently putting it to one side, perhaps planning to pick it up again later using a different tone. Whatever the reason, the pages on Kate Field were omitted by his son Henry before publishing the book after his death. C P Snow, in *Trollope: His Life and Art* (Macmillan Press, 1975) considered that *'there was no pain any time on either side'*; he had a good marriage, was also bound to the morality of the times, and clearly Rose had complete confidence in him.

He advised Kate Field to put matrimony before independence (unlikely advice if he was in the throes of an affair), and wrote in *Miss Mackenzie*:

> *I believe that a desire to get married is the natural state of a woman at the age of – say from 25 to 35, and I think also that it is good for the world in general that it should be so ... There is I know, a feeling abroad among women that this desire is one of which it is expedient that they should become ashamed ... But I confess to an opinion that human nature will be found to be too strong for them ... A woman's life is not perfect or whole until she has added herself to a husband.*

He added:

> *Nor is a man's life perfect or whole till he has added to himself a wife; but the deficiency with this man, though perhaps more injurious to him than its counterpart is to the woman, does not, to the outer eye, so manifestly unfit him for his business in the world.*

I think an argument for his not having an affair is summed up in the following:

> *If the rustle of a woman's petticoat has ever stirred my blood; if a cup of wine has been a joy to me; if I have thought tobacco at midnight in pleasant company to be one of the elements of an earthly Paradise; if now and again I have somewhat recklessly*

fluttered a £5 note over a card-table; of what matter is that to any reader? <u>I have betrayed no woman</u>. Wine has brought me to no sorrow. It has been the companionship of smoking that I have loved rather than the habit. To enjoy the excitement of pleasure, but to be free from its vices and ill effects, to have the sweet, and leave the bitter untasted, that has been my study. [My emphasis.]

Other Women

Trollope also corresponded with a wide range of lady friends such as Mary Holmes and Anna Steele, Mary Russell Mitford, Lady Lytton, Mrs Oliphant and Mrs Gerald Porter, and freely flirted (safely) on paper. One lady correspondent, Dorothea Sankey, received the following letter:

> My affectionate & most excellent wife is as you are aware still living – and I am proud to say her health is good. Nevertheless it is always well to take time by the forelock and be prepared for all events. Should anything happen to her, will you supply her place, as soon as the proper period for decent mourning is over?
>
> (Booth, *Letters*, I, 144)

This may be in questionable taste but is quite obviously intended as a joke.

In keeping with his sense of humour and ebullient character, when returning on the *Bothnia* from New York after his second trip to Australia, he wrote to fellow passenger Katherine Colman DeKay Bronson, an American hostess and friend of Browning: '*What of half a score of other interesting young ladies who liked autographs from old men and more tender acknowledgements from those who were younger?*' It appears that he considered such jollities to be normal behaviour (perhaps Victorian ideals of chivalry?) for what he described as 'old men'.

Trollope was also fond of his publisher John Blackwood's wife Julia and wrote '*When Mrs Blackwood is in town I will take her whist into my own keeping*' (Booth, *Letters*, II, 751).

Publications, Periodicals and Printers

Novels in the 1860s were considered too expensive for most middle-class English people, hence the rise of both popular periodicals and Mudie's lending library. The periodicals left readers eagerly awaiting the next instalment. Sometimes authors wrote an instalment without knowing themselves how they would write the next episode, and authors such as Trollope refreshed their own memories, as well as their readers', with a recap or refresher at the beginning of each new episode. Such magazines not only offered literature to a wider public and outlets for novelists, but also provided information on science, travel and culture. For fifty years Mudie's, with an office near the British Museum, censored the subjects, morals and scope they considered suitable for the public, and ultimately what authors wrote and what publishers produced. If Mudie's considered a book to be unfit for the public other libraries followed suit. They also influenced the rise of the three-volume novel, which often necessitated padding by authors. In its heyday, Mudie's had around 180,000 novels which could be distributed from subsidiaries around the country, assisted by the new railways. Its advance orders at special rates were vitally important to the novel trade, including for Trollope. *The Times* considered Trollope to be Mudie's ideal author (as quoted in the *Oxford Reader's Companion to Trollope*, edited by R C Terry, Oxford University Press, 1999), and when reviewing *The Bertrams* on 23rd May 1859, p. 12, said:

> *The wide world of authors and the wide world of readers alike regard ... [Mudie] ... with awe; nay, even the sacred race of publishers have been known to kiss the hem of his garments ... He is the mighty monarch of books that are good enough to be read, but not cheap enough to be bought ... This majestic personage, whom authors worship and whom readers court, knows that at the present one writer in England is paramount above all others, and his name is Trollope ... He writes faster than we can read, and the more that the pensive public reads the more does it desire to read. [He] is, in fact, the most fertile, the most popular, the most successful author – that is to say, of the circulating library sort ... and so long as Mr Anthony Trollope is the prince of the circulating library our readers may*

Doorway of Smith, Elder & Co at 32 Cornhill

rest assured that it is a very useful, very pleasant, and very honourable institution.

Trollope was familiar with publishers; earlier in his career he had acted as his mother's agent with Henry Colburn, John Murray and Richard Bentley, and at one time Fanny had asked John Murray (unsuccessfully) if he could be employed as a part-time proofreader. It was also Fanny who arranged for the publication of Anthony's first novel, *The Macdermots*, by Thomas Newby but, as mentioned earlier, it was 'unfashionable' and failed to make any money. Trollope was slightly more successful with Longman & Co for *The Warden* and *Barchester Towers*, but when both they and Richard Bentley declined to purchase *The Three Clerks* he turned to Chapman & Hall who eventually published twenty-two of his novels plus two collections of short stories and eight volumes of his non-fiction. After serialization, most novels were published in the three-volume format with the exception of *The Warden*, published in one volume. Other publishers were James Virtue, Alexander Strahan and Alexander Macmillan.

Frederick Chapman, George Smith, John Blackwood and Alexander Macmillan all became close friends, while James Virtue persuaded Trollope to edit the new *St Pauls Magazine* in 1866 until it failed in 1870. Eventually Virtue's printing and publishing company merged with that of Alexander Strahan. Trollope's relationships with Virtue and Strahan became more complicated after they commissioned and offered £1,000 for another novel, but then rejected the resultant *Rachel Ray* on the grounds of it being inappropriate material for the Christian evangelical readers of *Good Words*. After demanding and receiving half payment for non-publication from Strahan, Trollope then sold the book to Chapman & Hall.

In total, Trollope's novels were serialized in nine different periodicals from 1860 to 1876: the *Cornhill* (where for *The Claverings* (1867) he received £2,800, 'the highest rate of pay that was ever accorded to me'); the *Athenaeum*; the *Fortnightly Review*; the *Pall Mall Gazette*; *Blackwood's Edinburgh Magazine*; *Macmillan's Magazine*; *St Pauls Magazine*; *Good Words*; and *Harper's New Monthly Magazine*. Trollope and Frederic Chapman were among the founders of the *Fortnightly Review*.

It was *Framley Parsonage*, first published in George Smith's *Cornhill Magazine* in January 1860 (book published in 1861), which propelled Trollope to the first rank of British novelists. He also wrote many essays on subjects such as hunting, travelling and clergymen, and several on political topics, such as 'The Irish Church', a hotly debated topic for the election in November 1868. He also wrote 'Whom Shall We Make Leader of the New House of Commons?' and 'The Civil Service as a Profession', and campaigned for the rights of British authors against

Periodicals: *Cornhill* 1860 Vols 1 and 2, *Cornhill* 1864, *Good Words* 1861, and *Saint Pauls* Vol III

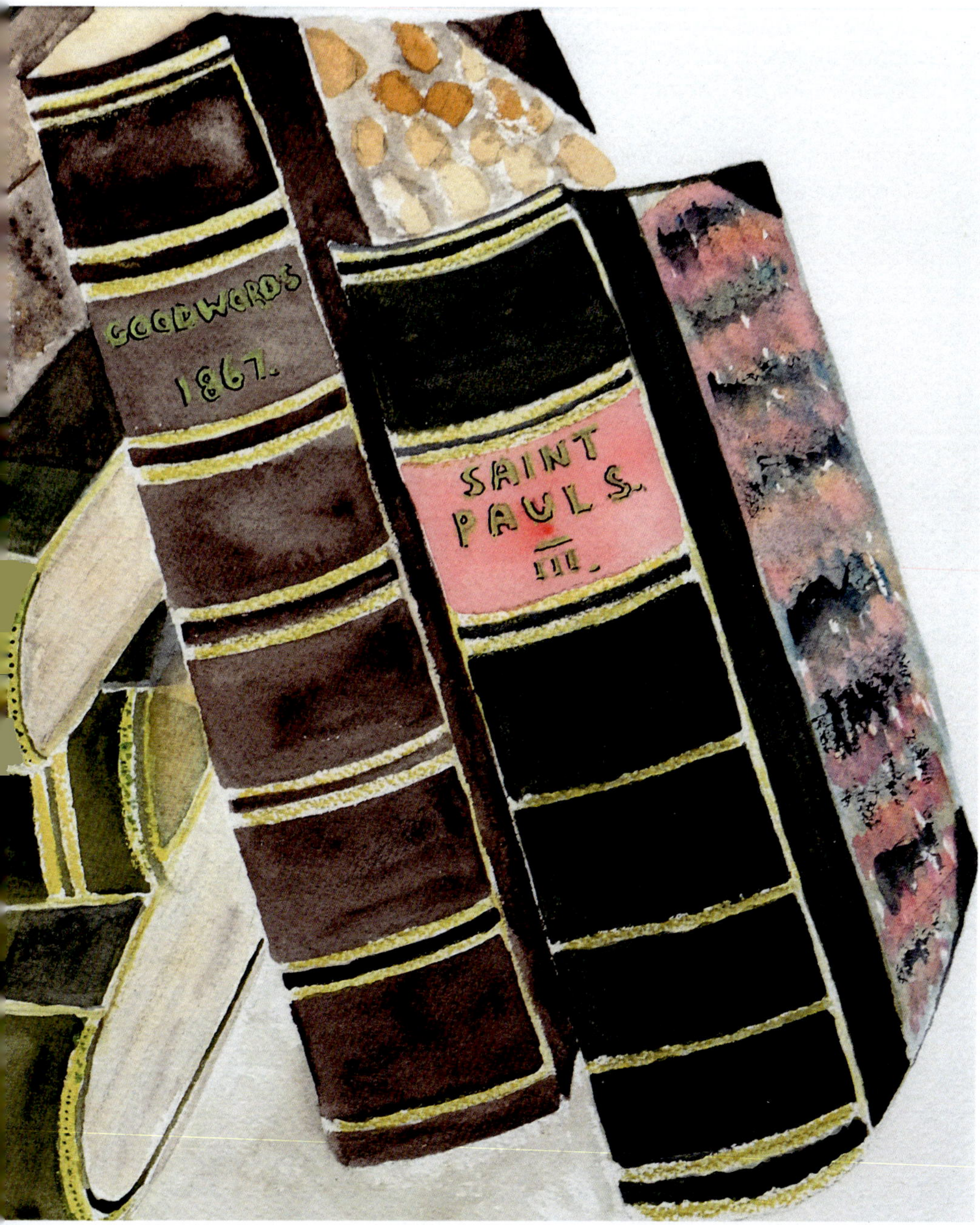
GOODWORDS
1867.
SAINT
PAULS.
III.

American literary piracy (based on the plagiarizing of Fanny's *Domestic Manners of the Americans*), with 'On the Best Means of Extending and Securing an International Law of Copyright' in *Transactions of the National Association for the Promotion of Society Sciences* (1867).

Mr George Smith held a sumptuous dinner in 1860 for all his contributors to the *Cornhill* and *Pall Mall Gazette* periodicals, which became memorable to Trollope in many ways: *'chiefly... because on that occasion I first met many men who afterwards became my most intimate associates. It can rarely happen that one such occasion can be the first starting-point of so many friendships!'* Here he met Thackeray, Sir Charles Taylor (*'than whom in later life I have loved no man better'*) Robert Bell, G H Lewes, Russell of *The Times*, and John Everett Millais, Sir Frederick Leighton, Sir Edwin Landseer, Sykes (designer of the *Cornhill* cover), Frederick Walker and Matthew Higgins, the 'Jacob Omnium' of the *Times*. George Augustus Sala, who was also at the dinner, wrote for the *Daily Telegraph* and *Illustrated London News* and founded the bohemian Savage Club affiliated to a masonic lodge, now housed at the National Liberal Club. Also there were Albert Smith, Billy Russell, Charles Lever, Fitzjames Stephen and many others (see London Clubs above).

Both Smith & Elder and Macmillan publishers frequently used Cambridge University Press as their printers of choice. According to Mike Petty in the *Cambridge News*, brothers Daniel and Alexander Macmillan began in Cambridge in 1850, moving to no 1 Trinity Street (now occupied by Cambridge University Press this continues to be one of the oldest occupied bookshops in Britain). Later they expanded into London at 23 Henrietta Street, keeping the main headquarters in Cambridge until 1863. They published many major figures such as Charles Kingsley, Lewis Carroll, Alfred Tennyson, Thomas Hardy, Herbert Spencer and Rudyard Kipling. Alexander Macmillan is buried in Mill Road Cemetery in Cambridge (his great-grandson, Harold Macmillan, became Prime Minister in 1957–63) and he and Trollope dined together the night before Trollope's final stroke.

I was fortunate to be included in a guided tour of the Cambridge University Press where I saw many historic printing presses such as the Columbian Hand Press (illustrated). This iron press was manufactured in 1860 by George Clymer of Philadelphia: it replaced the old wooden presses, with a platen size of 21" by 29". Each page was hand printed separately, and therefore changing proofs once set up was a difficult and lengthy process, which might account for some of the mistakes remaining in Trollope's novels after publication, such as a name appearing with one spelling on one page and a different spelling on another page. Even slight changes could alter the size of the printed page, thus making all subsequent pages obsolete and therefore too costly and time-consuming to be worth changing. Another hazard was the snapping of the iron band holding the pages together, and the *Cambridge Daily News* recorded one such catastrophe in 1908 when the '*nicely-arranged columns of print* [became] *a shapeless heap upon the floor*', such event being called a 'printer's pie'. It took several people forty minutes to sort it out. A slightly larger iron press, the Imperial, was manufactured c.1830 by John G Sherwin and installed at the CUP in 1840, followed by the Albion, manufactured in 1857 and installed in the 1870s. Some steam-powered machine presses were also introduced to the CUP in 1839, but in 1841 a complaint was received from a neighbour as to the rumbling and shaking of machinery. Thomas George Malcolm, Deputy Printer, responded that he had been employed for eleven years and considered the noise made was less than that of the men operatives, presumably chattering, and the CUP '*cannot in these times be altogether without the aid of machinery, and only wonders that its introduction was so long delayed*'.

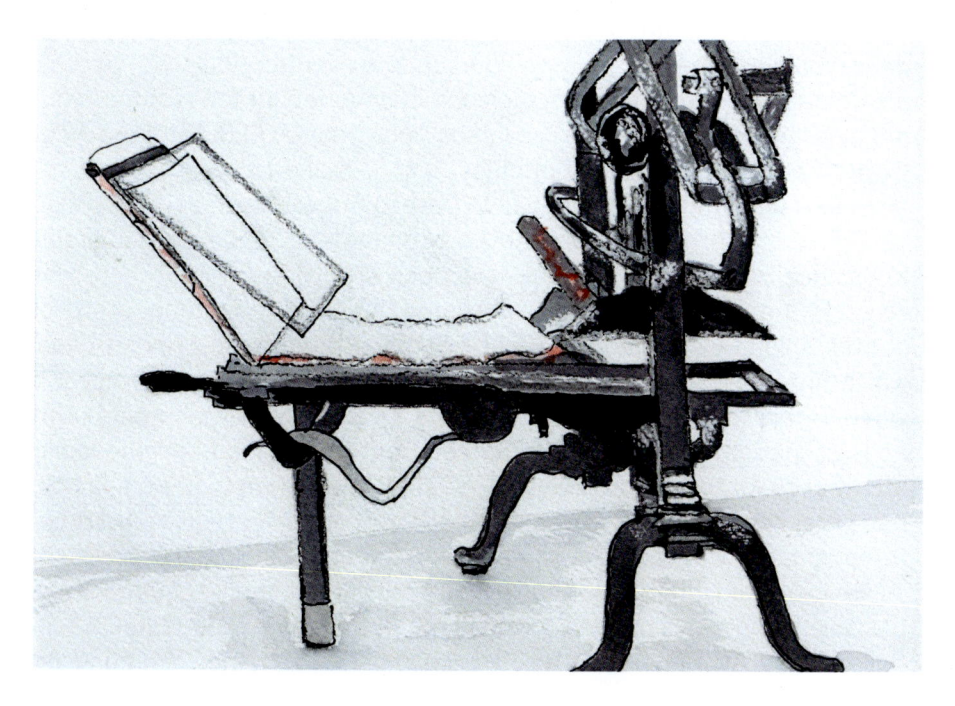

Columbian Hand Press at Cambridge University Press

Method of Writing

Trollope attributed his success to the *'virtue of early hours'*, a practice learnt from his mother. He was at his table every morning at 5.30 a.m. without mercy and, as previously mentioned, Barney was paid £5 per year extra during all those years, to take him coffee. Lighting would have been by candle and Barney would have lit a fire to boil the hot water, and also another one in Trollope's room on chilly days. Trollope wrote: *'I do not know that I ought not to feel that I owe more to him than to any one else for the success I have had'*. He felt strongly that working three hours a day would force the mind to concentrate: *'All literary men, working daily as literary labourers, will agree with me that three hours a day will produce as much as a man ought to write'*. He wrote with his watch before him, counting 250 words every quarter of an hour. He would spend the first half-hour reading the work of the previous day, *'weighing with [his] ear the sound of the words and phrases'*. This would equate to over ten (foolscap) pages of an ordinary novel volume a day which, if maintained for ten months, would produce three novels of three volumes each year. At 9.30 a.m. he would then dress and eat breakfast of meat, ham, fish and kidneys.

Once it became possible for him to travel by railway instead of horseback he decided to turn the hours to his advantage and made a writing-tablet to balance on his knee. It might have been slightly awkward if there were several other people in a small carriage, but after a few days' practice, he was able to write as quickly as he could at a desk. He wrote in pencil, which first Rose and later Bice copied out afterwards. The first novel he wrote in this way was *Barchester Towers* in 1857. Miss Mackenzie in the book of that name (1865) took her cue from Trollope, and as she looked after her sick brother in Gower Street, she used his method herself: *'She had brought a little writing-desk with her that she had carried from Arundel Street to Littlebath, and this she had with her in the sick man's bedroom.'*

Trollope said that once the art of writing had been acquired it was possible to write two or even three novels at the same time. When he had half-finished *Framley Parsonage* he went back to *Castle Richmond* and likened it to:

> ... when we go from our friends in town to our friends in the country, we do not usually fail to remember the little details of the

Method of Writing

one life or the other ... we are alive to them all, do not drive out of our brain the club gossip, nor the memories of last season's dinners, nor any incident of our London intimacies.

I have never found myself thinking much about the work that I had to do till I was doing it. I have indeed for many years almost abandoned the effort to think, trusting myself, with the narrowest thread of a plot, to work the matter out when the pen is in my hand. But my mind is constantly employing itself on the work I have done. Had I left FP [Framley Parsonage] or CR [Castle Richmond] half-finished 15 years ago, I think I could complete them now with very little trouble. Poor as the work is I remember all the incidents.

I may have boasted as to quantity but have not laid claim to any literary excellence ... but I do lay claim to whatever merit should be accorded to me for persevering diligence in my profession.

A typical Victorian writing desk

and

> *I have never been a slave to this work, giving due time, if not more than due time, to the amusements I have loved – but I have been constant – and consistency in labour will conquer all difficulties.*

He also said that he had never been troubled much about construction of plots, which would have been beyond his power, but that a novelist's aims should be to know his characters in order to:

> *... live with them in the full reality of established intimacy. They must be with him as he lies down to sleep, and as he wakes from his dreams. He must learn to hate them and to love them. He must argue with them, quarrel with them, forgive them, and even submit to them. He must know of them whether they be cold-blooded or passionate, whether true or false, and how far true, and how far false ...*

As a child he had kept a journal for ten years, although when looking at it anew in 1870 he destroyed it out of embarrassment, *'but [it had] habituated me to the rapid use of pen and ink and taught how to express with facility'*. He had also spent a great deal of time spinning stories in his head, for weeks, months even, year on year, carrying on the same tale, binding it together with events, morals and emotions.

Art and Illustrations

By the 1860s Trollope's standing as an author was so great that Luke Fildes and John Everett Millais were chosen to illustrate several of his novels. Both artists were already famous: Millais had been a Royal Academician since 1863 (and later President) and Luke Fildes, although not elected until 1887, was already so popular that railings were needed at the Royal Academy to hold back crowds at his exhibitions. Current artists of the same stature would be David Hockney, Anthony Gormley, Tracey Emin or Grayson Perry. Both Fildes and Millais were appreciated by Trollope for their sympathy and accuracy, but it was Millais who was particularly attuned to Trollope's work and became a close friend. Trollope wrote of him:

> *Altogether he drew from my tales 87 drawings* [for six novels], *and* [I] *do not think that more conscientious work was ever done by man ... In every figure he drew it was his object to promote the views of the writer and he never spared himself any pains in studying that work, so as to enable himself to do so. I have carried on some of those characters from book to book and have had my own early ideas impressed indelibly on my memory by the excellence of his delineations.*
> (Booth, *Letters* I, 104)

Millais' illustrations were representational and naturalistic, thus complementing Trollope's style of writing, often described as 'photographic realism'. This was an unusual partnership as Millais was also a member of the Pre-Raphaelite Brotherhood and I believe that, at the worst, Trollope disliked the Brotherhood, and at best mocked it. I believe such antipathy is shown by his aversion to red hair, using it to denote a fiery nature such as Lord Chiltern's. A part exception to his rule is Lady Laura Standish who, although not fiery, was a 'heroine' who had married the 'wrong' person and became nevertheless almost an 'outsider' described as: '... *in these days we have got to like red hair*' and '*Lady Laura's was not supposed to stand in the way of her being considered a beauty*'. Less subtly, her brother, the red-haired Lord Chiltern, was described thus:

> *The reader has been told that Lord Chiltern was a red man, and that peculiarity of his personal appearance was certainly the first*

> to strike a stranger. It imparted a certain look of ferocity to him, which was apt to make men afraid of him at first sight. Women are not actuated in the same way, and are accustomed to look deeper into men at the first sight than other men will trouble themselves to do. His beard was red, and was clipped, so as to have none of the softness of waving hair. The hair on his head also was kept short, and was very red – and the colour of his face was red. <u>Nevertheless</u> he was a handsome man, with well-cut features ... [My emphasis.]

I believe Trollope's inclusion of red hair was a humorous reference to the Pre-Raphaelite Brotherhood, founded in 1848 by William Hunt, Millais and Dante Gabriel Rossetti. Their models (Elizabeth Siddal, Janey Morris, Christina Rossetti and even Effie Millais) with their long dresses and long flowing red hair were associated with 'unrestrained', i.e. loose, morals, and were thought to represent the 'New Woman' campaigners for equal rights. A backlash to this fashion was depicted in opera and many novels, including Trollope's 'saving' of Carrie Brattle in *The Vicar of Bullhampton* (1870), and *La Traviata* (the 'fallen woman', 1848) by Verdi, adapted from *Lady of the Camelias* by Alexander Dumas. Trollope was actually a member of a counter art movement called 'The Clique' founded by several members of the Garrick Club and portrayed in a painting by Henry O'Neil, now hanging in the club billiard room. Also in The Clique was William Powell Frith who later, in 1881, similarly included Trollope (along with Gladstone, Browning and Huxley) in the left-hand bottom corner of his painting *Private View at the Royal Academy*. When Trollope featured the artist Conway Dalrymple in *The Last Chronicle of Barset* (1867) as a painter of society women in classical and biblical settings such as *The Three Graces*, he may have remembered Henry O'Neil and his satire on the Pre-Raphaelites, entitled *The Pre-Raphaelite* (1857). This portrait of a Britain two thousand years in the future depicts a frozen wasteland ruined by the lax morals of the Pre-Raphaelite Movement and consequent cultural decline. As already stated, if Trollope described a young lady as having brown hair and a dimple in her cheek, it was an indication that she would be the favoured heroine. In *Travelling Sketches* Trollope also mocks the prevailing fashion of dressing up for a tableau and thus almost foretells and parodies his own *The Last Chronicle of Barset* where Conway Dalrymple, a successful portrait painter, goes daily to Mrs Broughton's house to paint a tableau depicting Clara van Siever as Jael:

> The upshot of all this has been the creation of a distinct and new subject of investigation and study. Men and women get up painting as other men and women get up botany, or entomology

or conchology, and a very good subject painting is for the purpose. It is innocent, pretty, and cheap.

(*Travelling Sketches*, 1866)

Van Gogh would have been sympathetic to Trollope's style of writing: his paintings were described as 'reality more real than reality' and he is reputed to have stood in front of the windows of both the *Graphic* and the *Illustrated London News*, admiring their engravings and reports of urban poverty. He wrote to his brother, Theo, saying that English art had not appealed to him until he saw Millais' *Chill October* (1870), with its echo of his own *Autumn Landscape at Dusk*. He liked Dickens and George Eliot, Charlotte Brontë and Tennyson – whereas Trollope's characters, as we know, read Byron.

Trollope was a frequent visitor to private viewings at the Royal Academy, originally housed in Somerset House (home of *The Three Clerks* above) before moving to its present site at Burlington House. He was a frequent speaker at anniversary banquets, and at a function prior to the opening of the public exhibition on 4th May 1867, Trollope received a warm tribute from the President, Sir Francis Grant, who said that his novels appealed strongly to artists because they were graphic and faithful to nature. Two years later (but not published until 1871) Trollope wrote of young couples in *Ralph the Heir* meeting fortuitously at a Royal Academy exhibition. He also sometimes mocked the viewer:

Our art tourist … who flies from gallery to gallery, spending hours and often days in each, with a strong determination to get up conscientiously the subject of pictures … Pictures are the ever present subject of the English art tourist's thoughts, and to them and their authors he devotes himself throughout his holiday with that laborious perseverance which distinguishes the true Briton as much in his amusement as in his work'.

('The Art Tourist' in *Travelling Sketches*, 1866)

According to A M W Stirling in *The Richmond Papers* (1926 as quoted in R C Terry's *Interviews & Recollections*), he also met Millais at art and musical gatherings over a fruit shop in Jermyn Street, inhabited by Arthur Lewis, an artistic and influential captain in the Artists' Rifle Corps, where they met Leighton, Holman Hunt, and Sandys, amongst others.

The catalogue for the Tate Gallery's Pre-Raphaelite exhibition of 2007 praises Millais' illustrations and particularly *Guilty* in *Orley Farm* for contributing to the climax of Lady Mason's confession to Sir Peregrine Orme that, out of love for her son Lucius, she has forged her Will in his favour. Millais' depiction of her in a crouching position with unwieldy skirt demonstrates the drama of her emotions, and Sir Peregrine's compassion is shown by one hand resting on his heart, whilst his other outstretched arm foretells his subsequent rejection of her and the abandonment of their marriage. Millais paid equal attention to both his representations of Trollope's characters on the drawing board, and their transference onto the woodblocks, a function normally performed by the engraver brothers Dalziel, often cutting the blocks himself with a mixture of lavender and potash. When allowing the brothers to work the engravings, a typical instruction was to: *'Be careful with her head correction as above'*, later saying that *'aside from an eyelid that required shortening a trifle'* it was *'very satisfactory'*. The Tate's *Millais* also adds that although Trollope occasionally offered Millais some guidance *'he generally trusted Millais to choose the most dramatic points, as well as highlight the inner-selves of his novels' key protagonists'*.

Trollope and Millais' collaboration lasted for ten years, with nearly half the illustrations being for *Orley Farm*; two illustrations for each part of the original twenty monthly shilling-parts published by Chapman and Hall between March 1862 and October 1863, and later in two volumes in 1863. As periodicals included many adverts for perambulators and christening robes on both front and endpapers, it suggests they were aimed primarily at a female audience, and accordingly, Millais' illustrations for heroines included the most fashionable crinolines, to the occasional disapproval of Trollope.

Trollope was delighted to have Millais as his illustrator, both as a friend and knowing that his popularity could only encourage sales. He remarked specifically of *Orley Farm*:

> *I have never known a set of illustrations so carefully true, as are these to the conception of the writer of the book illustrated. I say that as a writer. As a lover of Art I will add that I know no book graced with more exquisite pictures.*

After illustrating *Framley Parsonage*, Millais was commissioned by Thomas Plint to paint watercolour versions of each illustration. Trollope remained intimate with him until his death in 1882, and after an alternative dinner invitation he wrote on 8th February 1880: *'I am very sorry but I have to dine with another artist on Saturday, very inferior, and no whist! I doubt the claret too!'* After illustrating *Phineas Finn* (1869) Millais was commandeered elsewhere to paint society portraits; Trollope's illustrations were subsequently produced by Mary Ellen Edwards and Marcus Stone. Millais also produced what were considered sensitive and detailed illustrations for Thackeray's *The Memoirs of Barry Lyndon* (1879),

Staircase and entrance hall of the former Royal Academy,
Somerset House, now the Courtauld Institute

Tennyson's *Poems,* and *Once a Week.* Burne-Jones also illustrated for *Good Words,* Holman Hunt for *Once a Week,* and Whistler for *Good Words* and *Once a Week.*

Perhaps part of Trollope's antipathy towards Dickens was due to his criticism (*Household Words,* July 1850) of Millais' painting of *Christ in the House of his Parents* when he described Mary as '*being so hideous in her ugliness that ... she would stand out from the rest of the company as a Monster, in the vilest cabaret in France, or the lowest gin-shop in England*'. Several articles in *The Times* sympathized with Trollope's belief that such a review was '*the lowest depths of what is mean, odious, repulsive, and revolting*' (*Anthony Trollope, His Work, Associates and Literary Originals,* by T H S Escott (The Bodley Head, 1913)).

Criticisms and Reviews

Express

Barchester Towers opens well, and the interest of the story is kept to the last ... The interest of the tale lies chiefly in the answer to the question, who is to be the new Warden of Hiram's Hospital? An office which Mr Harding had been compelled to resign on account of the attack made upon him in the columns of *The Jupiter*. This is it which connects ***Barchester Towers*** with a novel Mr Trollope had previously published under the name of ***The Warden***. It is difficult to continue a tale that seems already completed. Mr Trollope has done this, however, and done it well.

Saturday Review

Mr Trollope's success is wonderfully great ... The author is not a party writer, trying to run down the wrong party by painting it all black, and the right party all white. He sees and paints the follies of either extreme ... he has the merit of avoiding the excess of exaggeration. He possesses an especial talent for drawing what may be called the second class of good people – characters not noble, superior, or perfect after the standard of human perfection, but still good and honest, with a fundamental basis of sincerity, kindliness, and religious principle, yet with a considerable proneness to temptation, and a strong consciousness that they live and like to live, in a struggling, party-giving, comfort-seeking world. Such people are so common and form so very large a proportion of the betterish and more respectable classes, that it requires a keen perception of the ludicrous and some power of satire, to give distinctness to the types taken from their ranks by the novelist. Mr Trollope manages to do this admirably, and though his pudding may have the fault of being all plums, yet we cannot deny it is excellent eating.

Nathaniel Hawthorne

Have you ever read the novels of Anthony Trollope? They precisely suit my taste, solid and substantial, written on the strength of beef and through the inspiration of ale, and just as real as if some giant had hewn a great lump out of the earth and put it under a glass case, with all its inhabitants going about their daily business, and not suspecting that they were being made a show of … It needs an English residence to make them thoroughly comprehensive, but still I should think that human nature would give them success anywhere. (1860)

Tolstoy on *The Prime Minister*

Trollope kills me, kills me with his excellence.

The Globe

A fine healthful corrective to the injurious qualities of the religious novel is afforded in Mr Trollope's **Warden** and **Barchester Towers**. The latter is three times as long and three times as good as the former, of which, in some points, it is a continuation … Merely satirical sketches of persons, and sharp, witty observations on social or institutional absurdities, will not satisfy the most moderate man who takes up a book purporting to be a novel. But when we get hold of one which contains a good story told in unflagging, spirited English with a plentiful seasoning of allusive and direct satire, and not one-half-page of tediousness, we think it our duty to remind the reader to give honour to whom honour is due.

Henry James

The criticism, whether just or unjust, describes with wonderful accuracy the purport that I have ever had in view in my writing. I have always designed to 'hew out some lump of the earth', and to make men and women walk upon it just as they do walk here among us, with not more of excellence, nor with exaggerated baseness … recognize human beings like to themselves … If I could do this, then I thought I might succeed in impregnating the mind of the novel-reader with a feeling that honesty is the best policy.

Trollope's Response to Criticisms

Even whilst contributing to the *Cornhill* and enjoying success as a writer, in 1865 Trollope was insecure enough to feel that

> There were others who sat on higher seats to whom the critics brought unmeasured incense and adulation ... I felt that aspirants coming up below me might do work as good as mine, and probably much better work, and yet fail to have it appreciated.

and so in common with many authors who write under various (and sometimes several) pseudonyms, he published *Nina Balatka* (1867) and *Linda Tressel* (1868) anonymously. However, he was recognized by Mr Hutton of *The Spectator*, who analysed the repeated use of certain phrases and 'outed' him. '*Of all the critics he has been the most observant and generally the most eulogistic*'. Unfortunately neither book enjoyed much success.

—oOo—

> A critic must measure his work by his pay or he cannot live, shall review whatever book is sent to him and express an opinion ... [I] paid careful attention to the reviews which have been written on my own work; and I think that now I well know where I may look for a little instruction, where I may expect only greasy adulation, where I shall be cut into mincemeat for the delight of those who love sharp invective, and where I shall find an equal mixture of praise and censure, so adjusted, without much judgement as to exhibit the impartiality of the newspaper and its staff. Among it all there is much chaff, which I have learned how to throw to the winds, with equal disregard whether it praises or blames; but I have also found some corn, on which I have fed and nourished myself, and for which I have been thankful.

—oOo—

> An author can hardly hope to be popular unless he can use popular language. How may an author best acquire a mode of

writing which shall be agreeable and easily intelligible to the reader? He must be correct, because without correctness he can be neither agreeable nor intelligible. Without much labour, no writer will achieve such a style.

—oOo—

... [gave] accurately an account of Caesar's Commentaries, primary intention but also chief circumstances of his life. Beyond hard work got very little gratification, nobody praised it, one very old and learned friend, thanked [me] for 'Comic Caesar', but said no more.

—oOo—

Writing about *Orley Farm, Brown, Jones and Robinson,* and *The Small House at Allington,* Trollope wrote: 'If I had worked with one or the other [publishers Chapman & Hall and Smith, Elder & Co.] all might have been well but as worked with both became aware name too frequent on title pages. But work not inferior. In fact I believe that the work I did quickest has been done the best.'

—oOo—

Villino Trollope in Florence and Death of Fanny

After several attempts to find a permanent home, Fanny and Tom finally settled in the Villino Trollope, on what is now the Piazza dell'Independenza. Together they created a salon where they entertained scholars, writers, artists, thinkers and socialites of all persuasions. They both wrote novels and travel books, and Tom's first wife Theodosia also wrote poetry and translated articles. Trollope and Rose visited frequently, often staying for long periods of time, during which the brothers inevitably compared notes, causing Anthony to lament:

> *Sometimes my brother and I used to compare notes as to which of us had written the most. Unquestionably there are more volumes of his on the shelves than those which I am responsible for ... But then I have written and published such an inconceivable quantity of 'copy' in periodicals – quarterly, monthly, weekly, and daily – and in newspapers on both sides of the Atlantic.*

At the villa, with its octagon hall, double staircase, eight lancet windows of coloured glass, and eight niches between them, each with a full-sized panoply of a man-at-arms, Tom and Fanny created a 50ft library of 5,000 books (14,000 volumes) with unique and rare *Storia patria*, i.e. histories of the different municipalities and complicated petty medieval lordships (Italy was not unified until 1861). They also collected monographs of each previous municipality's codes of law, and many works on the topographical and legal antiquities of almost every Italian area. Anthony Trollope's similar interest in historical details of lordships and manors would account for the long descriptions of these given as introductions to many of his novels.

Fanny died on 6th October 1863, aged 83. For the last three years she lost her memory and mental faculties, for which Rose blamed her recent interest in clairvoyants. Prior to her death, Fanny exacted a promise that they would bleed her arm to prove that she was genuinely dead before burial.

Her last words were '*Poor Cecilia*' – remembering her last child to die before her. Here we must remember that she had first lost her mother when young and three of her siblings, then both her husband and five of her own children. She had also suffered her husband's lack of faculties, financial hardship and the fear of total loss of home and possessions in a society with no government fall-back except for a debtors' prison. At one time she had also feared for Anthony's life and had nursed him for months. Obviously, it had been difficult for Anthony as a teenager to understand why his mother had deserted him for three years leaving him with a bad-tempered father, but it is hard for us now to understand why he did not also mention any of her kindnesses, although he came to understand and appreciate her hard work in earning a living for the family (particularly difficult for a woman at that time). She had not only nursed him back to health but had also given him sound advice on how to prepare for a writing career, and organized publication of his first book. He did frankly say in his *Autobiography* that he told no lies and that no one should know all his business, but nevertheless it might be construed as heartless not to include some praise or understanding of her. Tom said: '*My mother the inseparable companion of so many wanderings in so many lands, the indefatigable labourer of so many years, found her rest ... in the beautiful little cemetery on which the Apennine looks down.*'

When Tom's wife Theodosia died two years later on 13th April 1865 and their 12-year-old daughter Beatrice needed looking after, Anthony introduced him to Frances Eleanor Tiernan, a musical student. Tom eventually married her, and they went on to spend many happy years together. Anthony's reply, when informed of the news, was '*Yes of course! I knew you would*'. Interestingly Frances Eleanor was the sister of the actress Ellen Terry, lover of Dickens, one of the strands in the two families' connections, and she also wrote novels and a biography of Fanny. She and Tom eventually sold the beloved Villino Trollope and moved to a new house at Ricorboli, with fifteen or more fair-sized rooms. As seems common with the Trollope family, they led a peripatetic life, constantly travelling for writing inspirations. Tom went on to be awarded the Order of Saints Maurice and Lazarus by Victor Emmanuel II of Italy.

Later, after Anthony Trollope's death in 1882, Tom and his wife Frances Eleanor (also known as Fanny) retired to Clifton, near Bristol, where Anthony and Tom's mother Fanny had danced so happily in her youth, and where they went on to enjoy long walks and local life.

Auguste Hervieux's portrait of Tom hangs in the National Portrait Gallery in London, and his portrait of Fanny hangs in the Ladies' Drawing Room of its outpost, Bodelwyddan Castle near Rhyl in North Wales.

Villino Trollope, Florence

Liverpool and SS *Great Britain*

In the spring of 1871, no longer tied by working for the Post Office, Anthony and Rose decided to sell the house at Waltham Cross and visit their younger son, Frederic James Anthony (known as Fred, 1847–1910), on his sheep station in New South Wales. They went for a full year and took their cook, Isabella Archer, with them. It was a hard decision to make as they had been very happy and sociable at Waltham, but the need to see Fred was strong. They therefore sold their furniture with *'heart-felt grief'* and *'many tears, and consultations as to what should be saved out of the things we loved'* and arranged to sell or let the house. When it remained unoccupied for two years before a sale, they lost £800 on the transaction. Trollope bemoaned the fact that he never made any money on anything but manuscripts, and even there, remunerations were declining. He said he lost money even when selling horses.

In addition to seeing Fred, they intended to explore the country and investigate institutions such as prisons, law courts, mines, schools, parliamentary sessions, processes for preserving meat, and of course post offices with postal routes and delivery times. This was in preparation for a book, *Australia and New Zealand* (1873), providing useful information for future emigrants, and for which Trollope had already negotiated terms. He recorded that he received almost half the price for non-fiction, even though such books *'Have an indominable tendency to stretch themselves'*, becoming almost twice the size of his usual fiction.

When the boys were young, Trollope had once described them as *'very nice boys – very different in disposition but neither with anything that I could wish altered'* (Booth, *Letters*, I, 31). As adults however, neither behaved in the way he and Rose expected. Both had attended St Andrew's College, Bradfield, near Reading, where, like his father at Harrow, Fred had been in a big fight with other boys. Harry and Fred were known as Paddy Major and Paddy Minor owing to their Irish brogues. Fred was more athletic than academic and, when not quite eighteen, decided he would like to become a sheep farmer in Australia (colonial careers had become popular after 1852 when unassisted, i.e. paid, passages encouraged over 16,000 emigrants to go to the colonies), possibly after gaining a love of sheep from his Trollope ancestors at Casewick. Trollope understandably described this as a *'great pang'*, but they eventually agreed to his going on condition that he return to England aged 21 to make a final decision on whether to stay at home or return to Australia. Accordingly, he came home in the winter of 1868 but after enjoying a season of hunting, still wished to return to his farm in the spring of 1869.

Meanwhile their elder son Henry (known as Harry, 1846–1926) had tried a variety of occupations: a spell at the Foreign Office arranged by his father's friend Lord Houghton of Sowerby: two unconsecutive periods of legal studies resulting in (eventually) a call to the Bar at Lincoln's Inn, although he never practised; a cornet in the Mounted Yeomanry, until finally in 1869 Trollope bought him a one-third partnership in Chapman & Hall for £10,000 (now equivalent to £1,198,150). This huge sum also quickly came to nothing as Henry soon quarrelled with Frederic Chapman, but fortunately not before he had successfully published some works for his father, including his later *Autobiography*. Henry also wrote a few unsuccessful novels of his own.

Being practical, as usual, before beginning the journey to Australia Trollope left the manuscripts of *Phineas Redux* (not published until 1873) and *An Eye for an Eye* (not published until 1879) with Henry to be published at suitable intervals with Chapman, and made arrangements to supply a series of articles to a London daily newspaper, plus twenty letters to the *Liverpool Mercury*. He also left the manuscript of *The Eustace Diamonds* (book not published until 1872) with the *Fortnightly* magazine. '*If therefore the* Great Britain, *in which we sailed for Melbourne, had gone to the bottom, I had so provided that there would be new novels ready to come out under my name for some time.*'

After leaving Waltham, Rose and Anthony, with Isabella, first journeyed to Liverpool to join the ship for Australia. They probably went by train from Waltham Cross to Liverpool Street station and from there to Manchester to join the new Manchester to Liverpool railway line, described by Tom as a train of fifteen carriages, with twelve passengers per carriage. The 52-mile journey took one and a half hours for first-class passengers paying 5s, and two hours for second class passengers paying 3s 6d. After a journey through Liverpool with Rose the previous year en route to America for six months, Trollope had written two short stories: 'The Two Generals' and 'The Widow's Mite' about the American Civil War, the former about two brothers fighting on opposing sides and vying for the love of the same girl, and the latter about lovers suffering the consequences of the cotton famine in Lancashire after supplies were cut off (both in *Good Words* 1863), and also the travelogue *North America* (1862).

The Merseyside Maritime Museum on Albert Docks, Liverpool, showcases the transatlantic slave trade as a triangular trade between Britain, West Africa and the Americas. By the 1780s Liverpool was considered the European capital of the American South and transatlantic slave trade, and by the 1840s/50s one of Britain's most important and prosperous cities. Liverpool ships sailed to West Africa and exchanged goods for enslaved Africans, who were traded as a commodity and transported brutally across the Atlantic on the 'Middle Passage' to be sold. These slave ships then picked up sugar, cotton and tobacco grown on plantations by enslaved African men, women and children, and brought them back to Britain.

The American Civil War (1861–5) was fought between northern American states and the slave-owning southern American states. After 1861 the South was against the idea of ending slavery and broke away to form the Confederate States of America leading to the Civil War. In Liverpool the valuable American cotton trade encouraged many people to support the South, where the cotton was grown. They flew Southern flags and held a fundraising bazaar at St George's Hall. Local shipbuilders designed and built ships knowing that, after leaving Liverpool, they would be converted to warships to attack the North's blockade of southern ports.

After accompanying Trollope on the earlier trip Rose had sailed home on her own after three months. Earlier, in 1866, Trollope had written about 'The Unprotected Female' in *Travelling Sketches* (possibly based on past journeys made by Rose), describing a man as having only a vague idea of his destination, whereas:

> *The unprotected female knows what she is about; she has something to do and she does it; she has a defined plan from which nothing moves her; the discomfort of a day will not turn her aside; nor will she admit of any social overtures 'till she has formed a judgement of their value, and has fair reason to believe that she will at any rate receive as much as she gives.*

After a delay of eighteen days (according to Gordon Trollope in *Trollope: Interviews and Recollections)*, Anthony, Rose and Isabella journeyed from Liverpool on the SS *Great Britain*, designed by Isambard Kingdom Brunel, the first iron steam ship with propellers, whose first voyage to Australia in 1852 was described by Nathaniel Hawthorne, then American consul in Liverpool, as generating:

> *... an immense enthusiasm amongst the English people about this ship, on account of her being the largest in the world. The shores were lined with people to see her sail; and there were innumerable small steamers, crowded with people, all the way out into the ocean.*

Although the ship was admired and an improvement on the packet (i.e. sailing ships, which took between ten weeks and four months), it was still an uncomfortable journey of about sixty days from Liverpool to Melbourne, and it took about six months to send a letter home. Once in the open sea the ship sailed primarily with wind power, switching to steam when necessary. The journey was crowded and hot, especially close to

Albert Docks, Liverpool

the equator, and passengers, attempting to keep cool, rigged hammocks on deck, whilst sudden storms would blow the ship around and roll it on the waves. Sometimes people fell out of bed, and many were seasick. Adding to the foetid atmosphere, hundreds of live sheep, pigs, cows and chickens were kept on board for milking, killing and eating along the way, their natural farmyard odour exacerbated by the heat. According to Joanna Thomas, Maritime Curator at the SS *Great Britain* Trust Museum in Bristol (*Trollopiana* no. 89, 2011) a passenger recorded 126 sheep, 4 lambs, 30 pigs, 2 bullocks, a cow, 510 fowl, 286 ducks, 65 geese, 32 turkeys and 6 rabbits on board in 1865, as well as tinned food, potatoes, flour, cheese, cooked meat and vegetables. Even more weight was added by a store of coal to provide steam when necessary.

The heat was also exacerbated by a ballroom on the top deck, which doubled up as the dining room, where people ate hot food, feted by musicians, with candles spreading their heat. After dinner people danced in their heavy Victorian evening attire, following which they retired to tiny windowless cabins leading directly off the ballroom. Inside was a set of two tiny bunk beds, one above the other, with a chair, washstand and mirror, and candles of course, such space usually being shared by two people. Rich people could share with a friend or family; second-class passengers shared with strangers, while single men often shared a cabin with five others. Poor emigrants travelled in third class, or steerage, and ate in their cabins. There were some sitting rooms for daytime use and walks could be taken up and down the deck.

Passengers provided their own entertainments with concerts, charades, chess, whist and backgammon and sailors sang sea shanties on deck; traditionally, when a new crew member 'crossed the line' for the first time an officer dressed up as King Neptune and issued 'orders', for example, insisting men shave their moustaches or have buckets of water thrown over their heads.

It was well known that many shipboard romances took place, often between people of different social classes, which usually ended upon arrival or stored up great trouble for the future; Trollope recalled his observations and memories from this trip and others for use several years later, for example *John Caldigate* as related above.

In addition to the publishing commitments arranged before travelling, Trollope also intended to write in his small cabin whilst on board, and therefore:

> ... succeeded in getting a desk put up in my cabin, and this was done ready for me in the *Great Britain*, so that I could go to work the day after we left Liverpool. This I did; and before I reached Melbourne I had finished a story called *Lady Anna*.

Lady Anna (published 1874) is about social class and jealousy and the heroine's love for a tailor. Although written on board ship, it was set in the Lake District, and in 2015 was adapted for the stage as *Lady Anna: All at Sea* by Craig Baxter, who incorporated aspects of Trollope's life into the story. Trollope also wrote *Harry Heathcote of Gangoil* (published 1874) in response to a request for a Christmas story (of which he disapproved) based on their adventures and the difficult life of sheep farmers such as Fred during the summer season of Christmas in the Antipodes. Years later

First-class cabin leading off ballroom of SS *Great Britain*

The Fixed Period, with its cricket match, is set in 'Britannula', a fictional empire between Australia and New Zealand. According to Neil Robinson, Library and Research Manager of Marylebone Cricket Club, Trollope was evidently a keen follower of cricket to judge by his comment in 1868 that:

> *One great merit which cricket has now, it had not always: I mean the absence of gambling. At one very sad time, when matches were made for money, and each side had its avowed backer, they were bought and sold as a natural consequence. This all died away, however, forty years ago. The game was not safe enough, and betters grew shy.*

Hull of SS *Great Britain*

Australia

Only one month after arriving in Australia, their cook, Isabella Archer, married and settled down to a new life, while Trollope and Rose enjoyed five or six very happy weeks on Fred's sheep farm, Mortray in New South Wales, where life was rough and primitive. Fred had married Susannah, a local girl who, it is said, Trollope loved to hear sing. He admitted later that Fred never made any money, and that several thousands of pounds were ultimately lost, but that it had not been Fred's fault as '*I never knew a man work with more persistent honesty at his trade than he has done*'. Ever alert to social hierarchy, even on raw settlements, he wrote:

> *The no. of sheep at states will generally indicate with fair accuracy the mode of life – 100,000 sheep will require man, cook, and butler – 40,000 cannot be shorn without a piano, 20,000 is lowest no. that renders napkins at dinner imperative, 10,000 require absolute plenty, meat, tea, brandy/water and wine, but not champagne, sherry or made dishes – must be content with miller?*

The only food offered seemed to be mutton washed down by lashings of tea (as mentioned earlier, both Trollope and Dickens' characters rarely ate anything other than mutton, the usual Victorian diet in Britain, the latter usually washed down by wine or half a pint of sherry). Although Trollope was in favour of mutton at home, even he tired of the monotony of it in Australia, and Rose arranged for soup and salad to be added to the menu, while Fred found some Australian wine as an accompaniment. Coincidentally, Dickens' sons Alfred and Edward also went to Australia, became friendly with Fred and dined at Mortray.

Such a person as Fred was called a 'squatter', a term meaning 'tenant of the Crown', detailed in Letter X *to the Liverpool Mercury* (this and other letters recounted in R C Terry (ed.), *Trollope: Interviews and Recollections*, St Martin's Press, Inc, 1987, and follow here, with their designated numbers):

> *it is intended to be understood that the rent which he pays is part of the public revenue of the colony ... [a young man] may own 20,000 sheep, lives and works on his own, and is perhaps*

40 miles from next town and half that from nearest squatter neighbour.

He has to shear, make fences, clear timber, tend to lambing, washing, and then in the middle of December (summer time) fires easily spring up. *'No shepherd, no stockman, no driver of a team of bullocks, stirs about the bush without a box of matches in his pocket, and very few rides miles to get to all the sheep'*. In Letter IX (eight pages long) of 13th November, he wrote of the hard work of running a sheep station, and *'very few travel far without a pipe in their mouths. In the middle of summer the slightest spark will set the dry grasses blazing'*. Again in Letter XIII, dated 25th September 1875, there was also the problem of the *'free selector'* who stole sheep and deliberately spread fires until the *'squatter'* was forced to buy him out.

After leaving Fred initially at Mortray, the Trollopes continued their travels around Australia, where Anthony's reputation had preceded him, and he was often feted and complimented. On 14th October 1871 he was guest of honour at a lunch in Gulgong and made a speech complimenting the locals on being *'more English than they are at home'* and thanked them for their warm welcome. They were also guests of the mayor for a performance at the Theatre Royal. However, on a visit to an asylum in Melbourne he wrote rather disparagingly of the Yarra River and that although he liked the fish barra mundi, he did not enjoy stewed wallaby. Travelling on horseback in the heat in what was often uncultivated bush territory was hard work, and particularly so for Rose, hampered by long skirts and petticoats and probably riding side-saddle. However, Trollope considered the Wiseman's Folly on Hawkesbury River to be *'more enchanting'* than either the Rhine or the Mississippi rivers, and could not *'paint the loveliness'* of Sydney Harbour. The Blue Mountains were like *'standing on the edge of a lofty cliff'* with an *'ocean'* of dense forest timber below, and astonishingly he climbed down a 450ft shaft into a mine to watch a quartz-crushing machine at work:

> *I do not know how far your readers may be aware of the difference between alluvial gold and gold got by the crushing of rock or of what is here called quartz. At the risk of some ridicule for attempting to teach that which is already well known, I will explain that alluvial gold is, or at any rate may be, got by the easy process of washing dirt, and that is the gold which the freaks of nature have placed in the soft soil; whereas the gold produced by crushing has to be extracted from the solid rock, which is pounded into dust and converted into mud in order that the gold may be extracted from it by chemical appliances.*

Additionally, in Letter IX above he described the gold diggers:

Since July, 1851, the date usually given for the discovery of gold in Victoria, up to the end of 1873, the value of the gold found in the colony has been £173,000,000, amounting to nearly three times the whole revenue collected in the colony during that period ... There are those in the colony now who say that all the gold in Australia has been raised at a cost greater than its value ... Men worked, not in large companies, but in small gangs – washing the gold out of the muddy gullies and small creeks; and no record was taken of the money which they brought with them, or of the labour which they expended. No wages were paid, as they were all masters. Many a well-born wretch from England was tempted out, with what money he could collect in his pocket, who instead of making his fortune died in abject want among the diggers. Who can compute how much such a one threw into the general stock of loss?'

But in Letter X he wrote:

But there is one class of workmen, or of intending workmen, who should never come to the colony. This is the young gentleman, who, finding that nobody wants him at home, thinks that he may as well emigrate. Neither will any one want him here.

Could this highlight anxiety about his own son?

In *John Caldigate* the hero was 'a well-born wretch' or 'a gentleman' and when he and two partners had been digging for about five weeks:

... about thirty feet from the surface, when they had already been obliged to insert transverse logs in the shaft to prevent the sides from falling in they had come upon a kind of soil altogether different from the ordinary clay through which they had been working. There was a stratum of loose shingle or gravelly earth, running apparently in a sloping direction, taking the decline of the very slight hill on which their claim was situated ... Handful after handful he washed, shifting and teasing it about in the pan, and then he cast it out, always leaving some very small residuum. He was intent upon his business to a degree that Caldigate would have thought to be beyond the man's nature. With extreme patience he went on washing handful after handful all the day ... he would not pause to eat, or hardly to talk. At last there came

a loud exclamation ... [his partners] were shown four or five little specks in the angle of the pan's bottom.

The Trollopes' trip was most successful, and their popularity continued until Trollope seemed to criticize *'boastfulness'*, i.e. locals constantly commenting that their meat or wine etc. was the best that could be found anywhere, when he wrote:

You hear it and hear of it every day: They blow a good deal in Queensland; a good deal in South Australia. They blow even in poor Tasmania. They blow loudly in New South Wales ... But the blast of the trumpet as heard in Victoria is louder than all the blasts – and the Melbourne blast beats all the other blowing of that proud colony.

Describing his embarrassment in Letter VIII of 21st August (five pages long), he pleaded that he had:

... admired so much of what I had seen, and had disapproved of so little; I had become so thoroughly convinced of their general well-being, and entertained so few fears as to their future; I regarded the whole enterprise as being so healthy in its tendency, that it was, I thought, impossible for me to write otherwise. And I am sure I did speak well of the colonies, and especially of Victoria.

Rose had also been known to make tactless remarks, and a supreme embarrassment must have been when Trollope was invited to a special evening reception as the guest of Mr E Landor and Mr Lochee, where Miss Lochee was to make her debut. He had refused to wear evening dress as expected and not only arrived wearing the wrong daytime attire, but also accidentally spilt a cup of coffee over Miss Lochee's new white silk grenadine frock (recorded by 'Gordon Trollope and Others' in R C Terry: *Trollope: Interviews and Recollections*).

In 1872 Rose returned to England, once again travelling on her own in what was still a perilous journey, while Trollope travelled home via Hawaii and the United States.

Alfred Dickens, aged 19, fourth son of Charles, came to the area after inheriting £7,000, but when he decided to move on to Melbourne to work in property management and sales of equipment, Fred wrote to Rose shortly after her return home, saying: *'Young Dickens has left the district ... [and] it makes one neighbour the less with whome [sic] you can exchange an idea'*. He also said that their baby (the first of eight) was *'growing a big fellow'*, indicating that she and Anthony had met their first grandson before their departure.

In 1869 Fred, with his parents' help, bought a sheep station 250 miles west of Sydney, and in 1875, Trollope went to visit him again, this time on his own and via Ceylon.

Dr Nigel Starck, writing in *Trollopiana* no. 97 (2013), chronicled how, in 1885 after Trollope's death, Fred lost his farm owing to drought and falling wool prices, and went to Wilcannia in New South Wales, 600 miles from Sydney, as chairman of the local Lands Administration Board. He did not enjoy living apart from his wife and children, and suffered greatly from the heat and dust storms. In letters to his brother and mother, Fred called the township *'one of those cursed places that no man over 30 years of age ought to be sent to'*, and *'A Worse place for children I cannot immagin* [sic]'. Dr Starck suggested that Fred's lamentations provide *'a vivid illustration ... of the rawness and hardness of colonial life, even for people with education and money'*. In another coincidence Fred's path then crossed with another of Dickens' ten sons: this time Edward, nicknamed 'Plorn'. He too had gone to Australia, aged 16, in 1868 and, after trying sheep farming, also opened an agency in Wilcannia, in 1883. A friendship grew between Fred and Plorn, as both were active in local sporting clubs, especially cricket, and both became honorary magistrates. *The Wilcannia Times* reported their involvement in a court case where Plorn was the presiding magistrate and Fred the chief prosecution witness.

Three years later in 1888 Fred managed to escape to a cooler coastal posting, while in 1889 Plorn became the MP for Wilcannia. Sadly, after the redrawing of boundaries, and the collapse of his agency interests, Plorn died five years later in 1902 of heat exhaustion in daytime temperatures at or above 105 degrees in Moree, in a similarly inhospitable climate.

Fred continued to enjoy modest prosperity, although his letters maintained a persistent mood of frustration and disappointment. His lasting achievement was to continue the Trollope line.

Montagu Square

In 1873, after returning from Australia and America, Trollope and Rose moved into 39 Montagu Square in Marylebone, a large terraced house built about 1815 around a central communal garden set with plane trees, where they stayed until 1880 when Trollope was aged 65. It was near Marble Arch and the Gower/Keppel Street area of his birth, and also to the British Museum where he was a Reader. According to *The History of the British Museum Library* by PR Harris, Trollope was included in an alphabetical readers' list from 1836 to 1843, alongside his brother Tom (confirming their closeness and Muriel Rose's assertion that he '*thought nothing of hurrying* [from Florence] *to London at short notice*', on one occasion with nothing more than a toothbrush), and also Charles Dickens, although Lyn Rees of the Central Archive has explained that the records for the 1870s have been destroyed.

Plaque on basement wall of 39 Montagu Square

Marylebone was a comfortable middle-class area: '*... not a gorgeous neighbourhood, but one which will suit my declining years and modest resources*'. It was not aristocratic like Berkeley or Belgrave Squares, so rather than living as a modest country gentleman as he had done at Waltham, he now lived as a modestly successful professional man and noted in his *Autobiography* that he hoped to spend the rest of his life here. They were even nearer to publishers, social functions and dinner parties than previously, and as the Garrick Club was about two miles away Trollope was able to ride there on one of his horses. Fellow members were impressed to see what Julian Hawthorne described as a '*fine-looking old gentleman*', dismounting outside the club, '*white-whiskered, ruddy-faced*'.

He initially returned to hunting three days a week, still always intending to give it up, stabling his four horses in one of the many local mews housing large numbers of horses. He was now able to travel back to the Essex meets (during the winters of 1873–5) by train, with a cab arriving at 7 a.m. to take him to the station, and home again for dinner at 8 p.m.

No. 39 Montagu Square, Marylebone

– this later time now being the fashionable hour. However, as he weighed sixteen and a half stone, with poor eyesight, it became difficult to continue at such a pace. He said: '*This* [hunting] *has been work for a young man and a rich man, but I have done it as an old man and a comparatively poor man.*' According to George Smith (R C Terry: *Trollope: Interviews and Recollections*) he was still energetic on non-hunting days and continued to drag around '*a garden roller at what might be called a canter*'.

On non-hunting days, he stayed in bed a little bit later, but continued to write between 8 and 11 a.m., after which the family ate breakfast. He began to suffer cramp in his writing hand, but as Bice had returned to live with them, she was able to write down in longhand from his dictation. Although he was said to tear up any pages she dared to criticize, they got on very well together. According to Hugh Walpole, their banter was the source of a family joke and Bice would be '*asked at breakfast if Trollope ever took a stick to her; she would smile, and he would laugh aloud and bang the table and, with his black eyes bright behind his spectacles, declare that some such punishment was sadly overdue*'. Tellingly, Cecilia Meetkerke described her as '*the tenderist and most devoted of daughters*'.

Many of the novels considered today to be his finest were written whilst at Montagu Square, such as *The Eustace Diamonds*, *The Way We Live Now*, *The American Senator*, *John Caldigate*, *Cousin Henry*, and the last of the Palliser or political novels: *Phineas Redux*, *The Prime Minister* and *The Duke's Children*. However, he began to notice declining health, thought to be heart problems and asthma, and he finally gave up hunting, a bitter blow. He also expressed humiliation or annoyance when writing '*I had humbly to crave* [the Speaker's] *permission for a seat in the gallery so that I might become conversant with the ways and goings of the House in which some of my scenes were to be placed*' after completing his research there.

Additionally, he would have felt keenly the knowledge that Fred preferred to struggle alone in Australia rather than settle nearby, the latter particularly being an echo and mirror image of the absence of his mother earlier. It was at this time of accumulated depression that he began his *Autobiography*, in 1875. Perhaps his bleak mood caused him to exaggerate his childhood adversities, or perhaps he intended to signal to Fred that he too could overcome struggles and adversity to be ultimately successful; even perhaps also send a message to all 16-year-old youngsters going out alone to seek their fortunes in the colonies. Such an explanation would fit with Trollope's sensitivity and prescience in writing about difficult themes. Perhaps looking back on his childhood, he began to understand more the family's difficulties (illness, deaths of children, severe financial worries, sheer hard work and father's recognition of the need for a good education), and while wishing to share any childhood unhappiness, transposed it into the hardship of walking and schooling, in an attempt to be chivalrous towards his family's difficulties.

The *Autobiography* has also been considered controversial for including references to Kate Field (see above) which were omitted by his son Henry. Trollope had stated in his publication instructions: '... *I leave it altogether to your discretion whether to publish or to suppress the word; and also to your discretion whether any part or what part shall be omitted*', and in his Preface, Henry justified this by writing: '*And I have made no alterations. I have suppressed some few passages, but not more than would amount to two printed pages has been omitted.*' As Trollope would have necessarily dictated the passages to Bice, which would ultimately have also been read by Rose, I cannot feel that the missing passages would have been particularly frank or upsetting to his family. Perhaps readers today would not have considered anything amiss: perhaps it is the omission itself that has caused a controversy.

Trollope told Millais: '*It is, I suppose, some weakness of temperament that makes me, without intelligible cause, such a pessimist at heart.*' Also, despite his prodigious output, he was aware of a loss of popularity leading to declining sales. Ten years previously in 1867 he had received £2,800 for *The Claverings* and even £3,200 for *Phineas Finn* and *He Knew He Was Right*, both published in 1869, but now in 1877 and 1879 he received only £1,800 each for *John Caldigate* and *The American Senator*. Additionally, *The Prime Minister*, in which he had '*for many years past, been manufacturing within my own mind the characters of the man and his wife*' was even dismissed with contempt. He was especially hurt by the criticism of *The Spectator*, as he said he loved his portrayal of Plantagenet Palliser as a perfect gentleman who devoted his life to fairness, politics and family, and who lived cleanly and frugally in spite of his great wealth. Palliser's gentleness allowed him to understand and accept Lady Glencora's extravagance and exuberances as misguided attempts to help him: '*If he be not, then am I unable to describe a gentleman. She is by no means a perfect lady; but if she be not all over a woman, then am I not able to describe a woman.*'

Trollope may not have been aware that other authors were also experiencing declining sales. Dickens was similarly upset when *Martin Chuzzlewit* didn't sell. Not all of the public were educated or prosperous enough or had time to read regularly, and some were disinclined or discouraged to read on the Sabbath, such as Laura suffering her husband Mr Kennedy's disapproval:

> '*I won't say that reading a novel on a Sunday is a sin,*' he said; '*but we must at any rate admit that it is a matter on which men disagree, that many of the best of men are against such*

> *occupation on Sunday, and that to abstain is to be on the safe side.' So the novels were put away, and Sunday afternoon with the long evening became rather a stumbling-block to Lady Laura.*

Additionally, the relatively small group of proficient readers were unable to keep up with the huge number of new novels produced by popular writers, first issued in instalments and later republished in book form.

Another contributing factor to depression may have been the need to make large cuts from his manuscript for *The Duke's Children*. Professor Steven Amarnick, in a new unabridged version of *The Duke's Children*, recently re-inserted 65,000 words from Trollope's original handwritten manuscript which had been indiscriminately edited out of the first publications. Readers today of the new full version of *The Duke's Children* can see Trollope's original intention of the development of Silverbridge's character from a hobbledehoy into a mature statesmanlike figure, echoing Trollope's own progression through life. It also shows a more complete portrayal and mature relationship of Lady Mabel Grex and Silverbridge, compared to the young Isabel Boncassen.

His later books reflected a constant 'looking back', such as *Cousin Henry* (1879), featuring the making and changing of Wills and the rearranging of a library by the main character's niece; *The Duke's Children* with the troubles heaped upon the Duke by his children; *Mr Scarborough's Family*, again detailing a family's obsession with Wills and inheritances, and Uncle Prosper of Buston Hall, Hertfordshire, probably modelled on Julians. Not only do his characters and their situations entirely resonate with us today, but he presciently wrote:

> *I do not think it probable that my name will remain among those who in the next century will be known as the writers of English prose fiction; but if it does, that permanence of success will probably rest on the characters of Plantagenet Palliser, Lady Glencora, and the Rev Mr Crawley.*

Trollope's granddaughter Muriel recorded that her mother, Ada Strickland, had also stayed with the family at Montagu Square for many years before she married their son Henry. '*She was devoted to him* [Trollope] *and they were great friends. She made him ride in the park with her when no one else would have dreamt of asking him to disturb his sacred sporting hours.*' Muriel went on to recommend Michael Sadleir's *Trollope: A Commentary* as '*a most excellent biography and a very sound piece of work*'. She also said that Sadleir, a contemporary of Trollope's, '*had lunched there on the previous Monday*' and that her father (Henry), had been very fond of him.

Library

Trollope had an extensive library. In his youth he had kept a Commonplace Book (an idea from Renaissance times of keeping a record of ideas, notes, quotations etc. for future use) in which he had written down his thoughts, ideas and records of his reading, which he had often read aloud to his family. He collected books wherever he went and in 1867, whilst at Waltham, had bought a collection of about four thousand works (at a fair price) from the executors of his friend and former colleague, Robert Bell (1800–67), a writer whose annotated edition of *The English Poets* remained unfinished at twenty-nine volumes. The purchase was made specifically to help the impoverished widow whom he also assisted in acquiring a pension. Trollope also wrote a tribute to Robert Bell, and later gave some of the books to Walter, the son of his friends Sir Frederick and Lady Pollock, the Queen's Remembrancer (historical judicial position) and future neighbour.

By the time they moved to Montagu Square, like his brother Tom, he had amassed five thousand books which he described '*as being dearer to me even than the horses which are going, or than the wine in the cellar, which is very apt to go, and upon which I also pride myself*'. Bice duly took all the books down to dust twice a year. The library was at the rear of the ground floor but overflowed upstairs into a recess at the end of the double drawing room and was said to be '*a quaint and quiet book room*', and '*more a workshop than a library*'. Occasionally visitors were allowed into the inner sanctum. One such visitor recorded that the library also had a cupboard filled with cigars '*stacked across each other as headers and stretchers like timber, so as to allow free circulation of air*'. These came once a year in a large consignment from Havana: they were used in strict rotation of eldest first, and, in accordance with accepted health ideas, the door was kept closed on wet days, and open on dry days. '*If I can not smoke a small cigar under eight pence, I will not smoke them at all*' (Booth, *Letters*, II, 573). He was said to smoke about four cigars a day, later cut down to three. Other visitors remarked on a store of different spectacles which he would rifle amongst to find an appropriate pair.

According to Bryan Welch in *Trollopiana* no. 97, Trollope organized the books according to the historic system of 'fixed shelf' locations, where a book's position is identified first by the bookcase and second by the shelf, sometimes also by its place on the shelf. This system has two problems: firstly, when the books are moved to new positions they need new shelf marks, and secondly, as they are not arranged by author or subject, they are difficult to find. Consequently, after the move to Montagu Square, a new catalogue was needed to fit the new space. This was duly organized by Bice and printed by James Virtue & Co. and is now in the Victoria and Albert Museum. It has eighty-six numbered pages and is inscribed '*John Forster with kindest regards from AT Ap.1874*'. There are 2,199 entries listing around 5,000 books on shelves ranging from A1 to T8.

Confusingly the catalogue does not list every volume individually. *The Complete Works of Voltaire*, for example, has a single listing although it consists of ninety-two volumes running along four shelves (T4,6,7 and 8). Another confusion is that although the catalogue entries are alphabetical, sometimes the books are listed by title and sometimes by author or subject, for example Macaulay's *Critical and Historical Essays* appears under 'Lord Macaulay' but Morley's *Voltaire* appears under 'Voltaire'. Some of the books are marked 'RB' perhaps relating to those previously belonging to Robert Bell.

When the Trollopes moved again a few years later, the process was duly repeated, and Trollope wrote to his son Henry on 23rd July 1880:

> *You may imagine what a trouble the library has been. At present though the bulk of the books are placed; and are placed on their old shelves and with their own numbers, still that which is not the bulk, but which forms a numerous portion, is all in confusion so that sometimes I am almost hopeless. I cannot describe to you the room. It is very much larger than the library in London, but still will not hold as many books. It is two shelves lower, and let a room be ever so long or broad you can only put books on the outside; round the walls. Now in London there was much wall space every inch of which was utilized. So it is here, but still there is not room for so many books. Nevertheless I hope to get them in order before you come, merely leaving for you the task of preparing the alterations in the catalogue. I fear that I must have another catalogue printed.*
>
> (Booth, *Letters*, II, 875)

Library

Trollope's bookplate for his personal library is listed in Egerton Castle's *English Bookplates* as F29845 dating from around 1860 and bearing the Trollope arms (vert three stags courant argent, attired or, within a bordure of the second), taken in descent from Sir Thomas Trollope, the fourth baronet (1691–1784). When Trollope died, he left all his books and pamphlets to Henry, whose bookplate, with single armorial, is similar to his father's except that the border at the top of the shield is straight.

The Trollope Collection at Winchester School includes a loaned bookcase, and one volume with the shelf label 'A3'; Trollope's bookplates are in the British Museum.

Trollope's bookplate

Former library at Waltham Cross

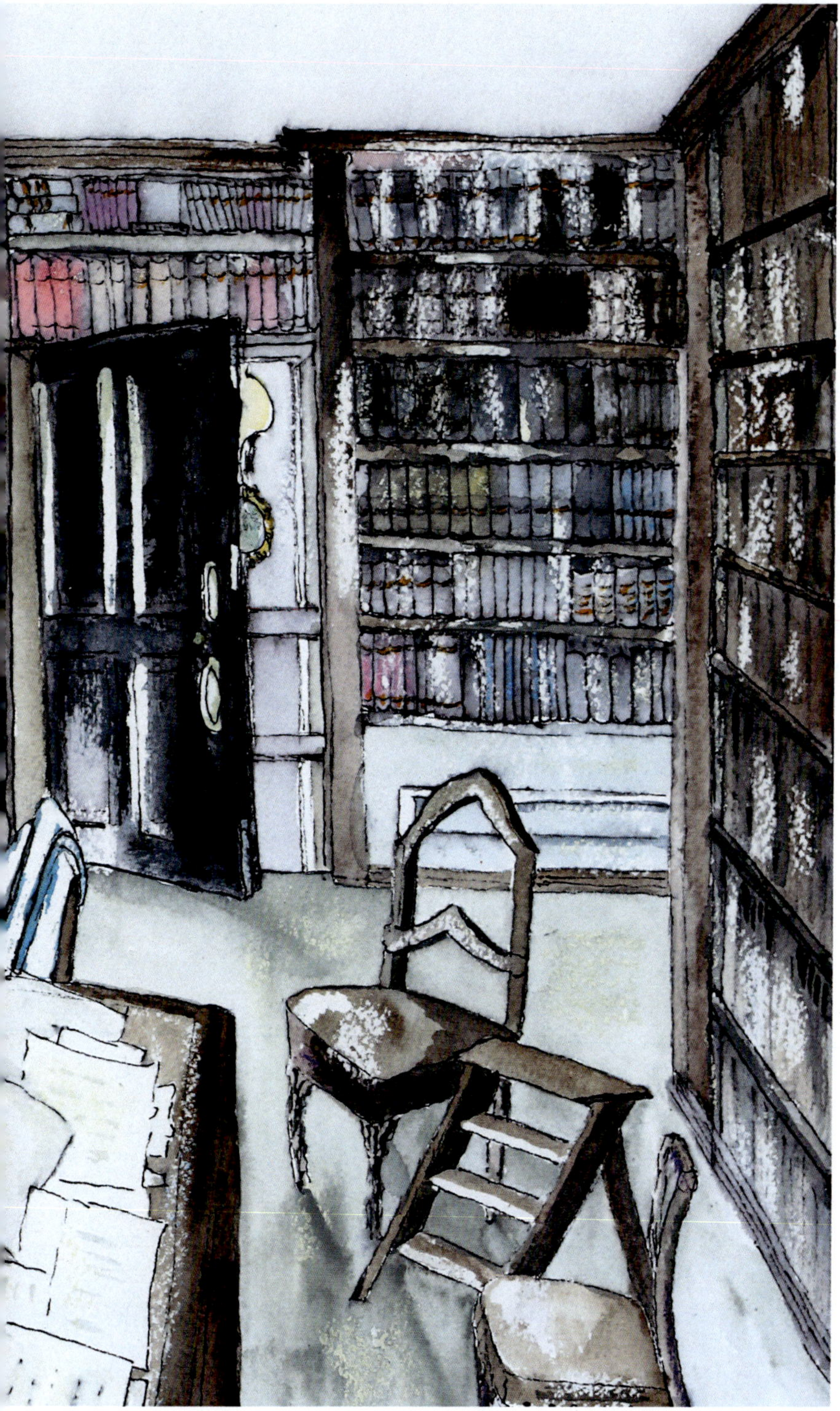

Further Travels

As we have seen, Trollope travelled widely, on Post Office business, and for research or pleasure, both on his own and with Rose, on journeys which would not have been as quick, comfortable or reliable as they are today, or even as safe.

Post Office Travels

Egypt and the West Indies

In 1851, whilst still based in Ireland, Trollope had been on a postal mission to the West of England and been inspired to begin the Barchester novels, and also to the Channel Islands, which resulted in his recommendation of the installation of pillar boxes in England.

In 1858, he went on a similar mission to Egypt to inspect postal systems from there to India and back again, after which he explored the Holy Land and Malta, Spain and Gibraltar on the way home. These travels added colour and background to the love affair between George Bertram and Caroline Waddington in *The Bertrams*, which he had begun writing in Egypt immediately after finishing *Dr Thorne*. In between, he fitted in a hurried visit to sort out postal problems in Glasgow, which he later blamed for the book's rather bland love scenes. Nevertheless, the book was well received by the critics.

The *Oxford Reader's Companion to Trollope* details how, on a visit to the West Indies later the same year on 17th November, Trollope similarly increased postal efficiency and reduced costs: he checked routes, devised economies, introduced changes, and negotiated the transportation of mail across Panama for an annual fee, and its shipping across the isthmus to the west coast of America. He recommended that Jamaica be the mail centre in the region, thus saving the packet company c.£16,000 p.a. He established local control of the post offices in Jamaica and British Guiana, and found Cuba and Puerto Rico needed '*to reduce their charges for local forwarding of mail sent from the United Kingdom*' and submitted his report a fortnight later, on 16th July 1859.

Almost immediately after completing *The Bertrams* on 18th January (not published until 1859), he began a travel book, *The West Indies and the Spanish Main*, on 25th January. This travel book criticizes animals roaming around slum areas but compares the scenic beauty with Switzerland. He liked the mangoes, breadfruits and cotton trees, but found the constant river crossings tiresome. He claimed it was *'not the best book that has come from my pen'*, but it was accepted as thoughtful and detailed. He perceptively evaluates people and racial characteristics and supports mixed marriages and multicultural societies: *'Providence has sent white men and black men to those regions in order that from them may spring a race fitted by intellect for civilization and by physical organization for tropical labour'*. He describes the honesty of his feelings as being *'to the eye of the reader, and to his ear, that which the eye of the writer has seen and his ear heard'*. He utilized the knowledge he gained in four of his short stories: 'Miss Sarah Jack of Spanish Town, Jamaica'; 'Aaron Trow'; 'Returning Home'; and 'The Journey to Panama'.

North America

Trollope made his first trip to North America, accompanied by Rose, whilst on holiday from the Post Office (despite disapproval from his superiors). They left Liverpool on 14th August 1861 although Rose travelled home on her own at the end of November. Before travelling Trollope had secured terms with Chapman & Hall for *North America* (published 1862) in which he reports on the Civil War. He also details its causes, the army, the price of wheat, the Constitution, the government, the Law Courts, lawyers, the rights of women (he approved of women working but hoped they would also seek husbands, as had been his advice to Kate Field above) and the price of food. He wrote: *'... the price of wheat in Europe will soon depend, not upon the value of the wheat in the country which grows it, but on the power and cheapness of the modes which may exist for transporting it'* and that *'the Protectionists ... will have grown sleek upon American flour before they have realized the fact that they are no longer fed from their own furrows'*. Typically noticing every detail, he refers to the unkempt hair of the North American army: *'No single trait has been so decidedly disadvantageous to the appearance of the American army, as the long uncombed, rough locks of hair.'*

He had no intention of emulating his mother's *The Domestic Manners of the Americans*, saying that while hers was *'essentially a woman's book'*, his would be less emotional and more systematic. The Civil War prevented his visiting the southern states, but he saw all the northern states except California. His mother had described vivid scenes and anecdotes, but he presented statistical tables of population and wheat production, and charts of army expenditures. He apologized for criticizing the women he saw, but nevertheless was uncomplimentary (and offensive by today's standards) in describing some on a bus as *'unclean animals'* with *'dragging trains of their filthy dresses'*, and *'blows from a harpy's fins'*, and *'loathsome as* snake's slime'. Whilst agreeing the Revolution was painful, he felt it was a necessary evolution of British colonialism and concluded that the North would win, that England would not recognize the South and France would follow. The book was published during the war but was considered tedious and confused.

He felt English people of his own class were treated better in England than in the States, but the reverse was true for those from a lower social hierarchy, both economically and psychologically, and that all people in America could *'walk like human beings made in God's form'*. He also included recommendations for visiting certain landmarks. Back in London, he gave a lecture advocating the Union's side, but his short stories in *Tales of All Countries* (1863) are more nuanced: 'The Two Generals' (see 'Liverpool and SS *Great Britain*' above) is about two brothers, each a general, on opposing sides. 'The Widow's Mite' exposes the so-called British 'cotton famine', with southern cotton being no longer available for British mills. A clergyman's family debate how best to aid the workers suffering the loss of their jobs, and one young woman decides to marry in her old clothes in solidarity with them. Others mock her decision as pointless, and the story ultimately leaves open the best way to aid the poor. 'Miss Ophelia Gledd' is an independent Boston beauty acutely sensitive to the cultural differences between her American and English lovers, considered by some people to refer to Kate Field, who may have provided useful information.

Trollope visited again in 1868 in order to negotiate a new treaty for postal rates and again in 1872 on his way home, via Hawaii, after visiting Fred in Australia; and one last time in 1875, crossing from west to east at the end of his tour of the Pacific, which resulted in an essay about California. Both America and American people occur frequently in several short stories and novels, such as the speculator Hamilton K. Fisker and the adventuress Mrs Hurtle in *The Way We Live Now* (1875). Unlike Trollope, Mrs Hurtle finds Britain to be *'an effete civilization'*, *'structured by inequality'* where everyone is either *'too humble or too overbearing'*. The novel also mocks *'trivial'* British attitudes to manners in gentlemen's clubs where members dislike a visiting American because *'his manners were not as their manners; his waistcoat was not as their waistcoat'*.

The garrulous Elias Gotobed in *The American Senator* (1877) from the fictional state of Mikewa, travels around England spouting unwanted views on everything he sees. The final chapter in *Dr Wortle's School* (1881) is set in America when Mr Peacocke travels to California to confront his wife's brutish husband who has threatened to expose them. William Blackwood, the publisher, had been reluctant to use the working title of 'Mr and Mrs Peacocke' because of Victorian sensitivity about a bigamous marriage.

South Africa

On 27th June 1877, Trollope began another arduous journey, this time to South Africa, following the annexation of the Boer province, then being debated in the House of Commons. He stayed in Cape Town for two weeks before travelling on. Again, even though he had only finished *John Caldigate* the day before his arrival on 21st July, he followed his mother's footsteps by writing a travel book, *South Africa* (1878), having previously negotiated terms of £850 from Chapman & Hall, and fifteen letters to provincial newspapers for £175,

He visited libraries, the botanic gardens and the Post Office (where he noted that his professional advice was, as ever, ignored!) and gave historical summaries of Dutch and English history. He gave his views on government, politicians, the police, ostrich farming, caves with stalactites and the happy sight of children playing kiss-in-the-ring in a park in Port Elizabeth. He took an 11-hour omnibus journey to Grahamstown to attend a conference of Kafir chiefs, where he heard a Siwani say that it would be best if the British all went away. He detailed the refusal of white labourers to work on an equal footing with Kafirs, was sympathetic to Bishop Colenso's views (who denounced the first five books of the Old Testament and doubted the accuracy of the Bible in general). He wrote a history of the Zulus, and travelled by railway, omnibus and cobb-cart, visited a diamond mine and slept in the veld. The *Oxford Reader's Companion to Trollope* opines that despite his increasing age and declining health: '*The quest for experience is undiminished. He records the grace of the Zulus, the lure of diamonds and gold, the decimating effects of the tsetse fly on the Limpopo river, racial characteristics, British acquisitiveness, statistics.*'

Holiday and Research Travels

Europe

Throughout his adult life Trollope, first with Rose and later with their sons and niece Florence Bland, travelled to Europe several times. They frequently visited Fanny and Tom in Florence for periods of a month at a time, and travelled extensively throughout Switzerland, the Rhine, Germany, Koblenz, Austria, Normandy, Brittany and Paris. Their granddaughter Muriel Rose (in *Interviews and Recollections*) recounted how Rose had told her that she had been four times over the St Gotthard: by diligence, by sleigh, by train and on foot, causing Trollope to tease that although she could walk in Europe she could not walk in London! Many short stories were inspired by these travels such as: 'Why Frau Frohmann Raised Her Prices', 'The Panjandrum', 'Relics of General Chasse', 'A Tale of Antwerp', 'The Chateau of Prince Polignac', 'The House of Heine Brothers in Munich', 'Miss Sarah Jack of Spanish Town, Jamaica', 'The Man Who Kept his Money in a Box', 'An Unprotected Female at the Pyramids', 'The Banks of the Jordan', 'John Bull on the Guadalquivir', 'George Walker at Suez', 'Aaron Trow' and 'Returning Home' collected in *Tales of All Countries*, Parts I and II.

Scotland

Scotland features prominently in both political and other novels, with young men going north for the annual shooting season beginning on 1st August. Since 1852 a train service from King's Cross reduced a stagecoach journey of several days to just ten and a half hours. Phineas in *Phineas Finn* (1869) visits Lady Laura (whose real love is Phineas himself) at Loughlinter, a vast *nouveau riche* pile in Scotland owned by her husband, the rich but grim Mr Kennedy, whom she had felt obliged to marry after gifting her own money to save her brother, Lord Chiltern:

> ... Loughlinter wanted that graceful beauty of age ... was all of cut stone, but the stones had been cut only yesterday. It stood on a gentle slope, with a greensward falling from the front entrance down to a mountain lake. And on the other side of the Lough there rose a mighty mountain to the skies, Ben Linter. At the foot of it, and all round to the left, there ran the woods of Linter, stretching for miles through crags and bogs and mountain lands. No better ground for deer than the side of Ben Linter was there in all those highlands. And the Linter, rushing down into the Louth through rocks which, in some places almost met together above its waters, ran so near to the house that the pleasant noise of its cataracts could be heard from the hall door. Behind the house the expanse of drained park land seemed to be interminable; and then, again, came the mountains. There were Ben Linn and Ben Lody – and the whole territory belonging to Mr Kennedy.

Ominously, after the season: 'A few men went down for the grouse shooting late in the season; but they stayed but a short time, and when they went Lady Laura was left alone with her husband' (an ominous phrase indeed!).

In *The Eustace Diamonds* (1872), Frank Greystock (a weak man engaged to governess Lucy Morris) could not resist the advances of his cousin Lady Eustace and her invitation to Portray Castle, on the banks of the Loch, and took his friend with him:

> He was what the world calls penniless, having an income from his father just sufficient to keep him like a gentleman. He was

not much known as a sportsman, his opportunities for shooting not having been great; but he dearly loved the hills and fresh air, and the few grouse which were – or were not – on Lady Eustace's mountains would go as far with him as they would with any man.

Not having much experience of shooting, he worried about the gillie: 'If a gillie means a lad without any breeches on, I don't mind; but I couldn't stand a severe man got up in well-made velveteens, who would see through my ignorance in a moment, and make known by comment the fact that he had done so.'

Ruins of Bolton Abbey, Yorkshire

Yorkshire and the Lake District

The River Nidd that runs through Knaresborough, Yorkshire, may have inspired Trollope to create Lord Nidderdale, the eldest son of the Marquis of Auld Reekie who appears briefly in *The Duke's Children*, and then becomes an important character in *The Way We Live Now* (1875), not only involved in Melmotte's financial schemes but also almost marrying his daughter. Not far from Knaresborough is the Skipton and Bolton Abbey area where the young Lady Anna of the book of that name is sent to stay with her aunt in the hope that she will be persuaded to marry her cousin Frederick, Lord Lovel, instead of the tailor Daniel Thwaite. On a family picnic at Bolton Abbey Frederick entices Anna to accompany him across the widely spaced stepping stones (hazardous in themselves) to the Strid where he encourages her to *'jump the Strid'*, an impossible feat as it is probably a 50ft-wide, deep gorge with mainly fast-flowing rocky water. However, there is one small obscure place where a person could conceivably cross on boulders, although still unlikely for a female in Victorian petticoats and skirts. This spot is known to have been taken by riders from the Pendle Forest and Craven Hunt who are still active in the area, and accept 'day membership', so it is possible that Trollope discovered this fact from a day's hunting.

> *The first thing to be seen at Bolton Abbey is, of course, the Abbey. The Abbey itself, is a ruin – a ruin not so ruinous but that a part of it is used for a modern church – is very well; but the glory of Bolton Abbey is in the river which runs round it and in the wooded banks which overhang it. No more luxuriant pasture, no richer foliage, no brighter water, no more picturesque arrangement of the freaks of nature, aided by the art and taste of man, is to be found perhaps, in England ... Nothing had ever been so beautiful as the Abbey – nothing so lovely as the running Wharfe! Might*

Stepping stones to the Strid

A typical commercial inn, opposite the Town Hall, Leeds

they not climb up among those woods on the opposite bank? Lord Lovel declared that, of course they would climb up among the woods – it was for that purpose they had come. That was the way to the Stryd [Strid] – over which he was determined that Lady Anna should be made to jump. But the river below the Abbey is to be traversed by stepping-stones, which, to the female uninitiated foot, appear to be full of danger.

In nearby Leeds, when the respectable Mr Dockwrath in *Orley Farm* (1861–2) asks to be shown into the commercial room of the Bull Inn, the waiter:

> ... looked at him with doubtful eyes ... feeling all but confident that such a guest had no right to be there. He had no bulky bundles of samples, nor any of those outward characteristics of a commercial 'gent' with which all men conversant with the rail and road are acquainted, and which the accustomed eye of a waiter recognizes at a glance ... All innkeepers have commercial rooms as certainly as they have taps and bars, but all of them do not have commercial rooms in the properly exclusive sense. A stranger, therefore, who has asked for and obtained his mutton chop in the commercial room of the Dolphin, the Bear, and the George, not unnaturally asks to be shown into the same chamber at the King's Head. But the King's Head does a business with real commercials, and the stranger finds himself – out of his element.

As the waiter anticipated, the usual occupants, Mr Moulder and Mr Kantwise, soon arrive. Mr Moulder immediately spots the intruder and, in a loud whisper, asks the waiter who he is. The waiter replies:

'Gen'elman by the 8.22 down'. 'Commercial?' asked Mr Moulder, with angry frown. 'He says so himself, anyways,' said the waiter. 'Gammon!' replied Mr Moulder, who knew all the bearings of a commercial man thoroughly, and could have put one together if he were only supplied with a little bit – say the mouth ... now began to be angry, for he was a stickler for the rights and privileges of his class.

Undaunted, Mr Dockwrath sits in the solitary armchair under the lamp with his glass of mahogany-coloured brandy and water and a cigar and calls for a pair of public slippers. Trollope's brother Tom, in his own memoir, wrote of walking in Wales and staying at a commercial inn where commercial gentlemen told him '*it was a herror to suppose that commercial men were hadverse to gentlemen making use of the commercial room provided they was gentlemen'*. In addition to their exclusivity, commercial rooms had strict rules: cigars were not allowed before 9 p.m., dinner was at 5 p.m. and a pint of sherry at 5s 6d was expected to be consumed, with three courses of salmon, chicken and venison, and three or four pastry dishes, for 2 shillings.

Norfolk and Suffolk

Trollope's detailed description of the area leads me to believe that he may have visited on Post Office business, but most certainly would also have been a guest in the area, either for hunting or purely social reasons. As stated earlier, trains had gone from London to Norwich at 36 mph since 1842: he would have been able to take hunters and probably been familiar with the villages of Great and Little Plumstead near Norwich Cathedral and also the Cathedral Close.

In *Can You Forgive Her?* (1864–5) the widow Mrs Greenow with her three suitors arranges a picnic at Yarmouth, and a large part of the action in *The Way We Live Now* (1875) takes place just over the border in Suffolk, particularly Bungay, Beccles, and Lowestoft. Young man-about-town Felix Carbury dallies with the farmer's daughter Ruby Ruggles who eventually safely marries the rustic John Crumb: the *'marriage-feast'* or '"bit of dinner" as John Crumb would call it …' takes place at the King's Head in

King's Head, Bungay, shortly before demolition

Bungay: the '*Bungay church bells rang merrily ... "What's the odds?" said Mrs Pipkin as they settled their bonnets in the room at the Inn just before they entered the church*'. St Mary's Church is indeed just opposite the substantial but now dilapidated King's Head Hotel which I was able to paint even as workmen began to demolish it for redevelopment.

In Bungay I also came upon a bridge and nearby building, fitting the description of Carbury Manor:

> The high road from Bungay to Beccles ran close to the house – so close that the gable ends of the building were separated from it only by the breadth of the moat. A short private road, not above a hundred yards in length, led to the bridge which faced the front door. The bridge was old, and high, with sundry architectural pretensions, and guarded by iron gates in the centre, which, however, were very rarely closed.

He then goes on to describe a different dwelling to the one near the bridge, but rather one in north Norfolk, suggesting that although not Tudor:

> [it] had the reputation of being a Tudor building. The windows were long, and for the most part old-fashioned panes; for the squire had not as yet gone to the expense of plate glass. There was one high bow window, which belonged to the library, and which looked out on to the gravel sweep, at the left of the front door as you entered it. All the other chief rooms faced upon the garden. The house itself was built of stone that had become buff, or almost yellow with years, and was very pretty. It was still covered with tiles, as were all the attached buildings. It was only two stories high, except at the end, where the kitchens were placed and the offices, which thus rose above the other part of the edifice. The rooms throughout were low, and for the most part long and narrow, with large wide fireplaces and deep wainscotings.

In *Ralph the Heir* (published 1871 but written 1869), a character (confusingly also called Ralph but not the heir) bought Beamingham Hall and Beamingham Little Wood, described in similar tones as the above, as an estate of 30 acres and being:

> ... built with considerable idea of architectural beauty. The windows were all set in stone and mullioned – long, low windows, very beautiful in form, which had till some fifteen years back been filled with a multitude of small diamond panes ... There

were three gables to the hall, all facing an old-fashioned large garden, in which the fruit trees came close up to the house, and that which perhaps ought to have been a lawn was almost an orchard. ...

It is possible that Trollope was describing Rainthorpe Hall, eight miles south of Norwich, a dwelling with a reputation for being Elizabethan, but which was built on the site of an earlier house. It has medieval stonework, latticed windows and old-fashioned 18-acre gardens 'close up' to the house and was the primary residence of the Hon Frederick Walpole (1868–76). Both the Hon Frederick and Trollope were members of the Garrick and the Athenaeum Clubs, and both had books published by Richard Bentley (the Hon Frederick several military works and one novel). They would also have recognized one another as Freemasons, as the Hon Frederick was Deputy Provincial Grand Master of the Norfolk Lodge from 1867 and became the Grand Master in 1875, as shown in the Norfolk Museum of Freemasonry. Both men had stood unsuccessfully for Parliament, but Walpole stood again and became Conservative MP for King's Lynn in November 1868 and remained so until his death. It is therefore very likely that they would have known one another sufficiently for Trollope to have at least visited Rainthorpe Hall, especially while in the area on hunting trips. Trollope would also certainly have known that the Hon Frederick extensively and expensively renovated the Hall during the 1850s and, as shown above, his sister Lady Dorothy Nevill, another novelist, had been involved in a scandal when discovered one evening in a greenhouse with a notorious 'rake', echoed by Lady Glencora meeting Burgo Fitzgerald in a folly. Lady Dorothy was a great friend of Joseph Hooker of Kew Gardens, renowned botanist and explorer, who in regular correspondence with Charles Darwin discussed their readings of Trollope, particularly *Can You Forgive Her?* I maintain that Rainthorpe Hall, together with the halls and follies situated around Waltham Cross, combined in Trollope's imagination to form Gatherum Castle and Glencora, and that Rainthorpe Hall was the seat from where he explored Norfolk.

Trollope also mentions that although Norfolk *'is a county by no means devoted to hunting'*, the character of Ralph is able to preserve foxes on his land, and I have been assured by present members of the Walpole family that the area was actually devoted to hunting at that time. The Cottesmore/Fitzwilliam website states that it has no boundaries and still holds meets far into the eastern area during the autumn hound exercise, and the Belvoir still hunts trails there every few years. It is even feasible Trollope could have hunted from Rainthorpe Hall's seven cast-iron stables encircling a cobbled yard.

Shelves of novels, travel books, short stories and biographies

Top shelf: *Sir Henry Hotspur, Cousin Henry, The Belton Estate, The Golden Lion of Granpere, The Eustace Diamonds, Marion Fay, Miss Mackenzie, La Vendée, Rachel Ray, The Small House at Allington, An Autobiography, The Claverings, The Struggles of Brown, Jones and Robinson, The Bertrams, The Three Clerks, An Old Man's Love, He Knew He Was Right, Linda Tressel, Kept in the Dark, Is He Popenjoy?, The American Senator, The Vicar of Bullhampton, Mr Scarborough's Family, The Way We Live Now* (the Folio Society)

Bottom Shelf: Short story collections, bottom to top: *The Journey to Panama, Tourists and Colonials, Courtship and Marriage, The Christmas Stories, The New Zealander, A Guide to Trollope, Thackeray, Hunting Sketches, Editors and Writers*

Left to Right: *The Life of Cicero* Vols I and II, *London Tradesmen, The West Indies and The Spanish Main* Vols I and II, *Lord Palmerston, Australia and New Zealand* Vols I and II, *North America* Vols I and II (The Trollope Society); *Dr Wortle's School, John Caldigate, The Fixed Period, Ayala's Angel, Dr Thorne, Orley Farm, Ralph the Heir, Nina Balatka, Lady Anna* (The Folio Society)

A memorable character in all the Palliser novels is the Duke of St Bungay from Longroyston, a fictional village near Bungay. He is an old friend and adviser to Prime Minister Palliser and considered *'the very front and head of the aristocratic Whigs of the country'*. Palliser feels unable to do much good in either *Phineas Finn* or *The Prime Minister* during political turmoil and consults the old Duke, whose advice is always the same: the Queen's government is the main object, he enjoys the support of the country, it is his sole duty to remain at his post. He must be patient until the agitators *'hang themselves with their own rope'*.

Lady St Bungay is obsessed with draughts and complains of her own home at every opportunity:

> *'I don't know how you manage in your house, but the staircases are so comfortable. Now at Longroyston we've taken all the trouble in the world, put down hot-water pipes all over the house, and everything else that could be thought of, and yet, you can't move about the place without meeting with draughts at every corner of the passages.'*

I was alerted by Jessica Finch and her sister Anne Frith who lived in the area, that just two miles out of Bungay is the tiny village of Barsham with Shipmeadow, where the Church of the Most Holy Trinity has a very old round-tower, and a stained-glass window of 'Christ Breaking Bread on the way to Emmaus'. This was a 'Thank Offering' from Major Napier Trollope, several times Mayor of Beccles and distant relative of Joanna Trollope and Anthony. It is said that at the equinoxes, for three days the sun, if out, comes through the window and half-door in the tower, to light up the heads of St Peter, the Virgin Mary, and possibly St John on the rood screen. Trollope's intimate knowledge of the area and its geography and distance from home indicate that rather than simply passing through he must have stayed in the area and, if not for Post Office business, then surely for social visits.

Iceland

In 1878 the well-travelled Trollope, alone this time, joined Mr and Mrs John Burns and other friends at their home at Wemyss Castle, for a two-month visit to Iceland in the *Mastiff*. Appropriately they called themselves the *Mastiffs* and Trollope accordingly wrote *How the 'Mastiffs' Went to Iceland*, published by Virtue & Co. (1878), with illustrations by fellow passenger Mrs Hugh Blackburn. There were fourteen guests in total, including two admirals, and a crew of thirty-two including an engineer, seamen, stewards and firemen:

> ... and thus being fifty on board, we started from just beneath the towers of Castle Wemyss on the evening of Saturday, the 22nd June, 1878: I presume it will be known to all who may read these pages that Castle Wemyss is the bode of our host, Mr John Burns.

Wemyss station, a very short distance away from Wemyss Castle, was useful for guests arriving for their journey, although at the time it was no more than a siding, as the present building (illustrated) was not built until 1903. Wemyss Castle is thought to be the model for Portray Castle featured in *The Eustace Diamonds*, and Mr Kennedy's Loughlinter is also based in the area.

At 6 p.m. on Saturday 22nd June 'the anchor was weighed, amidst the mingled cheers and lamentations of our friends on the shore, lamenting, not that we were going, but that they should not have been able to accompany us'. The *Mastiffs* travelled down the Firth of Clyde, passing the Cumbraes, Bute and Arran, arriving at Campbeltown on the Sunday where they found a church conducting two services simultaneously, one in English and one in Gaelic. Even though most of the party were from Scotland and would have spoken Gaelic the *Mastiffs* joined the shorter English service. Later, whilst travelling in thick fog during the night, a fracas erupted when the gentlemen commandeered a '*little snuggery*' for tobacco, whisky and water (in the manner of a gentleman's club). Alas, this was an area reserved for Mrs Burns and the ladies so when a cross Mr Burns tried to expel them, someone's head was '*liberated*' through the window. Alas, it belonged to a poor old gentleman who neither smoked nor drank. The booklet contains a humorous drawing of him being attacked by a rope, with another passenger standing on the roof with a bucket of cold water.

Next day in the picturesque island of St Kilda they felt they were '*a source of great delight ... [they] do not see much of their brethren from the mainland, and who are, in truth, in want of such help as their brethren can bring to them*'. The 70–80 inhabitants were very hospitable but lived as 'Robinson Crusoes' with only one small rowing boat between them. The *Mastiffs* were greeted by the Minister and Miss MacLeod, sister of the owner, and learnt that the schoolmaster and the Minister received £80 p.a. from the Scotch [sic] Free Church. The only two English speakers were unable to obtain supplies of books or newspapers. Trollope noted that there were twelve marriageable young women but only two marriageable young men; that many people were troubled by rheumatism and scrofula, and that many babies died at about eight days old. The *Mastiffs* felt they were a help by buying cloth and artefacts, and leaving presents of tea, sugar and much-needed rope.

The travellers then counted seventeen Faroe Islands, nearly halfway between the Shetland Islands and Iceland, where the basic language was a dialect of Old Norse, although the court, churches and schools spoke modern Danish. Trollope resisted the temptation to ask the Postmaster about his duties and salary.

On to Reykjavik: '*as we looked out upon the waters of the fiord in which we lay, and saw the islands and headlands around us, every Mastiff felt that he or she had done something memorable*'. Trollope wondered if an English Governor in the West Indies would give such a miscellany of sixteen men and women as friendly a welcome as did the Governor-General of Iceland. Again, the *Mastiffs* were welcomed as they bought souvenirs of leather goods and jewellery, but ate their own food as they thought it to be a '*fishy town*'. Trollope thought the Icelanders were mainly a '*healthy, comely race*' but with cases of '*scurvy, cutaneous diseases and even leprosy*'. Almost everyone could read and all were clean and pleasing, but they had no bank. On the Friday the *Mastiffs* invited fourteen local dignitaries to dinner (many wearing national costume) on board ship the following day, Saturday, even though the cook was busy preparing supplies for an imminent trip to the geysers. After dinner there were three toasts: the Queen, the King of Denmark, and the Governor.

The following day, Sunday, they joined a shipboard service where they '*sang ... hymns as printed in Reykjavik* [and] *went to the Reykjavik church*' for another two-and-a-half-hour-long service with probably five hymns. Again, girls wore full national costume.

Late-Victorian station at Wemyss as it is today

After the services their baggage was sent on ahead to the geysers. Trollope ordered:

> two great coats, a rug, a blanket, two or three changes of linen, a suit of clothes, a pair of boots, a pair of slippers, a brush, a toothbrush, a bit of soap, two towels, a mosquito net, and a big stick. Looking at the great mass which we carried I do not think that I was more unreasonable than others.

After breakfast at 4 a.m. they set off on the Monday, with sixty-five ponies, two each for themselves and servants, with tents, provisions and baggage. As no one dared choose the best horse, the guide Zoega chose for them:

> I believe that he gave me not only the worst pony in Iceland, but the most pernicious brute that ever was foaled in any country that ever possessed mares! ... Perhaps Zoega thought that no other man there was hero enough to ride such a brute!

Although Trollope had already seen geysers in New Zealand and been told that the Icelandic ones were inferior, he still wished to see for himself, although the journey was gruelling. There were many stops on the way when the men slept in tents, and the ladies sometimes in churches. On one night in a church the ladies slept by the communion table walled off by the ecclesiastical rail, and the men two and two together down the nave. There were giggles and titters: 'I had expected to find the minister indignant on the following morning, because of the desecration of his church; but the minister took it in good part, bell-ringing and all.' They were able to gallop back from the geysers in just two days.

Trollope describes a *'certain melancholy'* at the thought of going home to Wemyss Bay. They returned via the Hebrides and the coast of Sutherlandshire (nowadays called Sutherland), opposite Skye, then the west coast of Scotland, up the Firth of Clyde, and anchored in Wemyss Bay about 3 p.m. on Monday 8th July, after 16 days away.

> There was a little eating of cream and strawberries at Castle Wemyss, a little attempt at ordinary shore courtesies, a returning as it were to the dull ways of life on shore. But we all felt that this was to be done painfully, each by himself in solitude. And so with many pressings of the hand, but with few spoken words, we left our host and hostess and went away in melancholy humour to our own abodes.

Amusingly Trollope seems to have been prescient when, in 1866 in *Travelling Sketches*, he had included the short story 'United Englishmen who Travel for Fun':

> *The united Englishmen who travel for fun are great nuisances to other tourists, are great nuisances to the towns they visit and the scenes they disturb, are often nuisances in a small way to the police, are nuisances to people saying their prayers in churches, are nuisances to visitors in picture galleries, are nuisances to the ordinary travellers of the day, and are nuisances to the world at large ... but they generally achieve their own object, and have what the Americans call a good time of it.*

South Harting

When Trollope began to suffer respiratory problems, various reasons were given by doctors, such as asthma or angina and, like his siblings before him, he was advised by his doctor to move to the fresh air of the countryside. Consequently, on 6th July 1880, he and Rose left the smog (and social life) of London to live on the South Downs in the quiet little village of South Harting. Here they leased a collection of small cottages which they converted into a spacious house, then called 'North End', set in 70 acres of land, most of which they sub-let. It had seven bedrooms and a good cellar for wine, and they added a long glass porch as a covered way into the house from the gate. Indoor water was pumped by hand from the outside well into a cistern at the top of a special tower. This novel feature had been installed by the previous owner, Joseph Postlethwaite, and as it wheezed and squeaked when operated, Rose said she was 'a Postlethwaite's pump'.

The village, mentioned in the Domesday Book, had a population of 1,247 in 1871, with a church, school, and post office and general store. There were also four public houses, but today only one remains. It is a pretty village not far from the railway station at Petersfield, where the railway line from Waterloo had opened in 1859. Trollope of course was familiar with nearby Winchester, Salisbury and Exeter, and presumably with the novels of Jane Austen who had resided at Chawton, also nearby. On a good day, it is still possible to see the spire of Chichester Cathedral, a view painted by Turner.

The back of the house now has large bay windows similar to Julians at Harrow, and the French windows favoured by Trollope for sauntering through on summer evenings. Behind the house are views of the Beacon Hills, and a 2,500-year-old Beacon Hill Fort which, between 1796 and 1816, had been used as a shuttle telegraph connecting the Admiralty in London with stores in Plymouth and Portsmouth. Trollope probably had prior knowledge of this from his postal service work, hence his short story 'The Telegraph Girl', published in 1877.

The house, now called 'The Grange', is situated at the top of the hill above the village, facing a farm on the left-hand side and the manor house on the right, where their neighbour Lady Featherstonhaugh lived until her death in 1890. Being close neighbours, the Trollopes would surely have attended the many shooting and other social parties held in her house. She had been a 20-year-old dairymaid when she married the 71-year-old bachelor Lord Featherstonhaugh, who subsequently lived until he was ninety-one. The manor has been owned by the Featherstonhaugh family since 1746, who also owned the nearby Uppark Estate, now owned by the National Trust. The many memorials, effigies and stained-glass windows at the local Anglican church of St Mary and St Gabriel were donated by wealthy landowners living in the area. The church is large, and above a slight incline at the opposite end of the village, with the school, pub and store-cum-post office in the dip at the bottom.

Drinking fountain and horse trough said to be commissioned by Trollope

The church, known as the Cathedral of the Downs, had a state-of-the-art copper spire added in the 1820s and today houses several small Trollopian artefacts such as his pen, paper-knife and letter scales. Outside the church is a First World War Memorial designed by Eric Gill. The village has housed an artistic community over the years with writers Bertrand Russell, and H G Wells, and artist William Gunning-King. Jacob Epstein's son's painting *Summer Garden in South Harting* (1947) features a tower in the background looking very similar to Trollope's own water tower.

It is known that the Trollopes took an active part in the church life, and halfway up the long and steep hill to their house is a water pump which a local resident said had been designed by Trollope himself to refresh horses coming up on their way home from Sunday church. The large construction provides water for general drinking, with the addition of a bowl below for the horses to drink from. Although it is weather-beaten it is possible to see the Trollope coat of arms carved into the headpiece with a stag on the top. Trollope designed it for use after the well outside the school at the bottom of the hill became infected with typhoid.

According to Cecilia Meetkerke, Trollope wrote to her:

> Yes, we have changed our mode of life altogether. We have got a little cottage here, just big enough (or nearly so) to hold my books, with five acres and a cow and a dog and a cock and a hen. I have got seventeen years' lease, and therefore I hope to lay my bones here. Nevertheless I am busy as would be one thirty years younger, in cutting out dead boughs and putting up a paling here and a little gate there. We go to church and mean to be very good and have maids to wait on us. The reason for all this I will explain when I see you, although, as far as I see at present, there is no good reason other than that we were tired of London.

Life appeared to be happy and the friendly local vicar, the Reverend Henry Doddridge Gordon recorded that *'his genial frankness soon made him the honoured friend of us all. The sick poor in particular found him a staunch benefactor'* (R C Terry: *Trollope: Interviews and Recollections*). He recounted the story of Trollope being told that a labourer employed on his fences had nothing but bread to eat and so had stolen some fallen apples. When the gardener wanted to call a policeman, Trollope instead gave the man some slices of ham and cheese and was said to have thrown them into the man's lap saying, *'Eat and be better.'*

Trollope finished *The Life of Cicero* (published in 1880) just before moving to South Harting and on 18th August, just one month later, he began *Kept in the Dark* (published in 1882). In spite of failing health, he nevertheless completed *The Fixed Period* (published in 1882), *Dr Wortle's School* (1881), *Mr Scarborough's Family* (published in 1883), a biography of Lord Palmerston, a volume of short stories, *Why Frau Frohmann Raised her Prices and other stories*, and *An Old Man's Love* (published in 1884). He also began his final novel, *The Landleaguers* (published in 1883), for which he made two exhausting research trips of one month each to Dublin, accompanied by Florence Bland.

It is notable that in many letters he stressed how happy he was, whilst in reality being depressed, but when his health did not improve, he wrote, through Florence, to E A Freeman, the historian:

> I can't sleep, willing or not willing. I can't write, as you see, because my hand is paralysed. I can't sit easily because of a huge truss I wear, and now has come this damnable asthma! But still I am very good to look at, as I am not afraid to die I am as happy as other people.

In addition to missing Fred and the grandchildren, and in addition also to declining sales, he also missed Henry who was still living in London. Additionally, on Christmas Eve 1880 he heard from George Eliot's stepson Charles Lewes that she had died. He was shocked and grieved. George Lewes himself had died two years earlier and Trollope had attended his funeral four days before finishing *Cousin Henry*. Although he had enjoyed a good relationship with George Eliot, Trollope wrote matter-of-factly in his *Autobiography*: '*I doubt whether any young person can read with pleasure either* Felix Holt, Middlemarch *or* Daniel Deronda. *Finished* Kept in the Dark *and started* The Fixed Period.' Such curt abruptness was perhaps

Water tower at North End, South Harting

another symptom of his mounting depression as he and George Eliot had shared many aspects of their work.

The end of his life must have seemed to be a mirror image of its beginning: he now had plenty of money unlike his impoverished youth, but instead of his mother's absence and his own lack of money, it was his sons who were absent whilst he needed to provide them with money. He had felt the need for his family to be near him both in his youth and near the end of his life, although we can appreciate of course that at this time both Rose and Florence would have been very different company for him than was his father. Perhaps he took them for granted.

According to Victoria Glendinning in *Trollope* (1992), when Rose came to sell the house two years later, the auctioneer's brochure described: '*an Ornamental Conservatory, paved with Tiles, which is Heated by Hot-Water Pipes communicating with a Hot-Water Coil to give warmth to the Hall.*' Lady St Bungay would be impressed!

Garlant's Hotel, Suffolk Street

Whilst living at South Harting, Trollope probably missed the social life of London; the country air did nothing to improve his health; the cramp in his writing hand impeded his work, and he continued to feel dispirited. However, it was straightforward for him to visit London by train from Petersfield, or perhaps the village of Rogate, a mile away, for dinners, events and meetings with publishers. He usually stayed at the Garlant's Hotel (later called Garland's Hotel) in Suffolk Street, near the gentlemen's clubs in Pall Mall and theatreland. The hotel was in a cul-de-sac with windows looking down upon the stage door of the Haymarket Theatre where he would have seen actors, actresses, directors and visitors coming and going. This was when he wrote his last (and unfinished) novel, *The Landleaguers*, a political tale set largely in Ireland, but also featuring Rachel O'Mahony, the '*great singer*'. The novel was begun not long after *La Traviata* was adapted from Alexander Dumas' novel and *Carmen* was first performed in 1878. Both these operas were phenomenal and considered revolutionary at the time. As is usual with Trollope, his story mostly focuses not on the singer's career but on her lovers, their rivalries, their political aims and her financial difficulties, while her theatrical career remains in the background:

> *Rachel, before the end of March, received the following letter from her friend* [one of her competing lovers], *but she received it in bed. The whole world of Covent Garden Theatre had been thrown into panic-stricken dismay by the fact that Miss O'Mahony had something the matter with her throat. This was the second attack, the first having been so short as to have caused no trepidations in the world of music; but this was supposed to be sterner in its nature, and to have caused already great alarm. Before March was over it was published to the world at large that Miss O'Mahony would not be able to sing during the forthcoming week.*

Once again, we must remember that the time in which Trollope lived was very different to our own, and that he was often at the forefront of adapting to new ideas and milieus, such as the inclusion of theatrical characters into his novels. His brother Tom recounts in his own memoir how in his and Anthony's childhood the whole of the right-hand side of what we now

Stage door of Haymarket Theatre overlooked by Garlant's Hotel

know as Haymarket, from Piccadilly to the Opera House, was then lined with loads of hay, being literally a hay market. Carts were arranged close *'side by side with back parts towards the foot pavement crowded by the salesmen and customers'*. He testifies to the *'greatness of the purifying change which has been brought about in all the habits of playgoers and playhouses mainly and firstly by the exertions of my mother's old and valued friend Mr Macready'*.

By the 1850s the theatre had become respectable, supported by Queen Victoria and Prince Albert who attended productions and instituted Command Performances. New theatres were built, with opera in Covent Garden and pantomimes and melodrama in Drury Lane. In the 1870s and '80s, Trollope too acknowledged this new respectability: Lucy Graham in the short story 'The Telegraph Girl' allows her brother to take her to the theatre: she enjoys Hamlet at the nearby Lyceum, and the good-natured but brainless aristocratic Lord Dundreary in *Our American Cousin* written by Tom Taylor (1858) at the Haymarket Theatre. It is not feasible she would go on her own, and she certainly would not join her fellow workers watching saucy dancers at an unsavoury music hall. Euphemia Smith takes the stage name of Mlle Cettini when she comes to Cambridge to (almost) destroy the good fortunes of John Caldigate. Into this socially relaxing climate, Mr Toogood allows his daughter in T*he Last Chronicle of Barset* to choose to visit a pantomime.

Trollope had first-hand knowledge of the theatre as when young and ill in Northumberland Street, attended by his mother, he had listed five plays in his Commonplace Book, depicting *'Excellencies and defects of the modern English stage'*: Fanny Kemble's *Francis I* (1832), Sheridan Knowles's *The Hunchback* (1832), Henry Taylor's *Philip Van Artevelde* (1834), Joanna Bailey's *Henriquez* (1812) and Thomas Talford's *Ion* (1836). Later he had socialized with actors and singers in the Garrick Club, and had enjoyed seeing Kate Field perform in *Extremes Meet*.

His novels not only reflect the new respectability, but also highlight perceived lack of respectability. Examples include his disapproval in *St Pauls Magazine* of Boucicault's *Formosa* where the Oxford and Cambridge Boat Race includes a prostitute, while his Carrie Brattle in *The Vicar of Bullhampton* shows that *'the career of an English prostitute is the most miserable'*, thus deserving understanding and respect. He also suggested illegitimacy in *Is He Popenjoy?* and bigamy in *Dr Wortle's School*.

Although a successful novel writer, Trollope was not a successful playwright. Early in his career he wrote a play, *The Noble Jilt*, which he recycled later as the basis for *Can You Forgive Her?* He used it again in *The Eustace Diamonds* when Mr Carbuncle goes to see *The Noble Jilt* 'performed' at the theatre. The fictional critics are contradictory, which would have probably been the likely fate had the play been performed publicly. Trollope also had a serious but short-lived falling-out with his friend Charles Reade who, without permission, had turned Trollope's novel *Ralph the Heir* into a stage version called *The Shilly Shally Affair*.

As well as being frequented by Trollope, the hotel was also popular with Henry James, James Whistler and D H Lawrence, MPs and clergymen. In 1861 a delegation from the Confederate States during the American Civil War stayed there. Alas the hotel was bombed during the Second World War and has now been renovated into offices.

John Tilley

On one such visit to London on 3rd November 1882, when Rose accompanied him, Trollope dined first with Alexander Macmillan, the younger of the two brothers from the family publishing firm (see above), and the following evening both he and Rose went to dine with John Tilley, ex-colleague, brother-in-law and the person he called one of his *'oldest and dearest friends'*. John Tilley, now retired as Chief Secretary of the Post Office (and supporter of the introduction of Post Office Savings Bank accounts) had lived at 73 St George's Square, Pimlico since 1856, an unfashionable area at that time, with houses similar to those in Keppel Street. The houses are built around a large rectangular green space. Thackeray's daughter Anne Ritchie lived at no. 109 and later Bram Stoker and Dorothy L Sayers lived in the Square. When aged 63, John Tilley had written to Trollope for advice on whether or not to give up the Chief Secretaryship at the Post Office; Trollope had told him he had the health of a 40-year-old and should continue if he liked the work: *'You say of me: that I would not choose to write novels unless I were paid. Most certainly I would; much rather than not write them at all.'*

Sir John Tilley KCB (20th January 1813–18th March 1898), whose first wife Cecilia (Trollope's sister) had died in 1849 (after giving birth to five children), and whose second wife Mary Ann Partington, Cecilia's cousin, had died in 1851 after giving birth to another child, was now married to Susannah Anderson Montgomerie (later Dame) with three more children. He had eventually retired from the Post Office on 16th April 1880 aged 67 (ironically the age of Trollope's death and of the compulsory euthanasia recommended by him in *The Fixed Period,* 1882). He was as industrious in retirement as he had been in his working life, being Chairman of the Board of Guardians of St George's Church, Hanover Square; chairman of the Relief Committee for the distribution of outdoor relief to deserving poor; member of the Fulham Road Workhouse Committee (the largest workhouse in the country); and chairman of many other charitable institutions. In particular, he was a Churchwarden at his local St Saviour Church, when the Reverend Henry Washington was the vicar, and where in 1898 a window was dedicated to his memory.

Earlier in the day, before the dinner party and whilst still at the Garlant's Hotel, a band had started playing in the cul-de-sac below Trollope's window;

John Tilley's house at 73 St George's Square, Pimlico

he had become extremely angry and hung out of the window, shouting for them to go away. Later, guests remembered that during the dinner party he was again unusually animated and over-excited, and when one of the Tilley family read aloud a passage from Anstey's *Vice Versa*, a popular book at the time, he is said to have laughed particularly loudly and uproariously. The novel appealed to Victorian tastes, and perhaps particularly to Trollope as it involved a young man about to return to a boarding school run by Dr Grimstone, a sadistic cane-wielding headmaster – obviously a reminder of his own canings at school. When in the novel the father of the boy said he wished he was the person going back to school instead of the boy, his wish was magically granted and he changed into the son who went to the school, while the son changed into the father who went to work in the City, after which they both returned to their own bodies and better understood one another, in a fairy-tale ending.

Sadly, Trollope's over-enthusiastic laughing led to a severe stroke paralysing his right side. It is said that he never managed to speak again, although he was conscious and knew what was happening to him. In his own earlier and prescient words:

> *For what remains to me of life I trust for my happiness still chiefly to my work – hoping that when the power of work be over with me, God may be pleased to take me from a world in which, according to my view, there can then be no joy; second, to the love of those who love me; and then to my books.*

Kensal Green Cemetery

After a few weeks in a nursing home in Welbeck Street, Trollope died on 6th December 1882 and was buried three days later at Kensal Green Cemetery, where he and Charles Dickens and Robert Browning had attended the funeral of his friend and colleague William Makepeace Thackeray twenty years earlier. Many other literary figures such as Wilkie Collins, William Ainsworth and Baroness Byron (wife of Lord Byron and mother of Ada Lovelace), and more recently Harold Pinter, are also buried there. Trollope's mourners included Browning, Millais, Austin, Chapman and Rusden.

Kensal Green Cemetery was the first commercial cemetery in London, built in response to the increasing population and shortage of burial grounds. In response to a competition, a design in a Greek Revival style was chosen with two distinct areas: the consecrated Anglican area with a neo-classical Doric chapel, and the unconsecrated Dissenter area in the Ionic style for the non-conformists. Each chapel has catacombs; there is an entrance gateway with lodges, and a landscaped layout for monuments, linked by pathways wide enough for carriages to pass through.

The Fixed Period was set futuristically in the year 1978–9, suggesting euthanasia at age 67. Strangely, he finished writing it in 1881–2 (when it was serialized in *Blackwood's Magazine*), and then it was published in 2 volumes in March 1882. He died aged 67 in December 1882. In this futuristic book he foretold crematoriums (the first English one opened three years later in Woking), gears on bikes and protective clothing for cricketers (both now essential), and our present-day worries about bed-blocking, healthcare and pensions. In the book Trollope, as the narrator, explains: 'The Fixed Period ... *consists altogether of the abolition of the miseries, weakness and faineant imbecility of old age by the prearranged ceasing to live of those who would otherwise become old.*' The idea is opposed by the popular cricketer Neverbend, looking back over the fixed period of his own triumphs and failings, as Trollope must have reviewed his own life for his *Autobiography*: one son and family living in Australia (no telephones or zoom/Facetime calls, and letters taking weeks or months to arrive), his other son possibly not living up to expectations, unable to settle in a successful career, costing a lot of money in failing endeavours, and a first early wish to marry unsuitably. Perhaps, also, the wife of the narrator in *The Fixed Period* with her support of their son, Neverbend, the anti-euthanasia campaigner, resonated with Rose's support of Trollope's son. As we have seen, his memory of his childhood would not compare with the childhood he provided for his own sons: he had enjoyed financial success and stability as a novelist; he and Rose had been healthy and socially active, and therefore able both physically and financially to support them in their chosen careers. This contrast with his own childhood most likely

Tomb and inscription at Kensal Green Cemetery: 'He was a loving husband and a true friend'

contributed to depression and coloured his judgement about perceived neglect by his mother, lack of care by his father and a supposedly friendless time at school. In reality, of course, Trollope was a very popular man, and many kind words were spoken of him.

On his death, his brother Tom wrote to Henry: '*What will most remain in mind will be the pleasant strolling up and down in the orchard at Harting, as we watched and laughed at his dog humping for apples.*'

Although Trollope had some reasons to be depressed, as discussed above, in contrast he wrote in his *Autobiography* seven years earlier:

> *Since that time [arriving in Ireland] who has had a happier life than mine? Looking round upon all those I know, I cannot put my hand upon one. But all is not over yet, and mindful of that remembering how great is the agony of adversity, how crushing the despondency of degradation, how susceptible I am myself to the misery coming from contempt, remembering also how quickly good things may go and evil things come – I am often again tempted to hope, almost to pray that the end may be near.*

He also said: '*I have enjoyed the comfort for I may almost say the last twenty years, though no man in his youth had less prospect of doing so or would have been less likely at twenty-five to have had such luxuries foretold to him by his friends.*'

And finally: '*Now I stretch out my hand, and from the further shore I bid adieu to all who have cared to read any among the many words that I have written.*'

Recollections and Letters

As Anthony Trollope had set up postal systems around the world, introduced postal boxes, and used letters in his novels as a convenient way of moving the story forward, it is a fitting conclusion to highlight some of the letters that were written about him. As in the novels, 19th-century people generally wrote frequent letters to one another with gossip, invitations and instructions etc. These were often written last thing in the evening: in many novels people wait silently, sitting by the fireside (often while the man of the house is fast asleep), waiting impatiently until 10 p.m. when the staff could be summoned for prayers, after which all could escape to their bedrooms – and write their letters for posting the following day. A reply would often be received almost immediately.

R C Terry, in *Interviews and Recollections*, provides many quotations and letters testifying Trollope's character as being bluff and blustery:

> Julian Hawthorne: '… he was something of a paradox – an entertaining contradiction' and 'no man in London society was more generally liked.'

> Henry Johnston, Secretary of the Glasgow Athenaeum, invited Trollope to lecture at Glasgow: 'I met with Anthony Trollope by appointment at the Athenaeum Club, Pall Mall, on 15 July 1869. I … was seriously handicapped by the extremely limited amount of money placed at my disposal … I found waiting for me a tall, breezy, sun-tanned, farmer-like man with a hearty manner and an encouraging handshake. I had carefully intimated beforehand the object of my visit … but the delicate part of the negotiations had yet to come – his terms. … "Do not speak of terms," he said, "when a man has something to say, and a suitable place and opportunity are offered to him for saying it, that should be sufficient for him." The lecture was one of the most successful of a brilliant course.'

> Henry James: 'gross and repulsive' in face and manner, but 'he was *bon enfant* when you talked with him.'

> George Gissing: a 'big, blusterous, genial brute of a Trollope.'

> James Russell Lowell: 'big red-faced, rather underbred Englishman of the bald-with-spectacles type.'

> A M Cunynghame, a Post Office colleague, recalled a journey in late 1858 when Trollope suddenly announced 'Cunynghame, I must have a sleep. Wake me in 20 minutes, will you?' A passenger on a train also recollected his asking: '"Do you ever sleep when you are travelling?" Whereupon he donned a huge fur cap, part of which fell down over his shoulders, and proceeded to snore.'

> John Blackwood regarding noise on the golf course: '... his voice was heard all over the Links and when made a bad shot fell down with pretended agony, only to start up again with a real yell because he had fallen on a golf-ball in his pocket.'

> Wilkie Collins to William Winter: 'To me, he was an incarnate gale of wind. He blew off my hat; he turned my umbrella inside out. Joking apart, as good and staunch a friend as ever lived – and, to my mind, a great loss to novel-readers. Call his standards as a workman what you will, he was always equal to it .... In that respect alone, a remarkable writer, surely? If he had lived five years longer, he would have written fifteen more thoroughly readable works of fiction. A loss – a serious loss – I say again.'

> Cecilia Meetkerke: 'There was no kindlier or more genial man than Anthony Trollope, no one more hospitable and easy of access. Address him with a friendly word, and after a keen glance through his spectacles, under his heavy brows, you would have of his best in return. He had no idea of keeping his pearls for a chosen companion, but would lavish them freely for the entertainment of the hour and his chance companionships.'

Many letters written by the poet Edward Fitzgerald also attest to the popularity of Trollope's books:

To Stephen Spring (1860):

I am now awaiting another Box from Mudie: when some Novels of Trollope's will, I hope come. Have you ever read them? I was afraid my Power of Novel reading was gone: but living here all alone I am glad to go into Society so easily as one does in a good Novel. Trollope's are very good, I think: not perfect, but better than a narrower Compass of Perfection like Miss Austen's ...

To John Mowbray Donne (1867):

I fancied I could always read A. Trollope: but his last Barset (The Last Chronicle) *has made me skip here and there. The Account of Old Harding with his Violoncello in Volume II is – better than Sterne – in as much as it is more unaffected and true ...*

To John Allen (1868):

... in half an hour two Merchants are coming to eat Oysters and drink Burton ale. I would rather be alone, and smoke my one pipe in peace over one of Trollope's delightful Novels, Can You Forgive Her?

To W F Pollock (1873):

This is Sunday Night 10: p.m. And what is the Evening Service which I have been listening to? The Eustace Diamonds – which interests me almost as much as Tichborne. I really give the best proof I can of the Interest I take in Trollope's Novels, by constantly breaking out into Argument with the Reader (who never replies) about what is said and done by the People in the several Novels I say 'No – no! She must have known she was lying!' He couldn't have been such a Fool! Etc. ...

And earlier, in 1856, Trollope's mother had written:

Tom and I agree in thinking that you exceed in this respect [his industry] any individual that we have ever known or heard of – and I am proud of being your mother – as well for this reason as for sundry others. I rejoice to think that you have considerably more than the third of a century to gallop through yet before reaching the age at which I first felt inclined to cry ha ta la.

(Booth, *Letters*, I, 44)

Obituaries

The press at the time of his death was also appreciative:

> '... the most methodical romance writer of whom we have ever heard', [both for his] 'five o'clock in the morning genius' [and the] 'wonderful uniformity of quality in each of his novels' [which have] 'enriched our English fiction with characters destined to survive'.
>
> *The Times*

> 'No one was so representative of English fiction both by his books and by his personality.'
>
> Viscount Bryce in *The Nation*

> '... the most representative figure of contemporary literature and one who had achieved the rare distinction of having become an object of personal goodwill to uncounted readers.'
>
> Richard Littledale writing in *The Academy*

> 'He has enriched our English fiction with characters destined to survive.'
>
> *The Edinburgh Review*

> '... wholesome and innocent mental pleasure.'
>
> *The Graphic*

> [he was at his best in] *'kindly ridicule of the approved superficialities of life.'*
>
> The Athenaeum

> 'The readers of Good Words have had special links of connection with the friend whom we have all lost. Twenty years ago he began to contribute to these pages some of the short stories in which he was excellent ... Since then many a page from his hand has entertained our readers, and the last of his published stories had just appeared in Good Words when his life, too, ended; not without warning, nor prematurely, yet at an age when he was still in full vigour, and might still have lived and rode, and written for many a day to come. ... The great novelist is dead, at peace and in honour with all men, leaving nothing behind him that is bitter or painful, but an honourable man, a reputation which there is every reason to believe will increase rather than diminish, and the example of a life full of useful exertion. He did much in his life to restore character and credit to the literary profession, while at the same time he was no mere writer, but a man thoroughly experimented in the world, and knowing the life which he illustrated.'
>
> Mrs Humphrey Ward writing anonymously in
> The Times

Minchinhampton, Gloucestershire

After staying on at South Harting for a while and then having a short spell in Chelsea, Rose and Florence (Bice) moved in 1886, four years after Trollope's death, to what is now a Grade II* house called Greylands, in Minchinhampton, near Stroud in Gloucestershire. It is now no. 9 in the High Street and, according to Historic England, has three storeys and a basement. Eventually Henry and Ada, with their son, Thomas, and daughter, Muriel Rose, joined them, although Thomas was mainly away at school. The census lists three servants.

The town, which has a war memorial, a market every Thursday, and a number of local shops, is the birthplace of Joanna Trollope. It is near Gatcombe, the Princess Royal's estate, with its horse trials and rugby and golf clubs. A letter from Muriel Rose dated 7th August 1936 addressed 'Dear Madam' states: 'Perhaps I may be allowed to quote Mr Walpole [no relation to the Hon Frederick Walpole above] who described the autobiography as "one of the noblest-minded books in the English language".' She gave the address at that time as The Greylands, Minchin Hampton, Stroud, Glos.

According to Victoria Glendinning in *Trollope* (1992), Rose had sold the house at South Harting for £5,000 to Mr R W Oldham through Osborn & Mercer of Albemarle House, 28b Albemarle Street, Piccadilly, London. The brochure described the house thus: '... although situate close to the junction of two roads, is, in consequence of being on a higher level and there being but a small amount of traffic, perfectly secluded, while having at the Front Gate ample room for carriage approach.' It was described as a '*Comfortable Cottage Residence*', complete with stables, piggeries and cowsheds, a barn, wood-house, harness-room, coach-house, two enclosed yards and 70 acres, let out except for one meadow. It had five family bedrooms, two servants' bedrooms, one WC, front and back staircases, double drawing room and dining room and smaller sitting-room. There was also the book room which Trollope had earlier described as having two shelves fewer than at Montagu Square which he found awkward, but had said: '*If however I am in confusion with my books, I have got my wine into fine order, and have had iron bins put up in the cellar.*' The brochure also stated that '*The house will always possess a passing interest in having been the last residence of the popular author, the late Anthony Trollope.*

There are two Postal Deliveries daily and Telegraph Office at Rogate station.'

Trollope had made a Will about a year before his death, leaving all but minor bequests in trust for Rose, after which it was to be divided equally between Henry and Fred, with Henry his literary executor. The estate was valued for probate at £25,892s.3d – over three million pounds today – and as it was not the custom then to receive royalties instead of copyrights, it later earned another £10,000, roughly another million pounds. However, this was not as much as his colleague and rival Dickens, whose estate was worth £90,000 (almost £11 million today), although Rose was able to live comfortably but not extravagantly on £2,000 p.a. until her death in her mid-nineties.

Evidence of the declining popularity that Trollope had so feared was emphasised by Henry's difficulties in finding publishers for his final books. After he re-copied the manuscript for *An Autobiography*, omitting the pages on Kate Field and adding a Preface, he attempted to follow Trollope's instructions:

> *I should wish the book to be published by Fred Chapman if he is in business at the time of my death – but of course you will do the best you can as to terms, if not with him, then with some other publisher.*

Eventually, following his uncle Tom's recommendations, it was published by William Blackwood in January 1883 who knocked down the price to £1,000 for an edition of 4,000 copies and a royalty of two-thirds profits of any future printing. However, only 3,000 copies were printed, and Mudie's Library took 1,000 copies. Blackwood was reluctant to publish *An Old Man's Love* as they had sold only 877 copies of *The Fixed Period*, leaving them with a deficit. However, they eventually bought *An Old Man's Love* sight unseen for £200. Henry then sold the book rights of *Mr Scarborough's Family* to Chatto & Windus for £600 as he had done previously with *The Landleaguers*.

Rose maintained contact with a small group of journalists and literary people, who continued to appreciate Trollope's writings and brought in another small income. She died in 1917, having lived through most of the First World War, and now shares a grave in Holy Trinity Churchyard with Henry and granddaughter Muriel. There is an adjoining grave for Ada and her mother.

Greylands, Minchinhampton

Descendants

Not long after Trollope's death his son Henry, aged 37, married Florence's friend Ada Strickland. They had first a daughter, Muriel Rose, who died in 1953, and then a son, Thomas Anthony, who died in 1931. Both offspring were unfortunately childless and therefore the English line died out. Henry attempted to carry on the family writing tradition and published *My Own Love Story* with Chapman & Hall in 1887, but even his family found it uninteresting. He died at Greylands in Minchinhampton in 1926 aged 80. He corresponded with Michael Sadleir who, as almost a contemporary, wrote the definitive book: *Trollope: A Commentary*, published in 1927, dedicated to Henry's memory. After Henry's death Ada wrote to Michael Sadleir, saying: '*I was kind to my husband, and liked him because he was Anthony's son and only married him because he said if I refused him fifty times he would ask me as many times again!*' Muriel Rose in her later memoirs felt that, as her grandfather Trollope had always overworked and over-socialized, it was perhaps inevitable that his heart ultimately gave up, and she also remembered his great kindnesses. It is notable that no family members, who by now would presumably have read the omitted passage on Kate Field in his *Autobiography*, expressed anything but love and their happy memories of him.

The only direct Trollope family members today are descendants of Anthony and Rose's son Fred in Australia, whose wife Susannah Farrand died in 1909. They had eight children (Frank Anthony, Harry Reginald, Frederick Farrand, Frances Kathleen, Effie Madeleine, Arthur John, Clive Heseltine and Gordon Clavering (1885–1958), the eldest, who became the 15th Baronet). He married Mary Isabel Blacket (d. 1965) and had three children (Gordon Paul Clavering, Barbara Mary Clavering and Anthony Owen Clavering (1917–87), who married Jean Mary Alexis Gibbes. Their son is the father of one of the Trollope Society's Vice Presidents, Hugh Irwin Trollope. He and his wife Barbara have two daughters and one son, Andrew Ian Trollope. Hugh's older brother, Anthony Simon, is the 17th Baronet, married to Denise Thompson, with no son to continue the direct line.

More distant relatives are Angela Thirkell and Joanna Trollope, also renowned novelists. Joanna Trollope chronicles present-day situations and mores as did Anthony Trollope in his day. Angela Thirkell, also a granddaughter of the Pre-Raphaelite painter Edward Burne-Jones, whose painting *Amber Witch* features a dress later worn by her, wrote of a fictional county inhabited by descendants of Barchester characters, such as *The Duke's Daughters*, some published in the *Cornhill* magazine.

It was soon after Trollope's death and the failure of his sheep farm that his second son, Fred, became a clerk in the Lands Department in Sydney at a salary of £400 p.a. As we have seen, he did not enjoy travelling the roads as his father had done for the Post Office, and neither did he like the heat, social isolation or lack of facilities in Australia. Again, unlike his father he did not prosper financially and consequently his mother often sent him small amounts of money, and even his father's old coats, trousers, waistcoats and boots. The waistcoats were unsuitable for his lifestyle and the boots were a bit large, but he still managed to wear them saying they were '*not uncomfortable!*' He had the rest of his father's clothes altered to fit.

Researches by Dr Nigel Starck show that he did eventually gain success as Chairman of the local Land Board, President of the Horticultural Society and Vice-President of the cricket club in the small town of Hay; and named his Sydney house Clavering Cottage. His choice of the name 'Clavering' was not a reference to the large house in *The Claverings* with its troubled occupants, but instead to the comfortable Clavering rectory where the rector and his son '[sat] *in two easy-chairs opposite to each other,* [and] *lit each a cigar. Such was the reverend gentleman's custom in the afternoon, and such also in the morning.*' Fred's eldest son, Frank, came back to school in Margate and was unhappy (echoing the unhappy schooldays of his father and grandfather before him) and ironically was mocked for his accent, this time an Australian one. At seventeen he joined the British Navy to gain a free passage back to Australia. He then went on to South Africa and fought in the Boer War.

In 1903 Fred came back to England for the first time in thirty years, to see his mother. He died before her in 1910 aged 62.

Trollope also lives on in many biographies, some written soon after his death: the first of these being the earlier mentioned *Trollope: A Commentary* written by near contemporary Michael Sadleir. This was praised by Muriel Rose, Trollope's granddaughter, for being an informative and eminently trustworthy and reliable record of Anthony Trollope because he had looked beneath the surface. This was followed by T H S Escott's *Anthony Trollope, His Work, Associates and Literary Originals*; many others have followed later such as by C P Snow and Victoria Glendinning. Many playwrights have interpreted his work both for the theatre and radio such as Simon Raven and more recently Craig Baxter, David Witherow and Lord Julian Fellowes. TV adaptations by Alan Plater in the 1970s of *The Warden* and *Barchester Towers* became known collectively as *The Barchester Chronicles*, starring

Nigel Hawthorne as Archdeacon Grantly, Donald Pleasance as Mr Harding and Alan Rickman memorably as Obadiah Slope. Simon Raven's 1974 26-episode television dramatization of the six Palliser novels followed the characters over two decades. The stellar cast included Susan Hampshire, Clive Swift, Derek Jacobi, Jeremy Irons and June Whitfield, among others. Very recent television adaptations have been *The Way We Live Now* and *He Knew He Was Right* by Andrew Davies, starring David Tennant, Matthew Macfadyen and Anna Massey, and *Dr Thorne* by Lord Julian Fellowes, starring Tom Hollander as Dr Thorne.

Westminster Abbey

Although Trollope's writing career had been slow to start, his popularity grew during his lifetime: Queen Victoria herself wrote to her eldest daughter, the Crown Princess of Prussia, '*There is a very amusing book called* Barchester Towers *by A. Trollope*', to which her daughter replied, '*I like* Barchester Towers, *it makes one laugh till one cries.*' As often happens when ideas and social situations change, and also possibly because of the posthumous publication of his *Autobiography*, Trollope's popularity waned again immediately after his death, but his creation of a world of stability and comfort gave reassurance leading to a revival of popularity during the two World Wars and has continued to increase steadily until the present day. In response to this increased popularity, John Letts founded the Trollope Society in 1987 in conjunction with the Folio Society, and in 1989 they began a mission to republish the forty-seven novels at the rate of four each year. The Trollope Society has now grown exponentially with members around the world reading his novels in their own languages.

In 1991, in recognition of Trollope's contribution not only to English literature but to literature in general, Sir John Major, then Prime Minister and a staunch fan, as was Winston Churchill before him, was instrumental in arranging a memorial in Poets' Corner, Westminster Abbey where Trollope's memorial lies proudly in the last space on the floor, well over a hundred years after he had canvassed for an entry for his friend William Makepeace Thackeray. Poets' Corner, in the South Transept, is a Celebration of British cultural figures, including actors, philosophers, scientists, poets and writers, beginning with Geoffrey Chaucer in 1400 and including William Shakespeare, William Blake, Robert Burns, David Garrick, Lord Byron, Charles Dickens, George Eliot, Sir Isaac Newton and Stephen Hawking. Monuments are either stone slabs, carved monuments, hanging stone tablets or memorial busts. There is a special memorial for the Unknown Warrior.

In a ceremony, John Letts quoted Dean Stanley, in *The Monuments of Westminster Abbey*, who wrote:

> *Of all the characteristics of Westminster Abbey, that which most endears it to the nation ... is not so much its glory as the seat of coronations or as the sepulchre of kings ... as the fact that it is*

the resting place of famous Englishmen, from every rank and creed, and every form of mind and genius. It is not only Rheims Cathedral and St Denis in one; but it is also what the Pantheon was intended to be in France, what the Valhalla is to Germany, what Santa Croce is to Italy.

Members of the Trollope Society marked the bicentenary of Trollope's birth on 24th April 2015 with the 100th edition of *Trollopiana* and a series of lectures, discussions, dinners and exhibitions, and the publication of Professor Steven Amarnick's unabridged version of *The Duke's Children* published jointly with the Folio Society.

A concluding highlight of the year of celebrations was a special ceremony in Westminster Abbey on 4th December 2015 when HRH The Duke of Kent laid a wreath of pink roses on the memorial tablet. The service included music set to *The Barchester Prayer* by Alex Woolf (BBC Young Composer of the Year 2012) accompanied by Vivian Williams on cello. Michael Williamson, then Chairman of the Society, quoted a poem by Mowbray Morris Junior, published in 1883 following Trollope's death:

> *What though the man was rugged to the view*
> *And blunt of speech; no one who knew him knew*
> *A soul more gentle, generous and true*

and the Right Reverend and Right Honourable Dr Richard Chartres KCVO, then Bishop of London and President of the Trollope Society, concluded his Address:

> *At the end of a long life marked by early friendlessness and misery and later esteem and prosperity Trollope teaches us about the complexity of moral judgements and the beauty and the worth of an intense respect for the moral autonomy of others. He portrays urbanity and courtesy as lovely virtues but in the end they cannot do without the scaffolding of simple and direct moral teaching largely dealing with the restraint of our appetites and our propensity to wickedness.*

Doorway of Westminster Abbey

Acknowledgements

My voyage of discovery whilst writing this book has lasted many years, and along the way many extraordinarily kind friends have helped and supported me. I am eternally grateful and owe them all the utmost praise and thanks that it is possible to give.

First of all my heartfelt thanks to Quentin Letts for agreeing so readily to write a Foreword, and to the estate of Gwen Raverat (granddaughter of Charles Darwin) to allow a reproduction of her engraving. Also, I cannot thank my 'Trollope' friends enough for their help. Pamela Morgan accompanied me to Willesden Junction, the Houses of Parliament and Westminster Abbey searching out the best views to paint; Haruno Watanabe, Associate Professor at Atomi University of Tokyo, who inspired me during our illuminating exploration together of Buntingford, Cottered and Rushden, and an especial thank you to Nicky Barnes who drove me from Essex to South Harting in Hampshire where we enjoyed a very productive day. Almost every village member and householder we visited was incredibly enthusiastic and helpful when learning about the mission of a total stranger turning up in their midst. Michael Williamson knew my secret toils from the outset and was supportive.

Having edited *Trollopiana* for ten years I was also privileged to have access to many contributors' articles and research. Enormous thanks are therefore due to contributors Peter Blackmore, Dr Nigel Starck, Hugh Trollope, Teresa Ransom, Guy and Susan Robinson, Julian Stray, Peter Blacklock, the Very Reverend Keith Jones, Pamela Neville-Sington, Bryan Welch, Jessica Finch and her sister Anne Frith, Lucie Simms for her suggestion regarding maps of Barchester, Thomas Rawcliffe for financial knowledge and for his showing me round Wemyss station with Sarah Whitcher; Clare Munn for arranging a Trollope Society visit to Scotland and Wemyss Castle, Joanna Thomas, Maritime Curator at the SS *Great Britain* Trust Museum in Bristol; Peter Lee for introducing me to *How the Mastiffs Went to Iceland*, Allen Holliday for his recollections at Bruges, and Howard Gregg for guiding me around Carrick-on-Shannon. Also, the Reverend Bill Brett at Stotfold, Deborah Owen (who guided me to CUP), and Professor Rohan McWilliam were helpful, and the kindest of parishioners at Heckfield supplied information and even climbed a ladder to read the text of William Milton's memorial which had become obscured by building renovations.

I also received excellent advice from playwright Craig Baxter. David Wayman drove me to Heckfield and around the perimeter of Stratfield Saye, seat of the Duke of Wellington; Mike Petty of the local Cambridge newspaper provided useful information; and friend John Tordoff enthusiastically and skilfully brought Anthony Trollope to life in portrait form. A hearty thank you also to Paul Baker, London tour guide, for his fascinating insights and literary tours.

A special tribute is deserved to my kind brother Stephen Whitley who, after exploring Waltham Cross and Waltham Abbey with me and sourcing antique maps, drove me in his vintage car on old roads and pathways to the villages of Matching, Matching Green and Matching Tye at a slow stagecoach pace.

Special credits go to my husband, Alan, for enduring long train journeys and rambles along country lanes in driving rain and thunderstorms in pursuit of various properties (and his ability to spot them before me!). Also, to Dr Anne Pugh who proofread and corrected my typos, and to Dr Yvonne Siddle, Visiting Lecturer of Literature at Chester University, who also proofread and gave me invaluable advice.

Another special thank you must be given to the Earl of Leicester at Holkham Hall who tried to find a Trollopian connection, and particularly to The Most Hon David Cholmondeley, 7th Marquess of Cholmondeley of Houghton Hall who guided me to the nearby Walpole family at Mannington Hall, who in turn were incredibly helpful and led me to the Courtauld family at Barningham Hall, all of which eventually led in a straight line to the Hon Frederick Walpole at Rainthorp Hall.

Many thanks also to Ken Sewell, Barbara Legg and Tina Brand at Janus Publishing.

And lastly, I could not have completed this project without the support and photography of Dr Ros Ridley and Dr Harry Baker who took superb photographs of all my paintings (following which we consumed copious cups of coffee!).

Sources

I have read and re-read Anthony Trollope's own books for many years, and have benefited from discussions and seminars with friends and colleagues and their many academic books and papers absorbed over the years, together with the museums, galleries and places of interest related above. I have also relied particularly heavily upon the following:

Books and Periodicals

Booth, Bradford Allen (ed.), *The Letters of Anthony Trollope*, Oxford University Press, 1951

Escott, T H S, *Anthony Trollope, His Work, Associates and Literary Originals*, The Bodley Head, 1913

Glendinning, Victoria, *Trollope*, Hutchinson, 1992

Harris, P R, *A History of the British Museum Library 1753-1973*, British Library, 1998

Heineman, Helen, *Mrs Trollope, The Triumphant Feminine in the Nineteenth Century*, Ohio University Press, 1936

Hennessy, James Pope, *Anthony Trollope*, Jonathon Cape, 1971

Mullen, Richard, *Anthony Trollope: A Victorian in His World*, Gerald Duckworth & Co Ltd, 1990

Neville-Sington, Pamela, *Fanny Trollope, The Life and Adventures of a Clever Woman*, Penguin

Sadleir, Michael, *Trollope: A Commentary*, 1927

Snow, C P, *Trollope: His Life and Art*, Macmillan Press, London, 1975

Terry, R C (ed.), *Oxford Reader's Companion to Trollope*, Oxford University Press, 1999

Terry, R C (ed.), *Trollope: Interviews and Recollections*, St Martin's Press, Inc, 1987

Trollope, Anthony, *An Autobiography*, Goldstone Rare Books, 1946

Trollope, Thomas Adolphus, *What I Remember*, volumes I, II and II, Cambridge University Press, 2010

Trollopiana issues as detailed above

Other Sources

Cambridge University Library
Cambridge University Press
Garrick Club Library
London and Norfolk Museums of Freemasonry
Norfolk Records Office
Suffolk Records Office
Trinity Hall Library, University of Cambridge

List of Publications by Anthony Trollope

Title	Publisher	Date (book form after serialisation)
The Macdermots of Ballycloran	Thomas C Newby	1847
The Kellys and the O'Kellys	Henry Colburn	1848
La Vendée	Henry Colburn	1850
The Warden	William Longman	1855
Barchester Towers	William Longman	1857
The Three Clerks	Richard Bentley	1858
Dr Thorne	Chapman & Hall	1858
The Bertrams	Chapman & Hall	1859
West Indies and the Spanish Main	Chapman & Hall	1859
Castle Richmond	Chapman & Hall	1860
Framley Parsonage	Smith, Elder & Co	1861
Tales of All Countries: First series (collection of short stories)	Chapman & Hall	1861
Orley Farm	Chapman & Hall	Vol 1 1861 Vol 2 1862

Title	Publisher	Date (book form after serialisation)
North America	Chapman & Hall	1862
Rachel Ray	Chapman & Hall	1863
Tales of All Countries: Second series (collection of short stories)	Chapman & Hall	1863
The Small House at Allington	Smith, Elder & Co	1864
Can You Forgive Her?	Chapman & Hall	Vol 1 1864 Vol 2 1865
Miss Mackenzie	Chapman & Hall	1865
The Belton Estate	Chapman & Hall	1865
Hunting Sketches	Chapman & Hall	1865
Clerical Sketches	Chapman & Hall	1865
Clergymen of the Church of England	Chapman & Hall	1865
The Claverings	Smith, Elder & Co	1867
Nina Balatka (anonymously)	Blackwood	1867
The Last Chronicle of Barset	Smith Elder & Co	1867
Lotta Schmidt (collection of short stories)	Alexander Strachan	1867

Title	Publisher	Date (book form after serialisation)
Linda Tressel (anonymously)	Blackwood	1868
British Sports and Pastimes	Virtue & Co	1868
Phineas Finn	Virtue & Co	1869
He Knew He Was Right	Alexander Strachan	1869
The Struggles of Brown, Jones and Robinson	Smith, Elder & Co	1870
The Vicar of Bullhampton	Bradbury & Evans	1870
Sir Harry Hotspur of Humblethwaite	Hurst & Blackett	1870
The Commentaries of Caesar	William Blackwood	1870
Ralph the Heir	Hurst & Blackett	1871
The Golden Lion of Granpere	Tinsley	1872
The Eustace Diamonds	Chapman & Hall	1872
Phineas Redux	Chapman & Hall	1873
Australia and New Zealand	Chapman & Hall	1873
Lady Anna	Chapman & Hall	1874
Harry Heathcote of Gangoil	Samson Low	1874
The Way We Live Now	Sampson Law	1875

Title	Publisher	Date (book form after serialisation)
The Prime Minister	Chapman & Hall	1876
The American Senator	Chapman & Hall	1877
Is He Popenjoy?	Chapman & Hall	1878
South Africa	Chapman & Hall	1878
How the 'Mastiffs' Went to Iceland	(printed privately by Virtue & Co)	1878
An Eye for an Eye	Chapman & Hall	1879
John Caldigate	Chapman & Hall	1879
Cousin Henry	Chapman & Hall	1879
Thackeray	Macmillan	1879
The Duke's Children	Chapman & Hall	1880
The Life of Cicero	Chapman & Hall	1880
Ayala's Angel	Chapman & Hall	1881
Dr Wortle's School	Chapman & Hall	1881
Marion Fay	Chapman & Hall	1882
Kept in the Dark	Chatto & Windus	1882

Publications of Anthony Trollope

Title	Publisher	Date (book form after serialisation)
The Fixed Period	Blackwood	1882
Lord Palmerston	William Isbister	1882
Why Frau Frohmann Raised her Prices and Other Stories	William Isbister	1882
Mr Scarborough's Family (posthumously)	Chatto & Windus	1883
The Landleaguers (posthumously/unfinished)	Chatto & Windus	1883
An Autobiography (posthumously)	Oxford World Classics	1883
As Old Man's Love (posthumously)	Blackwood	1884
The Two Heroines of Plumplington (posthumously pirated)		1953
An Editor's Tales (short stories published as *Editors and Writers* by The Trollope Society)		1996

Index

Note: References in **bold** are to illustrations.

16, Keppel Street, Russell Square, 1–4, **3**, **4**

Albert, Prince, 131, 231
Albion press, 165
All the Year Round, 24, 106
Allen, John, 241
Allen, William, 76
almshouses, 24, 97–99
Amarnick, Steven, 198, 252
America, 11, 14, 38, 41–43, 155, 184, 205–206
American Civil War, 184
American Senator, The, 18, 111, 196, 197, 206
Anstey, F: *Vice Versa*, 235
Anti-Garrotting Cravat, 143
Apsley House, London, 28, 132
Archer, Isabella, 182, 183, 184, 189
aristocracy, 140–141
Aristotle, 140
Arnold, Matthew, 116
art and illustrations, 169–174
Athenaeum Club, 115, 116, **117**, 118, 134, 215, 239
Athenaeum, The, 93, 161, 244
Australia, 139, 182, 183, 184–185, 187, 188, 189–193, 206

Australia and New Zealand, 182
Autobiography, 1, 8, 24, 29, 32, 37, 39, 40, 50, 183, 194, 196–197, 236, 238
  AT's father, 42, 45
  AT's mother, 180
  childhood, xvii–xviii, xix
  farms, 14
  George Eliot, 227
  holidays, 74
  Kate Field, 156, 157, 246
  marriage, 82
  novels, 93, 97
  Parliament, 119
  Post Office, 65, 102
  publication of, 1, 197, 246, 251
  Rose, 92
Ayala's Angel, 50, 52, 72

Baker, Paul, 67, 68, 70, 71
Barchester Chronicles, The, (TV adaptation), 249–250
Barchester novels, 37, 97–100, **98**, 126, 204
Barchester Prayer, The 252
Barchester Towers, 10, 97, **98**, 102, 161, 166, 175, 176, 249, 251
Barney (stableman), 76, 106, 111, 166
Barry, Charles, 123
Barsetshire (map), **151**
Baxter, Craig, 187, 249

265

Baylis, Thomas Henry QC, 36
beards, 146
Bede, Cuthbert, 112
Bedside Barchester, The, **144**
Beer, Gillian, 99
Bell, Robert, 164, 199
Belton Estate, The, 61
Bent, Fanny, 29, 48
Bentham, Jeremy, 45, 46, 99
Bentinck, Lady Frederick, 91
Bentley, Richard, 161, 215
Bertrams, The, 69–71, 92, 159, 161, 204
Bessborough, Lord, 36
Betjeman, John, 15
Beverley, Yorkshire, 119–122, **120**, 123
Bianconi, Charles, 83, 86
Bice (Florence Bland), 105, 228
  adoption of, 81
  as amanuensis, 81, 166, 196, 197
  and AT's library, 199, 200
  at Greylands, Minchinhampton, 245
  travels, 207, 226
biographies, 249
Birch, Peregrine, 48
Bishop, Henry, 60
Blacket, Mary Isabel, 248
Blacklock, Peter, 99
Blackwood, John, 106, 158, 161, 240
Blackwood, Julia, 158
Blackwood, William, 246
Blackwood's Edinburgh Magazine, 161
Blackwood's Magazine, 154, 236
Bland, Florence see Bice (Florence Bland)
Booth, Bradford Allen: Letters, 106, 158, 169, 182, 199, 200

boots and shoes, 146–147
bouts rimés, 68
BPMA *see* Postal Museum Archives
Bray, Charles, 153–154
Brennan, Maeve, **120**
British Museum, 194
Bronson, Katherine Colman DeKay, 158
Brontë, Charlotte, 76
Brontë, Emily: *Wuthering Heights*, 93
Broughton, Rhoda, 141
Browning, Elizabeth Barrett, 14, 104, 155
Browning, Robert, 116, 155, 158, 236
Bruges, 48–51
  Chateau d'Hondt, 48, 49–50, **51**
Brunel, Isambard Kingdom, 126, 184
Bryce, Viscount, 243
Buckingham Palace, 131
Bulwer-Lytton, Edward, 141, 147
Buntingford almshouse, 24, 99
Burghley House, 15
Burnand, Sir Francis (Frank), 116
Burne-Jones, Edward, 174, 249
Burns, Mr and Mrs John, 219
Buxton, Charles, 119
Byron, Clara Allegra, 36
Byron, Lord, 118, 251

Cambridge, **56**, 127, 138–139, 156
Cambridge Daily News, 165
Cambridge University Press, 164, 165, **165**
Can You Forgive Her?, 92, 110, 125, 131, 132, 140, 144, 146, 213, 215, 231
Canal Museum, King's Cross, 103

canals, 103
Carey's Walk, 45, 46, **46**, **47**
Carlton Club, 115, 118
Carlyle, Thomas, 154
Carmen (opera), 229
Carrick-on-Channon, 118
Casewick, 15, **16-17**, 18, 112, 131, 134
Castle Richmond, 75, 79, 80-81, **84**, 110, 166-167
Chalmers, James, 60
Chamberlain, Neville, 28
Channel Islands, 60-61
Chapman, Frederick, 161, 183, 236, 246
Chapman & Hall, 161, 172, 183
Chartres, Dr Richard, 252
Chatto & Windus, 246
Chaworth, Mr, 118
Chesterfield, Lady, 95
Chetwode, Penelope, 15
Chuck, Neville, 19
Churchill, Randolph, 21
Churchill, Winston, 251
Claverings, The, 6, 102, 110, 112, 116, 126, 131, 141, 161, 197
Clergymen of the Church of England, 100
Cliffe Castle, 87
'Clique, The', 170
Colbourn, Mr, 93
Colburn, Henry, 161
Collins, Reverend W. Lucas, 106, 112
Collins, Wilkie, 14, 126, 141, 155, 236, 240
Columbian Hand Press, 164-165, **165**
Commonplace Book, 199, 231
Contagious Diseases Act, 143
Conyers, Henry John, 132, 134
Cook, A K: *About Winchester*

College, 38
Copped Hall, 134, **136-137**
Cornhill, 161, **162**, 164, 177, 249
Cosmopolitan Club, 116
Cottered, 18-19
  St John the Baptist Church, 18, 19, **19**
Cousin Henry, 196, 198, 227
Cowen, William, 87
Cox, Alan, 134
cricket, 188
Crimean War, 140
criticisms and reviews, 175-176
  Trollope's response to, 177-178
Crowther, Stan, 88
Cubitt, Thomas, 67, 131
Cumberlow Green, 21
Cunningham, Reverend John, 8, 9-10, 36, 37, 97
Cunynghame, A. M., 240

Daily Telegraph, 164
Dalziel brothers (engravers), 172
Darwin, Charles, 215
Darwin, Lady Ida, 156
Davies, Andrew, 250
Davison, Emily, 6
DeBurgo family, 86
Depression, (1840s) 88
descendants, 248-250
Dickens, Alfred, 189, 192
Dickens, Charles,
  AT's antipathy towards, 8, 115, 119, 174
  and British Museum, 194
  estate of, 246
  and government, 140
  in London, 4, 6, 71
  Poets' Corner, Westminster Abbey, 251
post box, 61

and railways, 126
  sons, 189
  at Thackeray's funeral, 236
  writing, 147, 197
Dickens, Edward (Plorn), 189, 193
Donne, John Mowbray, 241
Dr Thorne, 21, **98**, 102, 126, 250
Dr Wortle's School, 113, 145, 152, 206, 226, 231
Drought, Mr (Surveyor), 76
Drury, Arthur, 37
Drury, Charles, 67
Drury, Henry (Harry), 9–10, 32, 37, 50, 65
Drury, Herman, 65
Drury, Joseph, 32
Duke's Children, The, 29, 83, 103, 106, 111, 112, 120, 125, 131, 134, 138, 139–140, 154, 196, 198, 209, 252
Dumas, Alexander, 229

Eden Hall, 91
Edinburgh Review, The, 243
education, 32
  Harrow School, 7, 32–37, **33**, **35**, 39–40
  Sunbury, 37
  Winchester, 11, 37–40, **40**
Edward VI, 132
Edwards, Mary Ellen, 172
Egypt, 204
Eldon, Earl of, 46
Eliot, George, 103, 126, 141, 147, 152–154, 156, 227, 228, 251
Engels, Friedrich, 114
Epstein, Jacob, 225
Escott, T H S: *Anthony Trollope*, 249
essays, 161

Europe: holiday and research travels, 207–208
Eustace Diamonds, The, 6, 10, 125, 126, 143, 183, 196, 208–209, 219, 231–232
Evans, Mary Anne *see* Eliot, George
Examiner, 80
Exeter, 29–31, **30**, **31**
Exeter Cathedral School, 29
Express, 175
Eye for an Eye, An, 75, 82–83, **84**, 145, 183
Eyre, Vincent, 87

Famine Letters, 75
Faroe Islands, 220
Farrand, Susannah, 248
'Father Giles of Ballymoy', 75, 77
Featherstonhaugh, Lady, 224–225
Felix Holt, 152
Fellowes, Lord Julian, 249, 250
Field, Joseph M., 155
Field, Kate, xviii, 154–158, 197, 205, 231, 246
Fildes, Luke, 169
Finch, Jessica, 147, 218
Finn, Phineas, 172
Fitzgerald, Edward, 241
Fitzgerald family, 86
Fixed Period, The, 118, 188, 226, 233, 236–237, 246
Folio Society, 251, 252
Fortnightly Review, 110, 153, 161, 183
Foster, Suzanne, 38
Framley Parsonage, 21, 42, 97, 110, 161, 166, 167, 172
Freeling, Clayton, 50, 57
Freeling, Henry, 57
Freeling, Mrs Clayton, 50, 104

Index

Freeling, Sir Francis, 50, 57, 58
Freeman, E A, 226
Freemasonry, 76, 119, 141–143, **142**, 215
Frith, Anne, 218
Frith, William Powell, 170
Fulham, 28–29, 104
Garlant's Hotel, Suffolk Street, 229–232
Garrick Club, 115, 116, 134, 170, 194, 215, 231
Garrick, David, 115, 251
Gentleman's Magazine, The, 55
'gentlemen', 102
Gibbes, Jean Mary Alexis, 248
Gielgud, John, 115
Gill, Eric, 225
Gissing, George, 240
Glendinning, Victoria: *Trollope*, 228, 245, 249
Globe, The, 176
gold, 139, 190–191
Golden Lion of Granpere, The, 110
Good Words, 64, 161, **163**, 174, 183, 244
Gordon, Reverend Henry Doddridge, 226
Gower Street, 1, **3**, 4, 126, 127, 166, 194
Grant, Colonel, 14, 48
Grant, Sir Francis, 171
Graphic, The, 171, 243
Grascour, Monsieur, 49
Great Northern Railway (GNR), 18
Gregory, Sir William, 36
Gresley, Mary, 26, 27
guano, 127
Gunning-King, William, 225

Hampshire, Susan, 250
Hardy, Thomas, 126, 141

Harper's New Monthly Magazine, 161
Harris, P R, 194
Harrison, Frederic, 147
Harrow on the Hill,
  Illots Farm, 7–8, **9**, 10, 14
  Julians, 8, 9–10, **12-13**
  St Mary's Church, 36
Harrow School, 7, 32–37, **33**, **35**, 39–40
Harrow Weald, 10–11, 38, 41
Harry Heathcote of Gangoil, 187
Hastings, Ridley, 8
hats, 145–146
Hawksmoor, Nicholas, 4
Hawthorne, Julian, 194, 239
Hawthorne, Nathaniel, 176, 184
Hawthorne, Nigel, 250
Haymarket Theatre, **230**
He Knew He Was Right, 4, 29, **30**, 30–31, 45, 156, 197, 250
Headford House, Drumsna, xv, 76–77
Heckfield, Hampshire, 25–28
  Highfield Place, 28
  St. Michael's Church, 25, **26**, 27–28
Henry VIII, 132
Hervieu, Auguste, 7, 41, 54, 180
Heseltine, Edward, 87, 88, 127
Heseltine, Rose *see* Trollope, Rose
Higgins, Matthew, 164
Hill, Sir Rowland, 60, 107
Hiram's Hospital, 97
Hitchcock, Thomas Patrick, 127
Hogarth, William, 6
holiday and research travels
  Europe, 207–208
  Norfolk and Suffolk, **213**, 213–218
  Scotland, 208–209

Yorkshire, **209**, 209–213, **210**, **211**
Hollander, Tom, 250
Holliday, Allen, 49
Holmes, Mary, 158
Home Rule, 123
Hooker, Joseph, 215
horses,
   hunting, 76, 107, 111–114, **113**
   racing and Newmarket, 139–140
Houses of Parliament, 119–120, 123, **124**, 145
How the 'Mastiffs' Went to Iceland, 219–220
Hudson, Mr, 88, 127
Hugel, Charles, 68
Hunt, Holman, 174
Hunt, William, 170
hunting, 76, 107, 111–114, **113**
Huntingford, Bishop of Hereford, 99
Hutton, Mr (*Spectator*), 177

Iceland, 219–220, 222–223
Illots Farm, Harrow on the Hill, 7–8, **9**, 10, 14
Illustrated London News, 164, 171
Imperial iron press, 165
inheritances, 8
Ireland, xv, 75, 86, 155
   Banagher, 76
   Carrick-on-Shannon, 77, **79**, 79–81
   Cliffs of Moher, 82–83
   Clonmel, 83, 86
   Cork, 94
   Drumsna, xv, 76–77, **78**
   Freemasonry, 142
   Home Rule, 132–133
   Kingstown, *now* Dun Laoghaire, **81**, 81–82
   Mallow, 83
   novels, 75, **84–85**
   Post Office, xv, 46, 75, 76, 83, 86
Irons, Jeremy, 250
Irving, Henry, 115, 143
Is He Popenjoy?, 140, 146, 231

Jacobi, Derek, 250
James, Henry, 176, 240
Jebb, Lady Caroline, 156
Jockey Club, 118
John Caldigate, 58–59, 139, 186, 191–192, 196, 197, 207, 231
Johnson, Samuel: *Lives of the Poets*, 74
Johnston, Henry, 239
Jones, Keith, 99–100
Julians, Harrow on the Hill, 8, 9–10, **12–13**
Julians, Rushden, 20, 21–24, **22–23**, 131

Kellys and the O'Kellys, The, 75, **84**, 93
Kensal Green Cemetery, 236–238, **237**
Keppel, Admiral, 1
Kept in the Dark, 126, 226

La Fayette, General, 41
La Traviata (opera), 170, 229
La Vendée, 49–50, 53, 93, 97
Lady Anna, 92, 145, 186–187, 210
Lake District, 72, 187
Landleaguers, The, 75, 79, **85**, 226, 229, 246
Landon, Letitia 14
Landor, W. S. 155

Landseer, Sir Edwin 164
Larkin, Philip **120**
Last Chronicle of Barset, The, 45, 97, **98**, 110, 170, 231
Lawrence, Thomas, 115
Leighton, Sir Frederick, 164
letters, 239–242
Letts, John, xvi, 251
Letts, Quentin, xv–xvi
Lever, Charles, 164
Lewes, Charles, 153, 227
Lewes, George Henry, 106–107, 152, 153, 155, 164, 227
Lewis, Arthur, 171
libraries,
　Mudie's lending library, 159, 241, 246
　Trollope's library, 199–201, **201**, **202–203**
Life of Cicero, The, 226
Lifted Veil, The, 152
Lincoln's Inn xviii, 1, 10, 44–46, **46**, **47**
Linda Tressel, 177
Lindsey, Earl of, 15, 18
Littledale, Richard, 243
Liverpool, 183–185, *185*
Liverpool Mercury, 183, 189
London, 230, 231
　clubs, 115–118
　Garlant's Hotel, Suffolk Street, 229–232
　prostitution, 143
　violence, 143–144
London lodgings: Northumberland Street, Marylebone, 65–67, **66**, 71, 72–74
Longman & Co, 161
Lonsdale, Lord, 91
Lord Raglan (tavern), 58, **59**
Lowell, James Russell, 240
Lowick, 112–113

Lowther Hall, 91
Lyon, John, 32
Lytton, Lady, 158

Maberly, Colonel, 58
McAleese, Mary, 77
Macdermots of Ballycloran, The, xv, 75, 77, 79, **85**, 92, 93, 161
Macfadyen, Matthew, 250
Macleod, Donald, xix
Macmillan, Alexander, 161, 164
Macmillan, Daniel, 164
Macmillan, Harold, 164
Macmillan's Magazine, 161
McWilliam, Rohan, 141
Major, Sir John, 251
Malcolm, Thomas George, 165
Malthus, Thomas, 99, 123
　Essay on the Principle of Population, An, 123
maps,
　area local to Trollope, **150**
　Barsetshire, **151**
Marion Fay, 92, 146
Marx, Karl, 114
Mary Tudor, 132
Massey, Anna, 250
Matching Green, 111, 112, 131
Matching Tye, 111–112, 131
maternal ancestry,
　Exeter, 29–31
　Fulham, 28–29
　Heckfield, Hampshire, 25–28, **26**
Meetkerke, Adolphus, 21, 152
Meetkerke, Augustus, 8, 20
Meetkerke, Cecilia, xix, 152, 196, 226, 240
Meetkerke, Penelope, 20
Melton Mowbray, 112
Members of Parliament, 119–120
Merivale, John, 67, 76

Methodism, 88
Metternich, Prince, 69
Middlemarch, 153
Midsummer Night's Dream, A, 132
Mill on the Floss, The, 152
Millais, Effie, 170
Millais, John Everett, 4, 115, 164, 170, 197, 236
  illustrations, 169, 171–172, 174
Milman, Rev Henry, 14
Milton, Frances see Trollope, Frances (Fanny)
Milton, Henry, 26, 28–29, 119
Milton, Mary (née Gresley), 26, 27
Milton, Reverend William, 25–28
Minchinhampton, Gloucestershire, 245–246, **247**
Miss Mackenzie, 27, 45, 102, 110, 157–158
Miss Ophelia Gledd, 156
'Misteltoe Bough, The', 92
Mitford, May Russell, 158
Monken Hadley, 67–71
  Grandon, 70, **71**
  St Mary the Virgin Church, 68, **68**, 70
Montagu Square, Marylebone, 194–198, **195**
Montgomerie, Susannah Anderson, 233
Montrose, Duke of, 107
Morris, Janey, 170
Morris, Mowbray, Jr., 252
Motley, J L, 116
Mr Scarborough's Family, 21, 24, 45, 49, 118, 142, 198, 226, 246
Mudie's lending library, 159, 241, 246
Mullen, Richard, 116
Murray, John, 161
Musgrave, Sir George and Lady, 91

National Liberal Club, 115, 116, 164
Nevill, Lady Dorothy, 134, 215
Neville-Sington, Pamela, 29–30, 48, 49, 53, 55
New Zealander, 140
Newby, Thomas Cautley, 93, 161
Newmarket, 139–140
Nicholls, Arthur Bell, 76
Nicholson, Dr, 91
Nicholson, Fanny, 91
Nightingale, Florence, 156
Nina Balatka, 110, 153, 177
Noble Jilt, The (play), 50
Norfolk, 134, 213, 214–215
North America, 183, 205
Northumberland Street, Marylebone, 65–67, **66**, 72–74
Northwick, Lord, 7

obituaries, 243–244
'O'Conors of Castle Conor, County Mayo, The', 75
Old Man's Love, An, 156, 226, 246
Oldham, Mr R. W., 245
Oliphant, Margaret, 141, 158
Once a Week, 174
O'Neill, Henry Nelson: *The Pre-Raphaelite*, 115, 170
Orley Farm, 8, 45, 97, 105, 110, 114, 145, 171–172, 212
Orwell, George, 4
Osborne House, Isle of Wight, 131
Osborne, Jeremy, 26
O'Tingay, Lance, **144**
Oxford, 138–139, 156
Oxford Reader's Companion to Trollope, 204, 207
Oyler's Farm, 105
Pall Mall Gazette, 110, 161, 164

Palliser novels, 21, 28–29, 34, 58, 86, 112, 131–135, 140, **148–149**, 156, 197, 218, 250
Palliser, Reverend Bury, 83
Palmer, John, 60
Palmerston, Lord, 100
Partington, Mary Ann, 233
Partington, Sarah, 27
paternal ancestry, 15–16
  Casewick, 15, **16–17**, 18, 112, 131, 134
  Cottered, 18–19
  Rushden, **20**, 20–24, **22–23**, 25, 131
Payne, James, 141
Pen Photographs of Charles Dickens's Readings, 155
Penny Black, 60
Penrith, 91–93, **92**
Pevsner, Nikolaus, 15, 88
Phineas Finn, 50, 82–83, 110, 114, 118, 119, 125, 143, 144, 145, 146, 197, 208, 218
Phineas Redux, 45, 116, 118, 125, 144, 183, 196
Pickett, William, 24
Plater, Alan, 249
Pleasance, Donald, 250
Plint, Thomas, 172
Plumer, Sir Thomas, 46
Plumpton, 92
Pneumatic Despatch Company, 61, 64
police, 143
politics, 119–120, 123, 125
Pollock, Sir Frederick and Lady, 107
Pollock, W F, 241
Pollock, Walter, 199
Poor Law Amendment Act (1834), 99
Porter, Mrs Gerald, 158

post boxes, 60–61, **62–63**
Post Office career, xviii, 50, 57–58, 60–64, 65, 102, 153
  Eastern District of England, 105
  Egypt, 204
  examinations, 102
  Ireland, xv, 46, 75, 76, 83, 86
  North America, 155, 205–206
  Penrith, 91
  Salisbury, 99–100
  South Africa, 155, 207
  West Indies, 114, 204–205
Postal Museum Archives (BPMA), 60, 64
Postlethwaite, Joseph, 224
poverty, genteel, 2, 6
Pre-Raphaelite Brotherhood, 169, 170
Prime Minister, The, xvi, 83, 125, 126, 127–128, 131, 132–134, 143, 146, 176, 196, 197, 218
printers, 164–165, **165**
Private View at the Royal Academy, 170
prostitution, 143
publications,
  novels, 159, 161
  periodicals, 159, 161, **162**, 164
Pugin, Augustus, 123

Quiroz, Francisco de, 127

Rachel Ray, 105, 110, 154, 161
railways, 111, 126–130, **128**, 134, 183
  and speculation, 126, 127–128
  stations, 111, 126, **129**
  trains, 127–128, **128**

writing on, 129, 166, **167**
Rains, Colonel George, 105
Rainthorpe Hall, Norfolk, 134, 215
Ralph the Heir, 8, 29, 45, 103, 110, 112, 120, 171, 214–215, 232
Randall, John, 25
Raven, Simon, 249, 250
Reade, Charles, 232
recollections and letters, 239–242
Rees, Lyn, 194
Reform Club, 115, 118
Richmond Papers, The, 171
Rickman, Alan, 250
Ritchie, Anne, 233
Robinson, Guy, 92
Robinson, Neil, 188
Robinson, Susan, 92
Romola, 152
Rossetti, Christina, 170
Rossetti, Dante Gabriel, 4, 170
Rotherham, 87–90, **89**, 99
Royal Academy, 103, 171, **173**
Royal Gunpowder Mills, 105–106
Rushden, 20–21
  Julians, 20, 21–24, **22**-**23**, 131
  St Mary's Church, 20, **20**, 25
Ruskin, John: *Sesame and Lilies*, 154
Russell, Bertrand, 225
Russell, Billy, 164
Russell, Lord John, 4

Sadleir, Michael: *Trollope: A Commentary*, xix, 198, 248, 249
Sala, George Augustus, 164
Salisbury, 97–100
Sankey, Dorothea, 158
Saturday Review, 175
Savage Club, 116, 164
Sayers, Dorothy L., 233
school holidays, 44–46
Scotland, 208–209
Scott, Walter, 147
Shaw Lefevre family, 28
Sherwin, John G, 165
short stories, 64, 75, 77, 110, 156, 161, 183, 205
Shrimpton, Nicholas, 8
Siddal, Elizabeth, 170
Siddle, Dr Yvonne: *The Literary Encyclopedia*, 80
Sidney Sussex College, Cambridge, 138
Sir Harry Hotspur, 92, 110
slave trade, 183–184
sleigh, 95–96, **96**
Small House at Allington, The, 8, 72, **98**, 110, 126
Smith, Albert, 164
Smith, Elder & Co., **160**, 164
Smith, George, 161, 164, 196
Smythe, George, MP, 134
Snow, C P: *Trollope: His Life and Art* (1975), 8, 9–10, 21, 42, 72, 105, 156, 157, 249
Society of Merchant Venturers, 26
Somerset House, 102–104, 171, **173**
sources, 257–258
South Africa, 155, 207
South Africa, 207
South Harting, 224–228, *225*, **227**, 229, 238, 245–246
Soyer, Alexis Benoit, 118
Spectator, The, 93, 177, 197
Spencer, Herbert, 103
SS *Great Britain*, 183, 184–185, 186–187, *187*, 188
St Andrew's College, Bradfield, 182
St George's Church, Bloomsbury Way, 4–6, **5**

St John's College, Cambridge, 138–139
St Martin's le Grand, St Paul's, 57–58, 64, 75
St Paul's Magazine, 161, **163**, 231
St Vedast Church, 58
Stanley, Dean: *The Monuments of Westminster Abbey*, 251–252
Stanley, William, 87
Starck, Dr Nigel, 193, 249
Steele, Anna, 158
Stephen, Fitzjames, 164
Stirling, A M W, 171
Stoker, Bram, 233
Stone, Marcus, 172
Stotfold, Hertfordshire, 24–25
Strahan, Alexander, 161
Stratfield Saye House, 28, 131–132, 256
Stray, Julian, 60
Strickland, Ada *see* Trollope, Ada
strong women, 152, 158
  see also Eliot, George; Field, Kate; Meetkerke, Cecilia
Suffolk, **213**, 213–214, 218
Sunbury, 37
Swift, Clive, 250
Sykes, 164

Tales of All Countries, 206
Tate Gallery, 171
Taylor, Sir Charles, 164
'Telegraph Girl, The', 224, 231
Telegraph, The, 143
Tennant, David, 250
Tennyson, Alfred, 171, 174
Terry, Ellen, 91
Terry, R C: *Trollope: Interviews and Recollections*, 27, 171, 189, 192, 196, 226, 239–240
Thackeray, 69

Thackeray, Anne, 106
Thackeray, Georgina, 68
Thackeray, Marianne, 68
Thackeray, Reverend John Richard, 68, 70
Thackeray, William Makepeace, and AT, 164
  on aristocracy, 140
  and Dickens, 115
  family, 69, 233
  Garrick Club, 115
  Hadley, 71
  The Memoirs of Barry Lyndon, 172
  Poet's Corner, 251
  Reform Club, 118
  works, 2
  writing, 147
  death, 116, 236
theatre, 231
themes,
  aristocracy, 140–141
  Freemasonry, 76, 119, 141–143, **142**, 215
  hats, beards, boots and shoes/observations, 145–147
  horse racing and Newmarket, 139–140
  Oxford and Cambridge, 138–139
  violence, 143–145
Thirkell, Angela, 248–249
Thomas, Joanna, 186
Thompson, Denise, 248
Thomson, Christopher, 87
Three Clerks, The, 2, 45, 57, 72, 102, 103–104, 138, 161, 171
Three Graces, The, 170
Tiernan, Frances Eleanor *see* Trollope, Frances Eleanor
Tilley, Cecilia *see* Trollope, Cecilia
Tilley, Edith Diana Mary, 83
Tilley, John, 69, 107, 233–235

house in Pimlico, **234**
marriage to Cecilia Trollope, 69, 72, 83, 91, 93
Times, The, 93, 159, 161, 243, 244
Tolstoy, Leo, 176
Tordoff, John: *Anthony Trollope* (collage), **v**
Trades Guilds, 141
trains, 127-128, **128**
Transactions of the National Association for the Promotion of Society Sciences, 164
Travelling Sketches, 170-171, 184, 223
travels,
  America, 155, 205-206
  Australia, 139, 182, 183, 187, 188, 189-193, 206
  Egypt, 204
  Europe, 207-208
  holidays and research, 207-218
  Iceland, 219-220, 222-223
  Ireland, 75-86, 155
  South Africa, 155, 207
  West Indies, 114, 204-205
  see also Post Office career
Trevelyan, Sir Charles Edward, 102
Trevithick, Richard, 4
Trinity Hall, Cambridge: Modern Jerwood Library, **56**
Trollope, Ada (née Strickland), 81, 95, 198, 245, 246, 248
Trollope, Andrew Ian, 248
Trollope, Anthony (AT),
  birthplace, 4
  character, xvii
  descendants of, 248-250
  early years 1-6
  education, xviii, 32-40
  in Harrow, 7-14
  illness, 72-74

marriage to Rose (see Trollope, Rose)
plays by, 231
portraits of, **v**, 103
publications, **216-217**, 259-263
response to criticisms, 177-178
stroke, 235
Will, 246
death, 236, **237**
see also travels; works by name
Trollope, Anthony (grandfather), 18, 20
Trollope, Anthony Owen Clavering, 248
Trollope, Anthony Simon, 248
Trollope, Arthur John, 248
Trollope, Arthur William, xviii, 1, 7, 32
Trollope, Barbara, 248
Trollope, Barbara Mary Clavering, 248
Trollope, Beatrice, 180
Trollope, Cecilia,
  childhood, 1, 8, 11, 41, 48, 67, 68, 69
  marriage to John Tilley, 69, 72, 83, 91, 93
  death, 93, 179, 233
Trollope, Clive Heseltine, 248
Trollope, Effie Madeleine, 248
Trollope, Emily (1813), 1
Trollope, Emily (1818-36), 1, 8, 11, 41, 48, 49, 67-68, **68**, 72
Trollope, Frances Eleanor (née Tiernan), 41-42, 94, 180
Trollope, Frances (Fanny; née Milton),
  in America, 11, 14
  and AT's illness, 72-73
  and AT's writing, 54, 92-93, 161, 241-242
  in Austria, 69

in Bruges, 48, 49
childhood, 26, 27
in Florence, 93, 179
in London, 8, 71
marriage to Thomas Anthony, 18, 21
in Penrith, 91, 92, 93
and Rose, 88, 90, 92, 94–96, 179
visit to America, 11, 14, 38, 41–43
death, 93, 179–180
Trollope, Frances (Fanny; née Milton): publications, 1, 93
Domestic Manners of the Americans, The, 14, 42–43, 164, 205
Romance of Vienna, The, 69
Tremordyn Cliff, 49
Vicar of Wrexhill, The, 10, 37, 68
Vienna and the Austrians, 69
Trollope, Frances Kathleen, 248
Trollope, Frank Anthony, 248, 249
Trollope, Frederick Farrand, 248
Trollope, Frederick James Anthony
and AT, 227, 246, 249
in Australia, 131, 182–183, 189–190, 192–193, 196, 206
childhood, 81, 83
descendants, 248
Trollope, Gordon, 184
Trollope, Gordon Clavering, 248
Trollope, Gordon Paul Clavering, 248
Trollope, Harry Reginald, 248
Trollope, Henry,
in America, 41
in Bruges, 48, 49
childhood, 1, 2, 7, 11, 37
death and burial, 49
Trollope, Henry Merivale, 227
& AT's autobiography, 157, 197, 246
AT's executor, 246
childhood, 81, 83
children, 245, 248
in Greylands, 245
marriage to Ada Strickland, 81, 248
My Own Love Story, 248
occupations, 183, 200
writing, 86
death, 248
Trollope, Hugh Irwin, 248
Trollope, Joanna, 218, 245, 248
Trollope, Major Napier, 218
Trollope, Mary Anne, 28–29
Trollope, Muriel Rose, 95, 194, 198, 207, 245, 246, 248, 249
Trollope, Rose (née Heseltine),
and AT's work, 166, 237
family, 87
and Fanny, 88, 90, 92, 94–96, 179
at Greylands, Minchinhampton, 245
and Kate Field, 155, 157, 197
marriage to AT, 81, 228, 233
in Montagu Square, 194
travel to America, 184, 205
travel to Australia, 182, 183, 184–185, 189, 190, 192
travel to Europe, 207
death, 246
Trollope, Sir Anthony (1691–1784), 15
Trollope, Sir John, 15, 18, 112
Trollope Society, xvi, 49, 76, 77, 251, 252
Trollope, Susannah, 189
Trollope, Theodosia, 179, 180
Trollope, Thomas Adolphus (Tom),
and AT, 238, 246
in Birmingham, 65

childhood, 7, 10, 21, 27, 28–29, 44, 48, 50, 52, 55, 64, 67–68, 69, 103, 141, 230
  in Florence, 93, 179
  at Harrow School, 32
  in London, 57, 58, 71, 194, 230, 231
  marriage to Frances Eleanor, 94, 180
  marriage to Theodosia, 179, 180
  in Penrith, 91, 93
  and St Cross, 99
  visit to America, 42, 44
  While I Remember, xix, 1–2, 21, 31, 38, 212–213
  at Winchester, 11, 37–38, 39
Trollope, Thomas Anthony (son of Henry Merivale), 245
Trollope, Thomas Anthony, L.LB (father of AT), 42, 45, 52–53, 55
  in Bruges, 48, 49
  Encyclopaedia Ecclesiastica, 14, 53–55, **55**
  in Harrow, xviii, 2, 8
  in Harrow Weald, 10, 11
  marriage to Frances (Fanny; née Milton), 18, 21
  A Treatise on the Mortgage of Ships as Affected by the Registry Acts, ... 55
  visit to America, 42, 44
  death and burial, 49
Trollope-Bellew, Lady Dorothy, 18
Trollopiana, 29–30, 48, 53, 67, 99, 193, 252
TV adaptations,
  The Barchester Chronicles, 249–250
  Palliser novels, 250
'Two Generals, The', 183

Uffington Manor, 15

Van Gogh, Vincent: *Autumn Landscape at Dusk*, 171
Vicar of Bullhampton, The, 6, 24, 92, 110, 138, 143, 152, 170, 231
Victoria, Queen, 131, 231, 251
Villino Trollope, Florence, 179–180, **181**
violence, 143–145
Virtue, James, 161

Walker brothers (steelmakers), 87
Walker, Frederick, 164
Walpole, Hon. Frederick, 115, 116, 134, 215
Walpole, Horatio, 28
Walpole, Hugh: *Anthony Trollope*, 106, 196
Waltham Abbey, 105–106, 134, **135**
Waltham Cross, 105–110, 132
Waltham House, 105, **108–109**, 182, **202–203**
Ward, Bishop Seth, 24
Ward, Mrs Humphrey, 244
Warden, The, 24, 25, 26, 88, 97–99, **98**, 102, 115, 161, 176, 249
Washington, Reverend Henry, 233
Waugh, Evelyn, 21
Way We Live Now, The, 24, 45, 86, 88, 120, 126, 127, 134, 135, 144, 145, 196, 206, 209–210, 213–214, 250
Welch, Brian: *Trollopiana*, 199–200
Wellington, Duke of, 28, 132, 134, 143

Wells, H G, 225
Welsh Gold, 139
Wemyss, 219, **221**, 222
West Indies, 114, 204–205
West Indies and the Spanish Main, The, 204–205
Westminster Abbey, **253**
  Poets' Corner, 251–252
WH Smith & Sons, 126, **129**
Whistler, James, 174
Whitfield, June, 250
Why Frau Frohmann Raised her Prices, 226
'Widow's Mite, The', 183
Wilberforce, Bishop 'Soapy Sam', 116
Williams, Vivian, 252
Williamson, Michael, 252
Wills,
  AT's will, 24, 26, 246
  Reverend William Milton, 28
Winchester School, 11, 37–40, **40**
Winchester: St Cross/Hiram's Hospital, 98–99, **101**
Winter, William, 240
Witherow, David, 249
Wood, Mrs Henry, 126
Woolf, Alex, 252
Wordsworth, Bishop, 99
Wright, Fanny, 41
writing desk, 166, **167**
writing method, 166–168
Wythes, George, 134
Wythes, George Edward, 134

Yorkshire, 209–213
  Bolton Abbey, **209**, 210, **210**, 212
  Leeds, **211**, 212

Zoffany, Johan, 115